Accounting

DeMYSTiFieD®

DeMYSTiFieD® Series

Advanced Statistics Demystified	Math Proofs Demystified
Algebra Demystified, 2e	Math Word Problems Demystified
Alternative Energy Demystified	Mathematics Demystified
ASP.NET 2.0 Demystified	MATLAB Demystified
Astronomy Demystified	Microbiology Demystified
Biology Demystified	Microeconomics Demystified
Biophysics Demystified	Nanotechnology Demystified
Biotechnology Demystified	OOP Demystified
Business Calculus Demystified	Operating Systems Demystified
Business Math Demystified	Organic Chemistry Demystified
Business Statistics Demystified	Pharmacology Demystified
Calculus Demystified, 2e	Physics Demystified, 2e
Chemistry Demystified	Physiology Demystified
College Algebra Demystified	Pre-Algebra Demystified, 2e
Data Structures Demystified	Precalculus Demystified
Databases Demystified, 2e	Probability Demystified
Differential Equations Demystified	Project Management Demystified
Digital Electronics Demystified	Quality Management Demystified
Earth Science Demystified	Quantum Mechanics Demystified
Electricity Demystified	Relativity Demystified
Electronics Demystified	Robotics Demystified
Environmental Science Demystified	Signals and Systems Demystified
Everyday Math Demystified	SQL Demystified
Forensics Demystified	Statistical Process Control Demystified
Genetics Demystified	Statistics Demystified
Geometry Demystified	Technical Analysis Demystified
HTML & XHTML Demystified	Technical Math Demystified
Java Demystified	Trigonometry Demystified
JavaScript Demystified	UML Demystified
Lean Six Sigma Demystified	Visual Basic 2005 Demystified
Linear Algebra Demystified	Visual C# 2005 Demystified
Logic Demystified	Web Design Demystified
Macroeconomics Demystified	XML Demystified

The Demystified Series publishes more than 125 titles in all areas of academic study. For a complete list of titles, please visit www.mhprofessional.com.

Accounting
DeMYSTiFieD®

Leita Hart-Fanta, CPA

New York   Chicago   San Francisco   Lisbon   London   Madrid   Mexico City
New Delhi   San Juan   Seoul   Singapore   Sydney   Toronto

4 5 6 7 8 9 10   DOC/DOC   1 6 5

ISBN: 978-0-07-176373-8
MHID: 0-07-176373-2

e-ISBN: 978-0-07-177097-2
e-MHID: 0-07-177097-6

This publication is designed to provide accurate and authoritative information in regard to the subject matter covered. It is sold with the understanding that neither the author nor the publisher is engaged in rendering legal, accounting, securities trading, or other professional services. If legal advice or other expert assistance is required, the services of a competent professional person should be sought.

—*From a Declaration of Principles Jointly Adopted by a Committee of the American Bar Association and a Committee of Publishers and Associations*

McGraw-Hill books are available at special quantity discounts to use as premiums and sales promotions or for use in corporate training programs. To contact a representative, please e-mail us at bulksales@mcgraw-hill.com.

This book is printed on acid-free paper.

This book is dedicated to my generous, supportive, and loving husband Jeff.
You are the best, baby!

About the Author

Leita Hart-Fanta is a certified public accountant, certified government financial manager, and certified government audit professional. She is the author of a number of self-study courses for CPAs and auditors on auditing and accounting topics, including generating cash flow, basic audit skills, and government auditing standards. She also has taught over 1,000 day-long seminars and is a frequent keynote speaker at CPA conferences. To find out more about her, visit her Web sites at www.auditskills.com, www.happycashflow.com, www.leitahart.com, and www.yellowbook-cpe.com.

Contents

Acknowledgments

Thank you to my finance for nonfinancial manager students at Dell and the University of Texas who allowed me to perfect my teaching over time. That class became this book. I have heard it said that the first time you teach a class the students are teaching you, the second time you are teaching each other, and the third you are teaching them. I wish it only took me three runs to figure out how to convey complex topics simply!

By watching the light bulb go on or the light bulb go out on the faces of my students, I could tell whether I was on the right track or not. I thank them for their eagerness to learn and their thoughtful questions. The questions and live feedback taught me what nonaccountants want to know about accounting—but more importantly what they do not want to know about accounting. Thank you!

I also want to thank Susan Allen who gave me my first shot as a writing teacher and writing coach and believed that I could pull it off. Those first classes were rough, but she didn't fire me!

And lastly I want to thank my friend Michele Carlquist, who once said that I had potential and encouraged me to stick to my plan to write and teach over and over and over.

Introduction

Why Is Accounting Important?

I was out of school and had my CPA (certified public accountant) license for several years before all the debit and credit microdetail the professors stuffed into my brain started to make real sense. And only after teaching the language of accounting and finance to others did it really become clear. An old Japanese proverb instructs: "Those who want to learn must teach." Very true in my case.

When I was asked questions, I was forced to take all my technical, detailed knowledge and distill it so that I could answer the question in an understandable and clear way. And that is what this book is all about—answering your questions in an understandable and clear way.

I don't know why the professors choose to start the first week with a discussion of debits and credits. I have a sneaking suspicion that, at my alma mater at least, it was a way to weed out tentative, unsure students. You had to be pretty darn sure you wanted to be a business major to sit through and memorize all that stuff.

I am not going to put you through that experience. You bought this book hoping that I'd make the subject easy, and I am going to do everything I can to make it painless. I find that many learners like to start with the big picture first. Many like to know why they need to know something before they just memorize a bunch of rules. So in Part I, debits and credits are mentioned only once. The emphasis is on grasping the big picture.

In Part II, I go into more detail. There I discuss debits and credits and inventory valuation and exciting stuff like that. But I am not going to discuss obscure transactions such as the repurchase of preferred stock under stock option plans. (It is scary to just write that sentence!) I imagine that would entail more detail than 99 percent of the readers of this book need. If you want that sort of detail, please consult accounting standards [through the Financial Accounting Standards Board (FASB) and/or the Governmental Accounting Standards Board (GASB)], an accounting professor, or an advanced accounting text.

In Part III, I discuss how financial information is used in business and various business information systems. There I cover budgeting and cost accounting and how those systems differ from general ledger or financial accounting. I also talk about how governmental and not-for-profit accounting has its own special way of doing things.

And in the last part, I take everything from the first three parts and perform a high-level financial analysis of two competitors and raise some interesting questions about their performance.

So we go from the big picture, to detail, to practical application.

Why Should You Learn This Stuff?

Good question! It might seem easier to just leave all this technical stuff up to someone else so that you can focus on your job. Maybe you are in marketing, sales, product design, administration, quality—anywhere but the finance and accounting department! You have successfully avoided the topic so far, but it just keeps coming up in meetings and conversations. It is like a nagging grandmother—always there, always hoping you will call.

Not understanding the language of business and leaving money decisions in the hands of accountants are bad ideas for several reasons:

- Accountants don't know your job, the real goings-on of the business, as well as you do. They shouldn't tell you how things should be.

- Accountants might make bad decisions. I don't know how many times I hear managers complain of how they are being victimized by a stringent and unreasonable budget created by the accountant. Big mistake! The accountant shouldn't have created the budget; the manager should have done it.

- You are ultimately responsible for results. When things go well or go badly, it is you that upper management looks to. Accountants don't make sales, do marketing, or design new products; often, all they do is compile and report data. You'd do well to keep informed of what is going on financially so that you can answer tough questions or consciously bask in the praise.

- You want your career to go somewhere. Maybe you have noticed that the farther you move up the chain of command in your organization, the more you hear talk about money. If you can't talk the talk, you won't be promoted to walk the walk.

- Accountants and other financially savvy members of your team might be snowing or manipulating you. You might have a sneaking suspicion that things are going on that you don't know about because you don't know what you don't know. In other words, how can you ask about something you know nothing about? Information is power.

- You would like to stay engaged during management meetings where financial results are discussed. When computer experts talk to me, they can quickly tell that they have surpassed my level of understanding when I start nodding and smiling in a glazed manner. This does nothing to enhance my credibility or stature with that computer expert. Not knowing what is going on in finance can be a detriment to your credibility with upper management. Wouldn't it be nice to be able to participate in a discussion about money?

- Business is about making money. You might think it is about the product or marketing or sales. But it's all about money. The reason that you have a product and market and sell it is to make money. And accounting is the language of money.

- Accounting really isn't all that hard. It is just a system and a language. Hey, if I can learn it, so can you!

Accounting Is Just a System and a Language

You see, accounting is one of the oldest systems around for tracking data. In business, someone has always wanted to know how much money was made or lost. For centuries, accountants have kindly kept track of the dollars that flow in and out of organizations of all types.

The systems that have been set up to track this information can be—and I emphasize *can* be—difficult to use and interpret. The debit and credit stuff can get pretty confusing. With a little effort, though, I know that you will be able to extract some information that will help you to make decisions about what to do next in your business.

For example, most accounting systems will spit out data on how much it costs to create a product or provide a service. Now why do we care about this? Because we must price our product or service for more than we spent to create it. Selling something for more than you put into it is called a *business*. Selling something for less than you put into it is called a *hobby*!

You also might want to know how well your sales staff is doing at pushing your latest gizmo. Your accounting system should be able to tell you volume of sales per salesperson as well as the customers to whom your salespeople are selling the gizmos. This can be very useful data if you want to determine who to reward and who to send back to sales school.

Some Accounting Systems Are Real Time and Very Detailed

Any basic accounting system will tell you simple things such as how much cash you took in today and how much you paid out today. Accounting systems track all the money that goes in and out of the business and categorizes the ins and outs into useful groups so that you can judge where the money came from and what it was used for. Bottom line:

All accounting is *a counting*.

But some businesses believe that accounting can and should do more for them. For this extra bit of tracking, for this extra counting effort, if you will, they pay in both time and money.

One Fortune 500 company invested a huge amount of time and effort into creating a daily accounting report that told how many products it was selling, how it was selling the products (by phone, by Internet, or in stores), and what kind of profit each product generated. The company decided that it was worth it to get immediate feedback on whether the bells and whistles it was offering its customers were selling. If they weren't selling, the company changed its offerings immediately. The company didn't want to waste a week, a month, or a quarter hawking low-demand goods. The accounting system gave the company the power to make decisions quickly.

In most decisions in business, an evaluation has to be made as to whether the cost is worth the resulting benefit. The same must be said of accounting. What is the information worth to you?

But before you can even make that decision, you need to know what kind of information a basic accounting system can provide, and you need to understand the terminology behind it.

I hate to tell you this, but accountants are not working at changing their tunes—or their terminology—any time soon. Mohammed (that's you) is going to have to go to the mountain (that's accounting terminology, information, and accountants). I am glad you have decided to take this journey with me. I will make the mountains into little, tiny, bumpy hills for you.

Part I

The Big Picture

Chapter 1

Where Did All This Lingo Come From?

Business is very simple. Money flows into an organization, and money flows out. But we in the finance and accounting profession sometimes get a little out of hand giving fancy names to very simple concepts. This fancy lingo can cause more than a little bit of confusion. So it is helpful to envision accounting as a foreign language. Most of the rules and concepts are perfectly intuitive and simple; you just have to know what to call them.

The title of this book, *Accounting Demystified*, is very appropriate. It is definitely attributing too much romance and intrigue to the profession to call it a mystery, but it does probably sell a few more books than the title, *Clarifying Accounting Lingo*. (This is why I am writing and someone else is marketing this book!)

CHAPTER OBJECTIVES

- Describe the origin and general purpose of accounting
- Introduce the three key financial statements

I want to give you the ability to have an intelligent conversation with an accountant or finance person. I want you to be able to justify your actions in terms that the folks holding the purse strings can understand and appreciate. I want you to be able to go to meetings with your management team and understand what the heck they are talking about. I don't want you to have to nod your head like you understand when you don't, so I am going to give you the knowledge to ask intelligent questions regarding finance.

What I am not going to do is bore you or muddy the waters with a load of unnecessary detail. You know, I was out of college and already had my certified public accountant (CPA) certificate before all the detail the accounting professors had me memorize gelled together in my head to form a big picture. I am going to take the opposite approach with you. We are going to start with the big picture and then go into a bit of detail. We are not going to go into super detail. I think it is best to keep it at a high level.

I am not going to tell you how to handle an advance repurchase agreement on stock or how to calculate a bond discount. This is too much detail for 99.99 percent of the population—and probably you. However, if you do need this kind of detail, this book will give you the basis to start asking those questions and understanding what the finance person says in response.

As Glinda the Good Witch says in *The Wizard of* Oz, "It is always best to start at the beginning." So let's take a minute to get a sense of how this system we have in place began a long time ago. It actually started in a very romantic and sometimes mysterious and dramatic place—Italy.

The Birth of the Accountant

The system we use today to track money in business was invented in Italy during the Renaissance. An Italian merchant invented it so that he could easily summarize his results at the end of the day. The system had a simple method of checks and balances to make sure that everything he had recorded was done correctly.

The Italian merchant called his system the *double-entry accounting system*, and it was very simple to understand. Each and every transaction must balance. The "ins" had to equal the "outs." This is the root of debits and credits that we will talk about in more detail in Chapter 6.

For instance, let's say this merchant sold jewelry. When he sold a piece of jewelry, the jewelry went *out* of his business. In return something came *in*—some cash. Through a series of entries in his books, the ins would equal the outs.

With this system, the merchant could make sure that every transaction was recorded completely because the books had to balance. If the books didn't balance, the merchant knew that he had missed something.

This system also was useful in that it posted the information to discrete accounts or categories that could be summarized at the end of the day. The merchant could look at his cash account category and see how much cash he had brought in that day; he could look at his jewelry inventory category to see how much jewelry he had left to sell. All very convenient.

This system was so convenient and useful that the merchant decided to share it with his friends. His friends liked it, and because Italy was a trade center, soon businesses all over the world were using the system. (Don't ask me what they were doing previous to this; I imagine just keeping a list of cash on long sheets of parchment.)

But the folks who were the most excited about this new system were the lenders—the banks and financiers who gave merchants money to expand their businesses. Before this system, the banks and financiers had to rely on subjective information to decide who to loan money to. They made decisions based on family reputation, where they lived, or what kind of carriage they drove. Now they could decide based on some real hard data.

The only problem is that everyone's data looked a little different because they all used different rules. They chose how to treat a transaction according to how good it made their books look.

For example, let's say that you are a sales representative for the famous artist Michelangelo. Your job is to find him commissions so that he can concentrate on his art, not on selling. The head of the Medici family, a very influential and wealthy Italian family, has commissioned Michelangelo—through you—to sculpt a replica of *David* for the foyer of the family villa.

When do you record a sale in your books? When you shake hands with the head of the Medici clan and say, "We'll have it to you in three years"? Or when Michelangelo puts chisel to marble? Or when the statue is installed in the villa? Do you record a sale when you bill for the statue or when the Medicis pay in cash?

All these viewpoints have validity. The lenders didn't like this at all. They desired consistency. They wanted everyone to use the same rules so that their financial statements would be comparable. They wanted to know, when choosing to invest in one of three businesses, which business actually was doing better.

The lenders demanded rules so that everyone would be consistent. It was then that accountants were born. Accountants are just the folks who know the rules on how to keep the records consistent. A dark day in the annals of history, I know, but. . . .

Gaps in GAAP?

Nowadays accounting rules are voluminous. The standards that accountants use to create financial statements are called *generally accepted accounting principles* (GAAP). There is a set of GAAP that applies to most everyone, and then there is GAAP for specific industries. The oil and gas business has different transactions than a software developer, so we have to have different rules for each group.

GAAP is created by a rule-making body called the *Financial Accounting Standards Board* (FASB, pronounced "faz-bee"). Governmental entities such as cities and counties have their own rule-setting body called the *Governmental Accounting Standards Board* (GASB, pronounced "gaz-bee").

Unfortunately, GAAP is full of gaps or loopholes. GAAP is designed to make financial statements comparable and consistent. And generally, most transactions are treated conservatively, meaning that transactions are not recorded until we are absolutely sure that the transaction will occur or actually has occurred.

But some organizations take advantage of the gaps in GAAP just to make their financial statements look a little bit better than those of their competitors. Wealthy folks hire savvy tax accountants to find shelters for their wealth so that they don't have to pay so much tax. Corporations hire savvy accountants to enhance their financial results. In essence, the tax accountant is hired to take advantage of the loopholes in the tax code. Well, GAAP is also full of these loopholes. You can't think of everything someone would do.

In the early 2000s, Enron was caught taking advantages of these loopholes to puff up its financial results. Years after the scandal broke, many members of the Enron executive team were still roaming free. Enron saw a loophole in GAAP and took full advantage of it.

Now, WorldCom was another story. The leaders at WorldCom took a hard-and-fast GAAP rule and broke it outright. They were immediately arrested and jailed.

And now that it appears that the accounting profession did not do a very good job regulating itself with GAAP and licensing efforts, the federal government has stepped in to create even more rules and regulations for accountants to follow. Now the profession is adopting international accounting standards that will change the look and contents of traditional financial statements.

Have I turned you off from a career in accounting yet? Wait, there's more! No, actually, I'll stop. It is too depressing to go on.

Another related profession was invented at the same time as accounting. It is the group that comes in to make sure that you are following GAAP. Right—it's the auditors. Talk about some shakeups in a profession—but that is another story for another book.

One Huge Database

Now back to this double-entry accounting system. How many transactions do you think a behemoth organization such as IBM has per day? I don't even know, but I know it's plenty—tens of thousands at least.

All these transactions are captured in a huge database. Every company has one; it is called the *general ledger*. This general ledger, like any database, has fields of information. And according to how detailed you want to get, it can have dozens of fields of information. Information the general ledger captures includes

- Date of transaction
- Amount of transaction
- Debit or credit
- Account title and code
- Budget code
- Vendor
- Purchase order number
- Invoice number
- Payment date
- Payment method

And the general ledger, just like any database, can be sorted just about any way you want. Accountants will tell you that this is not true because they don't want to generate a bunch of different reports, but they can sort it by date, by amount, by account, by budget code, and so on.

So let's pretend that you and I work at IBM. You are a muckety-muck executive manager, and I am your accountant. I am not very customer-focused; I just enter transactions and tell people no all day. So I print out the general ledger for the week on that green-and-white striped general ledger paper with the holes in the side, and I load it on a dolly. It is sorted by date entered. How big do you think that stack would be? It easily could take me several dollies to deliver the report to you.

So I walk into your office and dump the report at your feet and say, "Happy decision making!" and walk out. My job is done.

Is this what you want? No, you don't want all this detail; you want a summary.

QuickBooks Hides the Unpleasant Theory

If you can believe it, QuickBooks is sometimes hard for old-school accountants to get used to. Old-school accountants were taught how to keep track of transactions using T-accounts, where we saw each side of the transaction and had to memorize the theory behind why a particular T-account was updated in a particular instance.

When you enter a transaction in QuickBooks, it doesn't show both sides of the transaction. It hides the unnecessary, messy, confusing theory. The old-school accountant has to trust that the software knows where to put the other side of the expense, the distribution to owners, the purchase of a new computer. And at the end of the year, QuickBooks allows you to push a button to clean the books up and prep them for next year. Again, you have to trust the software.

Programs such as QuickBooks threaten to put accountants out of business entirely because anyone with a mouse can keep track of his or her business intuitively using QuickBooks—all except old-school accountants, that is.

The Three Key Financial Statements Are Just Summaries

That is all the three key financial statements are—summaries of the general ledger from three different perspectives. They are the summaries that everyone is used to seeing and using. Every publicly traded company in the United States generates these three key financial statements.

The *balance sheet* (Figure 1.1) is the super summary of the general ledger. It is the general ledger rolled up into as few categories as possible.

Balance Sheet

Assets	Liabilities
Cash	Accounts Payable
Investments	Long-Term Debt
Accounts Receivable	
Inventory	**Equity**
Fixed Assets	
Intangibles	Stock
	Retained Earnings

FIGURE 1.1 • Balance sheet model.

The balance sheet is called the balance sheet because it has to balance, just like the general ledger does and just like every transaction entered into the general ledger does.

I also call the balance sheet the mother of all financial statements. The other two financial statements are the babies of this mother.

Over the centuries, someone said, "I appreciate your sharing this balance sheet with me, but I could use a little more detail. In particular, I could use a little more detail about how you generated earnings." So we put a little magnifying glass on retained earnings and tracked how earnings were generated with the *earnings statement.*

Some call it the *income statement* (Figure 1.2), some the *profit and loss statement*, the *P&L*, or even the *statement of earnings*. No matter what it is called, it picks out only transactions from the general ledger that contributed to the earnings or the profit that the organization generated. It is the baby of the balance sheet, giving us detail only on earnings.

Income Statement

Sales
Less cost of goods sold

Gross margin
Less operating costs

Operating margin
Less taxes, other

Net income or net profit margin

FIGURE 1.2 · Income statement model.

The third key financial statement was added to the bunch only recently. The FASB started requiring it after the savings and loan crisis. It, too, is a baby of the balance sheet because it takes one item off the balance sheet and gives us more detail on where it came from. It focuses on cash, my favorite business asset.

The *cash-flow statement* is very similar to your bank account statement that you get at home. It tells you how much money you started the month with, how much cash you paid out, how much cash you deposited, and how much cash is left at the end of the month (Figure 1.3).

Cash-Flow Statement

Beginning Cash
Plus Cash collected
Less Cash paid

Ending Cash

FIGURE 1.3 · Cash-flow statement model.

Cash is the lifeblood of business; without it, you can't pay payroll, pay bills, or buy any inventory to sell.

Each of these financial statements will be described in greater detail in later chapters. All the statements put together tell a story about the business—and every story is unique. The income statement for a service business will look entirely different than the income statement for a manufacturing operation. Okay, not entirely different, but different enough to make it interesting.

And these three key financial statements contain about 80 percent of the business lingo that finance and accounting folks throw around on a regular basis. So, if you get a grip on them, understand what they tell you and don't tell you, and know how they are related to each other, you will have mastered a good portion of business-speak.

Liquidity, Profitability, Growth, and Financing

Most stories of how well a business is doing focus on three main questions:

- How flexible or liquid is the organization?
- How profitable is the organization?
- How is the business financed?

Each of these questions can be answered by looking at the three key financial statements. Let's first look at the balance sheet and discuss liquidity and financing.

Summary

Luckily for me and for you, accounting isn't rocket science or molecular biology! Think of it as a foreign language—a language that seeks to categorize the ins and outs of resources in a business.

QUIZ

1. **Accountants were born out of the need for?**
   A. Lender's desires for consistent, comparable record keeping
   B. Acceptance of the double-entry system in business
   C. Knowing when to bill for long-term orders, say, a statue that was to be made
   D. A system that would improve Italy's trade with the rest of the world.

2. **Cities and counties have their own accounting standards board called the _____.**
   A. GAAP
   B. FASB
   C. GASB
   D. FAF

3. **Companies' daily financial transactions are captured in this huge database called _____.**
   A. an earnings statement
   B. the general ledger
   C. a profit and loss statement
   D. a cash-flow statement

4. **Income statement, profit and loss statement, the P&L, and the earnings statement are all different names for which of the following statements?**
   A. Earnings statement
   B. The general ledger
   C. Balance sheet
   D. Cash-flow statement

5. **FASB started requiring this financial statement after the savings and loan crisis of the 1980s.**
   A. Earnings statement
   B. Profit and loss statement
   C. Balance sheet
   D. Cash-flow statement

6. **The three key financial statements are _____.**
   A. unorganized lists of accounting data
   B. summaries of the general ledger
   C. too detailed to use

7. **The cash-flow statement is similar to _____.**
   A. a cash register receipt
   B. an income statement
   C. a balance sheet
   D. a bank account statement

8. **The bottom line on the income statement is called _____.**
   A. net income
   B. net worth
   C. owners' equity
   D. net assets

9. **Balance sheet components include _____.**
   A. fixed assets, net income, and cash
   B. fixed assets, cash, and accounts payable
   C. cash, cost of goods sold, and operating expenses

10. **Which of the following financial statements discloses the total amount of fixed assets held?**
    A. The income statement
    B. The statement of shareholders' equity
    C. The balance sheet
    D. The cash-flow statement

chapter 2

The Balance Sheet— The Mother of All Financial Statements

The balance sheet probably was the very first financial statement ever created. It expresses the relationship that is basic to the double-entry accounting system:

$$\text{Assets} = \text{liabilities} + \text{equity}$$

In this chapter, we will explore how this equation works in more detail.

CHAPTER OBJECTIVE

- Interpret and perform a basic analysis of a simple balance sheet

So, on one side of the balance sheet, we see the assets. On the other side, we see liabilities and equity.

Assets – Liabilities = Equity
☺   ☹   ☺ or ☹

This relationship among assets, liabilities, and equity actually makes better sense if we view it from another angle.

Assets, Liabilities, and Equity: Another Way to Look at Them

The basic equation of the balance sheet is

Happy – Sad = Either Happy or Sad
☺   ☹   ☺ or ☹

A more intuitive way to express this equation is shown in Figure 2.1.

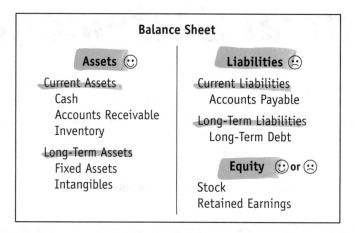

FIGURE 2.1 • Happy face balance sheet.

Or, in very simple language:

- Assets are happy things that you own.
- Liabilities are sad amounts that you owe to other people.
- Equity is the difference between the two—either a happy or sad remaining balance.

Equity is a concept that many of us are comfortable with because of our homes. We have equity in our homes because the amount that the house is worth is more than the amount we owe on it.

Have you refinanced your house recently? When you did, the lender asked you for all sorts of information on your financial health and ability to repay the loan. You probably created a personal balance sheet for the lender (Figure 2.2).

Personal Balance Sheet

Things You Own ☺	Amounts You Owe Others ☹
Cash in the bank	Home mortgage
Investments in brokerage account	Car #1 note
Retirement account	Car #2 note
House	Beach house mortgage
Car #1	Boat note
Car #2	Credit card debt
Beach house	
Boat	Happy Reminder ☺
Jewelry	Net Worth
Furnishings, art	

FIGURE 2.2 • Personal balance sheet.

The first thing you did was to list all of your assets—all the cool stuff you own that you could sell off for cash if you needed in order to repay the loan. Your assets would include the house, your car, some investments, your retirement account, a beach house, some jewelry, and so on.

Then you had to list all of your liabilities—the amounts you owed on all this stuff. So you had to list your mortgage, your car note, your beach house mortgage, and your credit card debt.

The difference between the two—assets and liabilities—is your equity or, in personal terms, net worth. You have heard the term *net worth* applied to wealthy folks. "Ross Perot has a net worth of $10 billion" or whatever. This does not mean that Ross Perot has $10 billion in a bank account in Switzerland; it means that his stuff is worth $10 billion more than he owes on it. He has equity in his real estate and business holdings.

Businesses are like this, too. They list their assets and then their liabilities. The remainder is the equity that has built up in the company.

By the way, in government, this remainder is called *fund balance* or *net assets*—but more about that in Chapter 12.

Two Mistakes in Reasoning

In teaching this topic live, I see my participants making two mistakes over and over, so I want to warn you about them. On the right-hand side of our balance sheet are two categories of items—a liability category and an equity category. Equity is not a subset of the liability category; it is an entirely different category unto itself.

The second mistake people make is that they want to link one side of the balance sheet to the other. For instance, they want to say that retained earnings is in cash. Remember that the balance sheet is the super summary of the general ledger. It rolls up the information in the general ledger—thousands, sometimes hundreds of thousands of transactions—and categorizes the data into just a few key accounts. So you can't and shouldn't try to link one side to the other.

Now, How Do We Use the Balance Sheet to Make Decisions?

The balance sheet tells us three crucial stories. First, it tells us who, in essence, owns the business. Second, it tells us how lean and mean the organization is running. And third, it tells us how liquid the organization is. Let's cover each of these stories in turn.

The First Question the Balance Sheet Answers: Who Owns the Business?

When you first open the doors of your business, you have two places to get money: either by taking out a loan or by selling ownership, or stock, in your business to others or to yourself. Look at the right-hand side of our balance sheet model (Figure 2.3). You will not have any retained earnings or accounts payable on day one because you have not created or sold anything.

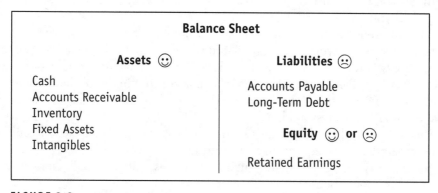

FIGURE 2.3 • Balance sheet model.

So let's first look at debt and stock.

When You Have Debt, the Lenders Own the Business

Long-term debt is loans that the business took out either to expand or to just plain operate. When you have a loan, in essence, the bank owns your business. Just as when you have a home mortgage, you don't really own your house until you pay the bank the final principal payment.

What do banks expect in return for doing business with you? They expect interest. So doing business with banks costs something. They expect to be paid on a regular basis. You cannot skip payments for a few years at your convenience. If you do that, they will call the loan and come take away the stuff you pledged as collateral.

And if you are what they consider a high-risk loan client, they might require you to do all sorts of things in the loan agreement. Clauses of the loan agreement are called *loan covenants*. Loan covenants are promises that you make to the bank in return for getting the money. The bank doesn't ever give you $10 million and say, "Go have a good time." There is always a catch.

I have seen loan covenants that require the borrower to keep a certain amount of cash in the lending bank at all times. Covenants might require you to keep inventory levels at a certain amount or limit debt with other lenders. If you fall outside its dictated parameters, you have "busted the covenants," and the bank can call your loan.

If you are super high risk, the loan covenants can require you to replace members of your board of directors with bank officers or require that you report to the bank on a daily basis the results of your operations. A friend of mine was a chief financial officer (CFO) of a company that had filed for bankruptcy. The bank decided to loan the company more money in the hope that the money the bank had already invested in the company would not go to waste. My friend had to create the three key financial statements plus a detail on sales prospects and inventory balances on a daily basis and send it to the bank. The bank also kicked the owners off the board and replaced them with a few business consultants that the bank believed could turn the company around.

If you take the money, you also take these terms.

When You Have Stock, the Stockholders Own the Business

Now, if you have stockholders as the owners of your company, you worry about a different set of issues. Stockholders expect two types of return on their investment: occasional dividends and/or rising stock price.

A company pays dividends in order to distribute the wealth it has accumulated to its owners. Many companies do not pay dividends. A dividend is usually declared on a quarterly or annual basis and is meant to take the profit that the company made and pay it out in cash to the shareholders. In growth companies, the stockholders prefer that the company, instead of paying them the cash, take the extra profits and plow them back into the company.

Still Struggling

Current Stock Price Has No Impact on the Financials

If the selling price of a stock triples because of a hot new product, the common-stock balance on the balance sheet doesn't move. As a matter of fact, the current selling price of the stock isn't disclosed anywhere in the 10-K [the annual financial report filed with the Securities and Exchange Commission (SEC)]. If you want to know it, you can use information disclosed about total shares outstanding and market capitalization on the face of the 10-K—but the organization is not going to calculate it for you.

Why? The value of common stock on the equity side of the balance sheet reflects how much the stock sold for when it was issued, not what it is worth today. So, if the stock sold in 1956 for $3 a share—it is still on the books at $3 a share, even though it might be selling for $130 today.

Then why does the company work so hard to get stock prices higher? A variety of reasons: High stock prices allow the company to raise more capital easily if it needs it, or the company may be setting aside part of its cash and investing in its own stock instead of the stock of other companies. But the main reason the employees work so hard to get stock prices to rise is that the executives and board members are shareholders. And when the stock goes up, their personal wealth goes up, too.

This will give the investors the second type of return they are looking for—growth of the value of the stock. If the company plows the profits back in and grows in market share or creates exciting new products, the worth of the stock goes up.

The shareholders have a lot of power. They have the right to vote anytime the articles of incorporation of the business are changed. You can liken the articles of incorporation to the U.S. Constitution. The articles spell out how the business is organized, how many folks are on the board of directors, how often they meet, what the mission of the organization is, if the organization pays dividends and when, how many shares of stock can be issued, and so on.

Even more important, though, is the shareholders' power to choose the leaders of the corporation. They get to choose who sits on the board of directors. The board of directors chooses the executive management, and executive management chooses every other player in the organization. It is not uncommon for the shareholders to get together and vote new directors in, thus influencing the future of the company. So the shareholders are at the top of the food chain.

Corporations, then, end up doing things to please their shareholders that might not be beneficial to the internal operations of the company. I was teaching a finance for nonfinancial managers course at a Fortune 500 company a few years ago on the day that the company announced its quarterly results to Wall Street. Unfortunately, the company did not make its projected revenue figures, and it expected that its stock price would plummet as a result.

So, to prove to Wall Street and the shareholders that the company was serious about maintaining profitability, it laid off thousands of people on the same day it announced the quarterly results. I was told that the team that had hired me had been eliminated and that I was welcome to finish the day's training, but the company wasn't sure when they would have me back. (I was back after the next quarter, by the way.)

This move did indeed stabilize the stock price. It only decreased by pennies; the stockholders loved the move. Internally, however, this Fortune 500 company was in turmoil for half a year. Morale went down the toilet. So, what looked good from the outside, to investors, may not have been the best move internally.

To summarize, by financing your organization with stock, you may be taking on an obligation to pay dividends on a regular basis *and* you give up some control of your business because shareholders are at the top of the food chain.

When You Have Retained Earnings, the Business Owns the Business

Now, when you have retained earnings, the company owns the company. Retained earnings are the earnings or profit that the company made that it holds and doesn't pay out as dividends.

What Can You Do with Profits?

When you make a profit, three things can happen to your money. The first is mandatory: You have to pay out a good chunk of your profit in taxes. With the remainder, you can either pay the owners or stockholders dividends or retain it in the company and do with it as you please. The amount that is held is accumulated in the account called *retained earnings*. Many companies do not pay dividends. The shareholders prefer that the earnings be kept to fund growth.

Retained earnings, in general, are the best way to finance your company's operations. Think of this in personal terms. You do not want to take a loan out from your parents or go into major credit card debt to finance your life. We can equate this to long-term debt. You also do not want to sell parts of your body (or your soul to the devil!) to finance operations. You can very loosely equate this to stock or equity financing. You prefer to make your own money and pay your own way. In this way, you are not beholden to anyone. This can be equated to retained earnings.

What Is Venture Capital?

Venture capital is a contribution of money or resources by someone who believes that your company will grow and prosper. Venture capital is usually structured in part like debt and in part like stock or equity. Venture capitalists may expect that you repay their contributions in periodic payments. This is structured like debt and would be accompanied by a corresponding set of debt covenants. Venture capitalists also may expect to own a piece of your company for the long run. They may expect dividends and the right to vote on important company matters. They even may want to put one of their own people on the board to keep an eye on things. This is structured like equity or stock financing.

Usually, venture capital is combo financing—a little bit of debt and a little bit of equity. All the terms of the contribution—the interest rate, the dividend rate, and the amount of control the venture capitalist has—are negotiable. In the quest for additional resources, however, some companies will agree to almost any terms.

The Second Question the Balance Sheet Answers: How Lean and Mean Is the Organization Running?

The best business in the world is one where you put a dime in and get a dollar out. The less we waste our resources, the more return we will generate, and this makes business worthwhile.

One of the most important things to examine to determine whether a company is running lean and mean is how it manages working capital.

What Is Working Capital?

There is the traditional view of working capital and the innovative view of working capital. Many accountants will tell you that they like to see a large balance in working capital. I will argue that the balance of working capital should be as small as possible. A small working capital balance indicates good management of resources.

The Textbook Definition of Working Capital

The formal, textbook definition of working capital is

$$\text{Working capital} = \text{current assets} - \text{current liabilities}$$

Now, you ask, what are a *current asset* and a *current liability*?

Generally, we segregate our assets and liabilities into groups: One group is long term, and one is current (Figure 2.4).

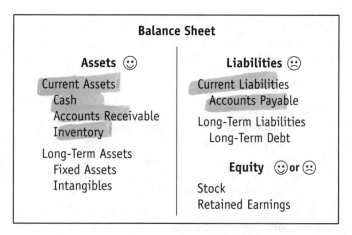

FIGURE 2.4 · Balance sheet model showing current and long-term assets and liabilities.

Long-term assets would include fixed assets. These are things that we are going to hold onto for a while, generally at least a year, such as land, buildings, machinery, and furniture. Long-term liabilities would include a 10-year bank loan.

Current assets and current liabilities, on the other hand, are assets and liabilities that will generate or use cash in the current or near period, within a year. For example, we consider accounts receivable to be a current asset because we believe that we will collect on our receivables in a month. We consider accounts payable to be current liabilities because they will use cash in the near period.

Back to our definition of working capital (Figure 2.5):

Working Capital = Current Assets – Current Liabilities

Cash	Accounts Payable
Accounts Receivable	
Inventory	

FIGURE 2.5 · Working capital formula.

Let's put cash aside for a minute. Let's talk about the other components of working capital.

Should Accounts Receivable Be Large?   Do we want our accounts receivable balance to be large? No, we don't. If it were, that would indicate that our customers are getting to use our products and services without paying for them.

They are using our money, and we like to minimize that. We would prefer to be paid up front for our services and products. At the least, we want to be paid as soon as possible after we provide our products and services.

Should Inventory Be Large?

Do we want our inventory balances to be large? No. Because that would mean that we have tied up our cash in stuff, and if we needed our cash, we might not be able to get it quickly. We want to be as liquid as possible.

Should Accounts Payable Be Large?

Looking at the other side of the equation, we want to have a relatively large accounts payable balance. This would indicate that we are using other people's money—vendors' money—as much as possible. Isn't that tricky? We want our cash up front, but we prefer to pay our vendors later. This allows us to have as much cash on hand at all times as we can.

So, given this selfish "I'd rather have the resources than you!" principle and leaving cash out of the equation for a minute, if we have a small accounts receivable balance and a small inventory balance and a large accounts payable balance, we would necessarily have a small working capital balance.

The Real Meaning of Working Capital

Now let's go beyond the textbook definition of working capital to the real meaning. Working capital is the resources you have tied up in your business that are working for you. Working capital is the money you have tied up in your product or service.

Another way to look at this is: How many resources do we have to keep plowed into the business to make our product or service? How much do we have to invest on a regular basis in inventory; how much in payments to vendors and employees; how much in granting our customers credit; and how much in rents, utilities, and other day-to-day necessities?

In the ideal world, this investment of resources is minimal. The best businesses in the world are the businesses where we put a little in and get a whole lot out. Wouldn't it be great if you could just invest 10 cents in a business yet make 5 dollars when you sold your product?

So, now let's consider the cash component. I see cash in two categories: day-to-day cash and rainy-day cash. Rainy-day cash is sort of like your reserve in case of emergency or in case of some cool business opportunity. Some organizations may have millions, even billions of dollars of rainy-day cash. On the balance sheet, the cash balance will be enormous. This does not mean that such companies need this much money to operate on a day-to-day basis. The cash they may need working for them every day may be minimal.

So, a true calculation of working capital should take out rainy-day cash and look only at the cash needed to operate on a regular basis and the resources tied up in receivables, inventory, and payables. If day-to-day cash needs are minimal, if receivables and inventory are minimal, and if payables are maximized, then working capital will be as small as possible. A small working capital balance is one key indication of a lean, mean operation.

The Third Question the Balance Sheet Answers: How Liquid Is the Organization?

One of the best things to do to understand the financial health of an organization is to see how the balance sheet would shake out if the company liquidated.

Liquidity is one of the more intuitive business terms. Have you ever seen those Oriental rug liquidation sales? What are the company owners trying to do? They are trying to convert all the rugs into cash so that they can buy some new rugs.

When your organization is liquid, it means that you are like water. Water is flexible and strong. Liquid organizations have assets that can flow wherever they want them to go. Cash—the most liquid asset—can be used for anything. Other liquid assets can be sold for cash easily and without significant loss in value.

If you have $100,000 in your pocket today, you can do whatever you want: Go out on the town and have a rip-roaring time, buy a new car or two, take your friends to a fabulous meal. If the same $100,000 is tied up in your house, enjoy cable—you aren't going anywhere.

Let me give you a story of how illiquidity can hurt a business. When I graduated from the University of Texas in Austin, one of the top employers in Austin was a company called Tracor. Tracor was a defense contractor, and I knew many engineers who worked there and were very happy. Tracor had a huge campus with about 10 buildings with underground parking and a snazzy cafeteria. Deer ran through the campus, and the test labs were full of fabulous equipment that would make any engineer proud.

Tracor was growing and doing great—until the political environment changed. When the Democrats came into office, spending on weaponry slowed. And Tracor—which had all its money tied up in those wonderful facilities, expensive engineer salaries, and long-term, slow-paying government contracts—choked. The company was illiquid, and the layoffs began. Every day my engineer friends would go into work not knowing whether they'd still be employed at the end of the day. Now Tracor is gone, and other companies occupy its buildings.

Contrast this with the largest employer in Austin now—Dell. Dell is highly liquid. It does not have fancy buildings or equipment. I've never seen a deer on Dell's campus, but the cafeterias are nice. Dell has billions of dollars in pure cash! Very few of its resources are tied up in inventory or facilities. When the market turns down, as it does every so often, Dell is able to withstand the downturn because of all this extra cash. The company is liquid and can respond to opportunities in the marketplace faster than competitors that do not have so much cash.

A Pretend Liquidation

So let's pretend that we are a simple manufacturing operation. All of a sudden, our owners have decided that they are tired of striving to make shareholders happy and want to start a spiritual retreat center in the mountains of Montana. They plan on liquidating the business, giving all the employees a nice severance package, and moving as soon as possible.

So the first thing the owners do is stop paying utilities and rent. Next they give the employees a severance package and pay off vendors.

Then they start selling all their goodies. What could a manufacturer sell?

- Finished inventory
- Raw materials inventory
- Headquarters building
- Manufacturing building
- Manufacturing equipment
- Office equipment
- Accounts receivable
- Investments
- Patents or designs
- Brand name of the company or product lines

Factoring Accounts Receivable

When you need cash fast, you might consider selling your accounts receivable—the amounts that others owe you. Instead of waiting 30 or more days for your customers to pay you, you can get cash on the receivables right away by selling them to someone else. This is called *factoring*, and the person who buys them is usually a bank or a factoring agent.

The factoring agent gives you 85 cents for each dollar of receivables. You walk away with the cash in hand, and then the factoring agent collects from the customers in a month or two.

The advantage of factoring your accounts receivable is that you don't have to wait to get your cash—you can have it now. The disadvantage is that you have to pay a pretty steep fee for doing so, often around 15 percent. So you get less cash than if you had waited. (Also, the customers are notified that instead of paying you, they will be paying this factoring agent. This might cause them some confusion or concern.)

Let's organize that list of goodies from most liquid to least liquid. Why don't you make up your list first and then check it against what I have in Figure 2.6?

Cash — **Most Liquid**
Investments
Accounts Receivable
Raw Materials Inventory
Finished Goods Inventory
Office Equipment
Manufacturing Equipment
Headquarters Building
Manufacturing Building
Birdbath Designs
Brand Names — **Least Liquid**

FIGURE 2.6 · Scale of liquidity.

Why is raw materials inventory before finished goods inventory? Raw materials are more liquid because you can simply send them back to the vendor.

Why is office equipment before manufacturing equipment? Because there are more people in the world who would want to buy your office chair and desk than your custom widget-making machine.

Buildings are near the bottom of the list because they might take months, possibly years to sell depending on their desirability.

Intellectual property such as patents and brand names is even less liquid than buildings because any number of businesses might move into your building, but only a few people in the world would want to buy a brand name or a patent.

So, as you are looking at this list, think of your own organization. Are most of your goodies at the top of this list or at the bottom? If they are at the bottom, your organization may not be very liquid.

Dell is very liquid. It has miniscule amounts tied up in intellectual property or real estate property. Many of its buildings are leased. It has billions in cash, minimizes its receivables by asking its customers to use credit cards, and holds only three days' worth of raw materials and finished goods inventory. Its holdings are at the top end of the list.

Why is liquidity important to a company such as Dell? Well, if the market changes, if a competitor acts, Dell can respond easily. If all its resources were tied up in intellectual property or real estate, it would have to let the opportunity pass.

So back to our scenario, liquidating our company. Now that we have paid everyone their severance pay, paid off our vendors, paid our last payments on utilities and rents, and sold off all our goodies, we should have a big pile of cash in our hands.

After Liquidating Our Assets, We Pay Off the Owners

Now it is time to pay off the owners with this money. This is the story that the right side of the balance sheet tells us. It tells us who owns the business. After we have paid off the vendors, our accounts payable, we have three accounts with which to work.

So, in paying off the owners, who do you think gets the money first?

The bank. As part of the loan covenants, the bank stipulates that, in case of liquidation, it gets its money first.

Next come the stockholders. Any funds that are left are given to them. If, after the company pays off the bank, only one dollar is left, the shareholders split the dollar and cry about their mediocre return.

The Difference Between Preferred and Common Stock

Preferred stockholders pay a premium for their stock and in return get special privileges. These privileges vary by company but commonly include more voting rights per share, a higher dividend rate, and first claim on the resources in case of liquidation. Common stockholders get the leftovers but usually pay a lower price for their stock.

What happens if the company doesn't even have enough cash to pay off the bank? This is called *bankruptcy*, or "rupturing the bank." In this case, the shareholders or owners of the company get nothing, and it usually means that they have to dig into their own pockets to make up the difference to pay the bank. Banks don't often walk away from such a sad situation and passively let the business owners hit the road. They often will pursue the owners for the remainder.

In Texas, we allow the bankrupt to keep their homesteads up to a certain dollar limit. Texas also allows you to keep your mule (in modern terms, a car) in case of bankruptcy. The bank can't touch such items. However, it can get to everything else—your coast house, your second car, your savings account, and so on. So, in the early 1990s, when the economy in Texas was in such bad shape and folks were going bankrupt left and right, those under the counsel of a law-yer went out and bought a Mercedes and the best home they could afford before declaring bankruptcy. Such tactics don't play as well 15 years later. The banks are serious about getting their money back and are calling for repeal of this law.

Where Do You Want the Balances on the Balance Sheet to Be?

Look at the balance sheet model again—at the assets (Figure 2.7). What kind of balance do you want to see in cash, large or tiny? Large!

What kind of balance do you want to see in receivables, large or tiny? You want this number to be as lean as possible. A disproportionate balance might indicate that the company has a hard time collecting from its customers.

Balance Sheet

Assets	Liabilities
Cash	Accounts Payable
Investments	Long-Term Debt
Accounts Receivable	
Inventory	**Equity**
Fixed Assets	
Intangibles	Stock
	Retained Earnings

FIGURE 2.7 · Balance sheet model.

How about inventory? You prefer that the company have a minimal investment in inventory. If your resources are tied up in inventory, they aren't tied up in cash, which is where we want the majority of our resources, right?

How about fixed assets? Again, minimal.

How about intangibles? Again, minimize if you can. One of the main types of intellectual property is patents. Ideally, you only get patents that will have a value down the line or patents that allow you to protect yourself against competitors. Patents are expensive to create because of legal fees and documentation costs and should not be undertaken just for the sake of having them.

Cheap Can Be Good

Two of my clients in Austin, both high-tech companies, are a study in contrasts.

One is a high-tech telecommunications company. The company paid me an enormous amount of money to come in and do what I do. I was thrilled with my fee. I was also thrilled with the facility where I taught. It had this white board on a track that I could pull anywhere in the room. It had a fabulous projection system. Two of the walls were floor-to-ceiling windows that looked out on the beautiful Texas hill country. I was in trainer heaven.

With the other client, I have a hard time getting a flip chart, much less a projection system or a white board on tracks. The rooms are cramped and noisy because their facilities are cheaply made. And a window? Forget it! The fees I make out there are nothing to write home about.

When the economy took its inevitable periodic nosedive a few years ago, my fancy telecommunications client was hit hard. The company was spending too much money on facilities, equipment, and meetings. I haven't worked out there in years, and the folks who hired me were laid off. In contrast, my cheap client is still going strong, and I do work with that company every month. Cheap can save you in hard times!

I remember reading an interview with the CFO of Southwest Airlines. He was asked why the company made it after 9/11 when other airlines were struggling. He said it was because Southwest Airlines always assumes that it is in a financial crunch, the company is never extravagant, and the company always makes decisions that are as frugal as possible. Interesting.

Cheap does have its price, however. As large organizations and American consumers continue to pressure suppliers to work cheaper and cheaper, it has negative consequences on our economy and our environment. But that is a discussion best had in *Economics Demystified*.

An engineering friend of mine works for a company that once was part of Motorola. He was expected to produce two or three patents a year. Motorola divested itself of his division in part because it did not respond quickly enough to market changes and changes in technology. Getting all those patents slowed it down.

Another thing about patents is that they are hard to sell or get value from. Technology changes so rapidly that your patent today may not be worth anything tomorrow. Or there may be only one or two folks who would want to buy your patent, and they may not be interested in buying it when you are looking for that extra cash.

Some industries are going to have heavy balances in some of the less liquid categories and can't help it. For instance, the airlines are going to have huge fixed asset or equipment balances and can't help it. Department stores might be forced to hold huge inventory balances and can't help it. (I feel that it is important to point out here that industry leaders are often the ones to break the mold. Walmart, the leader in retail, has minimized its inventory balances by essentially holding its entire inventory on consignment. If the product doesn't sell, Walmart doesn't pay.)

It is very important to know that you cannot compare balance sheets between industries. You can't compare, for example, an airline's balance sheet with the balance sheet of a department store. The comparison is just not meaningful.

For comparison sake, it is best to stay within the industry. But even that presents challenges because different businesses within the same industry have different business models.

Now look at the other side of the balance sheet. What kind of balance do you want to see in debt? You want it to be reasonable. You don't necessarily want to see zero debt. Debt can be a wonderful tool in many circumstances.

Again, back to your personal life. If you didn't have debt in terms of a home mortgage or a car loan, you couldn't live near enough to your job to get to work on time each morning. To live debt-free, you might have to live in the country in a trailer eating beanie-weenies every day—not a pretty picture.

Often, debt allows a company to expand and take advantage of opportunities it otherwise might have to pass up. So some debt is fine; we just don't want the burden to be too much to handle.

Now, down the balance sheet to equity. The balance for stock generally is fixed at the price that the shareholders paid for the stock on the first day of the company's inception. Occasionally, the company might issue more stock to finance growth or special projects.

Ideally, in a highly evolved company, the stock balance would be decreasing over time because the company was buying back its stock. This does several happy things. It increases the value of each remaining share of stock out on the market because there are fewer shares in fewer hands, and it concentrates control of the company into fewer hands. You end up with fewer people outside the company telling you how to run your business.

Finally, the figure for retained earnings, of course, should be healthy. However, if the company pays dividends, the shareholders may prefer that the company, instead of retaining earnings in the company, distribute the wealth to them. The ideal balance of retained earnings therefore depends on the philosophy of the organization. The company might prefer to share the wealth with the owners by paying dividends rather than keeping the money inside the company and using it to grow.

A Quickie Analysis

One of the most useful techniques for analyzing a balance sheet is to create a pie chart of each side. Very simple, very visual, and very informative.

What you do is take the left-hand side of the balance sheet—the assets—and total all the assets up. Let's say for simplicity's sake that total assets equal $100 million. Then you total up the liabilities and equity. It better also be $100 million. (If not, your balance sheet does not balance: You did something wrong.)

Now take each asset component and determine how much each one represents in relationship to the total. Let's say that cash is $20 million, inventory is $40 million, receivables are $30 million, and fixed assets are $10 million. Now you can create a simple pie chart showing the proportion of each of these items (Figure 2.8).

Looking at the pie chart, does this balance seem reasonable or wise? One key way to determine this is to compare this year's pie chart with pie charts from previous years. Is the pie chart looking better or looking worse? For instance, a decrease in inventory might make us smile. Why? Remember, inventory is not as liquid as cash—and we love cash.

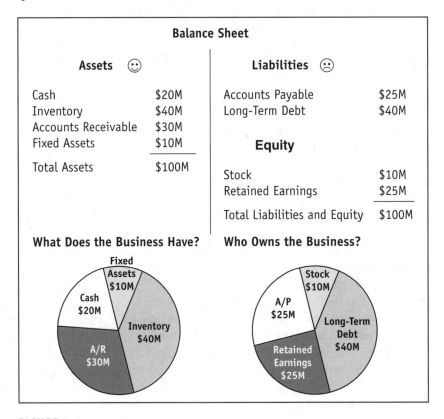

FIGURE 2.8 • Pie chart balance sheet. *(continued on next page)*

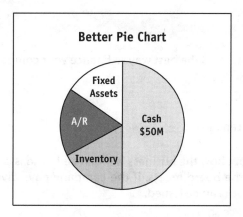

FIGURE 2.8 · Pie chart balance sheet. *(continued)*

On the other side of the balance sheet, we can do the same thing. Let's say that long-term debt is $40 million, accounts payable is $25 million, stock is $10 million, and retained earnings are $25 million. What would a better pie chart look like? Well, we might see a decrease in long-term debt, an increase in retained earnings, and a slight decrease in stock because the company is buying its stock back and retiring it.

Summary

The balance sheet is rich with important information about a business. It tells us where the organization got its money and what it did with it. It tells us who owns the business, whether the organization is fat or lean, and whether the organization is liquid.

QUIZ

1. **What, in general, is the best way to finance your company?**
   A. Bank loan
   B. Earnings
   C. Stock
   D. Venture capital

2. **This spells out how the business is organized, who is on the board of directors, how often the board meets, if the company pays dividends, and how many shares of stock can be issued.**
   A. The balance sheet
   B. Articles of incorporation
   C. Loan covenants
   D. Financial statements

3. **Some accountants like to see a large balance in working capital, but wise financial managers like to see a small working capital balance. Why?**
   A. It shows that you manage resources well.
   B. It shows that you have lots of cash.
   C. It shows that you have only long-term liabilities.
   D. It shows that you are debt-free.

4. **When talking about working capital, in which of the following do we want to have a large balance?**
   A. Accounts receivable
   B. Accounts payable
   C. Inventory

5. **Working capital = current assets − current liabilities. Which of the following is not a current asset?**
   A. Cash
   B. Accounts receivable
   C. Accounts payable
   D. Inventory

6. **If day-to-day cash needs are minimal, if receivables and inventory are minimal, and if payables are maximized, then working capital will be very small. True or false?**
   A. True
   B. False

7. **Assets** =
    A. liabilities plus cash.
    B. liabilities plus equity.
    C. liabilities plus net income.

8. **Busting the covenants is when you**
    A. ignore the classic accounting equation.
    B. run afoul of the agreement you made with the bank on a loan.
    C. stop tithing at church.

9. **Equity is a similar concept to**
    A. net working capital.
    B. net income.
    C. net worth.

10. **Factoring is when you sell your accounts payable to a third party. True or false?**
    A. True
    B. False

Chapter **3**

The Income Statement—A Focus on Earnings

The top four concerns of businesses are liquidity, profitability, growth, and financing. The income statement focuses primarily on profitability and growth.

CHAPTER OBJECTIVES

- Define profit
- Define cost terminology

The income statement has many aliases. Some call it the *P&L*, some the *profit and loss statement*. Governments are so opposed to the word *profit* that they call the income statement the *statement of revenues and expenditures*. I also have heard it called the *statement of earnings*.

Memorize This Formula!

What is common to all income statements, no matter what their name, is that they follow a very basic formula:

$$\text{Revenues} - \text{expenses} = \text{profit}$$

This makes perfect intuitive sense. Profit is what you have after you subtract expenses from sales revenue. Profit also has aliases. It is called *earnings, income,* and *net income*.

The income statement would be so simple if we had only three numbers: revenue, expenses, and profit. But, of course, we don't stop there. We want more information. The income statement is broken down into categories and subtotaled several times before we get to the final profit or net income figure. And the subtotals are focused primarily on segregating costs into categories.

To understand the subtotals, we need to first tackle some cost terminology.

Cost Terminology

Accountants are not happy just naming something a *cost*. It is useful to us to categorize and subcategorize costs. The two most common ways that we discuss cost center around the way a cost behaves and the way a cost is applied. Let's do the behavior breakdown first.

The Way a Cost Behaves

Costs can behave as variable, semivariable, or fixed. A *fixed* cost remains the same no matter how many units you produce or how many employees you have. It is stable. If we graphed it over a period of a year, it would look like this:

A good example of a fixed cost is rent. It stays the same no matter what month it is or how many units you produce.

A *variable* cost goes up and down depending on something else. It might vary with production or number of employees. If we graphed it over a period of a year, it might look like this:

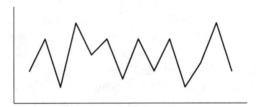

A good example of a variable cost is parts. The more products you manufacture, the more parts you need.

A *semivariable* cost is somewhere in between. It might be fixed for awhile and then jump, like this:

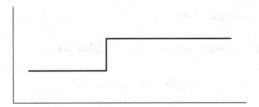

Or it might have a fixed component at its base and then vary on top of the fixed component, like this:

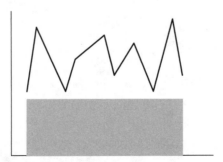

A good example of the first type of semivariable cost would be labor. If you employ six people, you are at the bottom level. As soon as you hire a new person, your cost jumps and stays high.

A good example of the bottom graph is electric utilities. You pay a fixed cost just to have the service turned on and then the usage changes month to month—a more variable behavior.

Now, all this is just shades of gray. A fixed cost—even rent—would look variable if you graphed it over a 10-year period. And if you compress the scale of your graph, a variable cost can look fixed.

So what should you take away from this? That there is no textbook definition of what qualifies a cost as fixed, variable, or semivariable. When someone starts talking this lingo with you, you need to ask him or her to clarify what costs he or she is lumping into what category. Folks have told me that component costs are fixed because they are the same per unit. This is one way of looking at it, but it does not take into account that you use varying amounts every day. So the caveat here is to be careful how you use and interpret this terminology. And you thought accounting was exact and precise? Surprise!

The Way a Cost Is Applied

The next way of discussing costs is by how they are applied to a product or service. The cost can be applied either directly to the product or service or indirectly.

Direct costs are costs that you logically and easily can trace to the creation of the product. Let's say that we are making birdbaths. The cost of the components (the wire and the cement) and the labor to create the birdbaths are direct costs. You can easily determine how much cement and wire go into each birdbath. You also can determine how many labor hours it took to mold and finish the birdbaths. Direct link, direct costs.

Indirect costs are all the other costs incurred in marketing, selling, and designing the product. Here is a partial list of items that might be considered indirect costs:

- Marketing
- Advertising
- Utilities
- Rent
- Travel
- Sales
- Legal
- Executive
- Security
- Accounting
- Auditing

- Packaging design
- Product research
- Reception

These costs are harder to trace directly to the product. For instance, if you have seven product lines and you asked members of the executive team how they contributed to each product line, you most likely would get a blank stare in return, or team members would say that they contributed to each product line equally. Of course, this isn't true.

So what we do in accounting to keep it simple is to allocate these indirect costs to the product using what we like to call an *indirect cost-allocation method*. Some companies call it a *burden rate*.

We take all the expenditures for the executive team and put them into what is called an *indirect cost pool* (a fancy way of saying a "lump of costs"). We then come up with a way to easily allocate them to the products or product lines. For instance, we might have allocated the costs based on volume of sales. Whichever product line generated the most sales got the largest chunk of the executive costs.

Is this fair and accurate? No. But it is easy for the accountant and normally it works.

So, if you are a project manager and are trying to sell a particular project, you might hear back from the accounting department that, in addition to the direct costs of your project, such as the new equipment and additional labor, you also must add in a burden rate. The accountants may say, "Yes, we understand that your project will cost the company $460,000, but we also want you to factor in an additional 20 percent to take into account organizational support." The extra 20 percent may push you right over the edge and make your project seem unprofitable.

Know that this burden rate or indirect cost-allocation rate is created by the accounting department and is subject to debate and change. The folks at one company I teach for seem to change both the rate and the components of their indirect cost allocation every six months. They keep refining it and adding different components or taking some out.

Something to be aware of here is that you may be able to argue successfully that your particular project should not be weighed down by all the costs the accountants calculated. If you ask the accountants for their allocation methods, you actually may be able to find some costs that should not be attributed to your project.

Now why do we go through all this rigmarole anyway? Why calculate the direct and indirect costs of creating a product or service? Because we want to make sure that we are making a profit on each sale. If we don't know the cost of our products or services, we might very well be selling them for less than it costs us to make them, and that would be bad.

Activity-Based Costing—Cost Accounting on Steroids

Activity-based costing (ABC) takes cost accounting to new levels of detail. The creators of ABC rightly argue that allocating cost based on production volume or dollar sales volume is not accurate or fair. They instead recommend that a detailed study be made of each function in the organization. In this study, all cost categories are scrutinized and their activities documented. The cost then is allocated based on activities, not volume—hence, the name *activity-based costing*.

Here is a rather silly example to show you how hard ABC has been for many organizations to implement. Back to our executive team example. The accounting department helps detail the activities of the executive team to better determine how to allocate costs. The executives document that they spent two hours on a conference call with management, two hours lunching with a key client, one hour responding to a request from a stockholder, one hour signing documents, and so on. This still might not get us any closer to coming up with a better allocation for the cost of the executive team to the product lines.

Some other costs are a bit easier. Take, for example, the cost of a supervisor in the manufacturing plant. We might have, using simpler cost accounting methods, allocated his time to all product lines based on volume. By studying his activities, we find that he spends more time every day working with a particularly troublesome product and the employees who manufacture it. In this way, we would uncover two pieces of information—one, that this troublesome product is taking up more time than we thought and therefore might need to be redesigned or even canned, and two, that if we decide to keep manufacturing the product, we might need to charge more for it because as it is, we might be selling it at a loss.

Now that we have covered the two main ways that accountants talk about cost—in terms of how cost behaves and the way cost is applied—we can look more closely at the income statement and the way it is broken out.

The Significance of Gross Profit Margin and Operating Profit Margin

Notice that the income statement (Figure 3.1) is subtotaled in two places before we get to the final profit figure.

The first subtotal is the result of taking sales and subtracting the cost of goods sold. This subtotal is called *gross profit margin*. I also have heard it called a variety of other things, so check out your own company's financials to uncover your company's terminology.

```
┌─────────────────────────────────────────┐
│           Income Statement                │
│                                           │
│   Sales                                   │
│   Less cost of goods sold                 │
│   ─────────────────────────────────────  │
│   Gross margin                            │
│   Less operating costs                    │
│   ─────────────────────────────────────  │
│   Operating margin                        │
│   Less taxes, other                       │
│   ─────────────────────────────────────  │
│   Net income or net profit margin         │
└─────────────────────────────────────────┘
```

FIGURE 3.1 · Income statement model.

The next subtotal is the result of taking gross margin and subtracting out operating expenses. This is called *operating profit margin*. This margin, too, has aliases, so check your own financials.

Where do you think direct costs go? In cost of goods sold or in operating expenses? Right! In cost of goods sold. So gross profit margin is the result of subtracting the direct costs of creating your product or service from total sales.

Indirect costs go in operating expenses. So operating profit margin is the result of taking both indirect and direct costs out of sales revenue.

This is the line that most of us need to pay attention to and manage—operating profit margin. It is the profit we garner from operating, from the day-to-day creation and sales of our product or service.

The items below this line generally are out of the manager's control—such things as taxes and the gain or loss on the sale of a business segment. These are called *nonoperating items* and are classified at the bottom of the statement. We put these at the bottom so that we can trend operating profit margin from year to year without any strange, nonrecurring, or unusual jumps.

For instance, I just read a company's financials that revealed a negative operating profit but a positive net income because of a gain on a foreign currency transaction. Will the company realize a gain on a foreign currency transaction next year? Who knows? Will the company be able to pull its operating profit out of the dumpster? We hope so.

The Income Statement Tells a Story about Profitability

Look at the information in Figure 3.2. The very bottom line—the net income—is the same for both years, but something happened in the second year that should raise our concern. The cost of goods, or the direct costs, went up by 10. Thankfully, we were able to cut operating expenses by enough to make up the difference.

Income Statement		
	01	**02**
Sales	100	100
Less Cost of Goods Sold	70	80
Gross Margin	30	20
Less Operating Expenses	20	10
Operating Margin	10	10
Less Taxes/Other	5	5
Net Income or Net Profit Margin	5	5

FIGURE 3.2 • Income statement trended percentage.

Now, instead of looking at those figures as dollars, look at them as percentages. It is always good practice to convert dollar figures into percentages. Both dollars and percentages tell a story. While you may be impressed with the sheer dollar size of the net income, you may be missing the story that it is only 5 percent of sales.

Still Struggling

Profit, Profit, Profit!

Yes, you are right. There isn't much point in having a business unless you get more out of it than you put into it. However, if all you care about is profitability, you will end up making some bad business choices. Profit is just one of the facets of a healthy organization. You also need to grow safely, remain liquid, maintain ready access to capital, realize that profit in cash, and I could go on.

The International Accounting Standards re-format the income statement to move profit off the bottom line of the income statement, making it a little harder to find. Investors and analysts often have unrealistic expectations regarding profitability—expecting double-digit growth in profits every year. A very rare company can achieve double-digit growth year after year, and to get there, a company may sacrifice overall health.

I remember many years ago seeing the grandson of Henry Ford on MSNBC warning that he was going to disappoint investors by retooling and rethinking his company. He would not be able to respond to Wall Street's demands for high profits. He said that he would not let his grandfather's company die on his watch. Ten years later, Ford was the only U.S. carmaker that didn't need a federal bailout. Long-term thinking demands a healthy balance between profit, profit, profit and other equally important concerns.

The P&L Tells Us What We Have Left

Try this analogy: Turn total revenues into a bar of Ivory Soap, and whittle the bar of soap to see how much you have left after you pay all your expenses. Your expenses whittle away at your revenue. Are you going to be left with a soap ball or with a generous hotel-sized bar of soap? How about a soap flake?

For instance, one high-tech manufacturer I work with has an income statement that breaks out as shown in Figure 3.3.

Dell Inc. Income Statement		
	Dollars	**%**
Revenues	41,444	100%
Cost of Goods	33,892	82%
Gross Margin	7,552	18%
Operating Expenses	4,008	10%
Operating Margin	3,544	9%
Other	899	2%
Net Income	2,645	6%

FIGURE 3.3 · Dell's income statement—fiscal year ending
January 30, 2004 (in millions).

So we start out with $41 billion in revenue. This is our total bar of soap. Now we take four-fifths of it to pay for cost of goods (82 percent). Ouch! We now have a hotel-sized bar of soap. We have 18 percent of our bar of soap left. Next, we take out operating expenses. This takes the remaining half and halves it again. Now we have half a hotel-sized bar of soap. After we take out taxes and other unusual stuff, we get to keep 6 percent of our bar of soap—a sliver of a bar of soap. But 6 percent of $41 billion is $2.6 billion—nothing to sneeze at.

EBIT and EBITDA

What are EBIT and EBITDA? These are hip little acronyms that are fun to pronounce. EBIT is pronounced "e-bit," and EBITDA is pronounced "e-bit-dah" (sounds like we're talking Latin!). EBIT stands for "earnings before interest and taxes." EBITDA stands for "earnings before interest, taxes, depreciation, and amortization."

These are just two more ways of cutting or subtotaling the income statement, very much like our gross and operating margins. For EBIT, you take the bottom line of earnings—the net income—and add back in interest and taxes. For

EBITDA, you take the net income and add back in interest, taxes, depreciation, and amortization.

EBITDA is a number that many organizations hold their managers to. If the EBITDA number makes targets, the managers are rewarded. This makes more sense than bonusing the managers on bottom-line net income because bottom-line net income is the result of factoring in a lot of costs that are not under the managers' control. Interest paid on debt is not generally under the control of front-line managers; they do not make decisions on how the organization is financed. Taxes, depreciation, and amortization are also not under the control of front-line managers.

So there are two more fancy acronyms you can use to impress your boss.

Summary

The income statement tells a story about profitability. It tells us how the organization earned revenues as well as which expenses whittled away at those revenues. Expenses on the income statement are described in terms of how they behave and how they are applied to the product or service.

QUIZ

1. Income statements focus primarily on
   A. liquidity and growth.
   B. profitability and financing.
   C. liquidity and financing.
   D. profitability and growth.

2. This is what you have when you add profit and expense.
   A. Revenues
   B. Net income
   C. Earnings
   D. Total cost

3. A variable cost may vary with levels of production. True or false?
   A. True
   B. False

4. Which of these is likely not categorized as a direct cost?
   A. Parts
   B. Raw materials
   C. Office security
   D. Labor

5. A good example of a fixed cost is
   A. materials cost.
   B. overhead labor costs.
   C. rent.
   D. utilities.

6. The income statement includes which of the following?
   A. Cash transactions
   B. Fixed asset purchases and long-term investments
   C. Revenues and expenses

7. If sales − cost of goods sold = A, and A − operating expenses = B, A and B are which of the following?
   A. Gross profit margin and net income
   B. Gross profit margin and operating margin
   C. Operating margin and net profit margin
   D. Net income and net profit margin

8. **This line item on the income statement generally is out of the manager's control.**
   A. Nonoperating items
   B. Net income
   C. Gross margin
   D. Revenue

9. **EBIT and EBITDA stand for earnings before interest and taxes and earnings before interest, taxes, depreciation, and amortization. To calculate EBIT, you take _____ and then add back interest and taxes.**
   A. revenues
   B. gross margin
   C. operating margin
   D. net income

10. **Governments call the income statement**
    A. the P&L.
    B. the revenue projection.
    C. the deficit indicator.
    D. the statement of revenues and expenditures.

Chapter **4**

The Cash-Flow Statement—Do We Have Enough for Payroll?

The cash-flow statement performs very much like your bank account statement at home. It tells you how much cash you had at the beginning of the month and how much cash you had at the end of the month. It summarizes how much cash you collected and how much cash you paid out.

CHAPTER OBJECTIVES

- Describe the purpose of the cash-flow statement
- Differentiate between cash and profit
- Classify cash flows into three categories

The cash-flow statement is often confused with the income statement. Some people figure that the final balance of cash will be the same number as your net income. This is never true when you use the accrual basis of accounting—and you probably do.

Cash versus Accrual Method of Accounting

The cash method of accounting is used by very few businesses because it takes such a simple view of transactions. Most of us use the accrual method of accounting.

The cash method of accounting works well if you have a very simple business. Let's take as an example a hot dog vendor on a college campus. Every weekday morning, the hot dog vendor wakes up, hitches her hot dog cart to the back of her truck, and drives over to Sam's Warehouse and buys hot dogs, buns, condiments, and sodas. She pays cash. She drives over to campus and sets up shop. She sells her hot dogs and sodas for cash. At the end of the day, she eats the leftovers. The next morning, she starts all over again.

The hot dog vendor's business is all about cash. She doesn't owe anyone money, and her customers don't owe her any money. There are no receivables and payables. Her business is very simple—unlike most businesses.

Most businesses operate with receivables and payables and keep track of their transactions using the accrual method of accounting. The accrual method records everything that happened in the business, whether or not it has an impact on cash.

You can make a sale and record it on your books but not collect payment in cash from your customer for 30-plus days. Using the accrual method, you accrue—or record—the income on your income statement. But nothing has happened over on the cash-flow statement. What you have just done is create an account receivable.

You also can incur an expense but not pay it in cash. For instance, when I do a training for a university, the university is getting the benefit of my services on the day that I do the training, but it won't pay me for a few months. (Universities are notoriously slow in paying their vendors.) So the university records an expense on the income statement for my fee and records an account payable. Again, there is no immediate impact on cash.

So, because of timing differences, the final net income—or the bottom line—on the income statement will never be the same as the ending cash balance on the cash-flow statement. Under the accrual method, you record things before they have an impact on cash (Figure 4.1).

```
┌─────────────────────────────────────┐
│         Cash-Flow Statement          │
│                                      │
│  Beginning Cash                      │
│  Plus Cash collected                 │
│  Less Cash paid                      │
│  ─────────────────────               │
│  Ending Cash                         │
│                                      │
└─────────────────────────────────────┘
```

FIGURE 4.1 • Cash-flow statement model.

A Real-Life Example of How Profit and Cash Differ

An engineer friend of mine once started a business with several of his engineer friends. They made global positioning systems and were geniuses in regard to the product. However, none of them knew how to run a business.

My friend was given the responsibility of keeping the books and records and negotiating contracts. His title was *Engineer in Charge of Finance*. (Do you smell trouble here?)

After much suffering, he came to me and confessed that his partners were upset with him and that he was worried that the business was going to fail. He said that his partners expected the net income on the income statement to be in the bank account, and they were very disturbed that they had to keep reaching into their own pockets to cover payroll. Indeed, on the income statement, the company was very profitable, but the company didn't have any cash. The partners thought that my friend had made a major error in the way he was keeping the books or that he had misplaced huge amounts of cash.

None of them understood the accrual method of accounting and the importance of cash flow.

The company was indeed very profitable because it had landed a juicy contract with the Coast Guard to equip its boats with global positioning systems. So, on the income statement, the company recorded a $400,000 sale. But does the Coast Guard pay fast? No! And the Coast Guard was paying in little bitty installments. My friend would install a global positioning unit on a boat and eventually bill the Coast Guard. The Coast Guard took several more months to pay. The cash was dripping in, not flowing.

Another mistake my friend made was to allow all his partners to buy whatever they wanted. He didn't think it was kind to place restrictions on what the partners purchased, so he left it up to their discretion to buy what they needed. They had a lovely company boat—to test the global positioning equipment, of course—and art in the boardroom, fancy test equipment, and way, way too much raw materials inventory. And because he wanted to have good credit with all his vendors, he paid every bill that hit his mailbox immediately. Ooh!

So no money was coming in and a whole lot was going out. No wonder he was out of cash.

I introduced him to the cash-flow statement and instructed him to watch it over the next few months. I asked him to plot out exactly what money was coming in each day and how much money was going out each day. In this way, he would know, ahead of time, whether he would have enough money to cover payroll.

At the moment, all his partners were tapped; they had no more money to contribute to the company. So he did what anyone would do and went to a bank for a loan. Any guesses what the bank told him? The bank turned him down because he was too much of a risk. Obviously, he knew nothing about running a business or cash flow.

Instead, the bank offered to factor his accounts receivable. *Factoring*, as explained in Chapter 2, is selling receivables to the bank or a factoring agent for cash. The buyer pays much less than the receivables are worth, but then the buyer is the one waiting for payment.

My friend walked away with 87 cents on the dollar for his Coast Guard receivable in cash and was happy to have it. The interest rate was steep, but he had the money the company needed to stay in business.

Unfortunately, as part of the factoring arrangement, the bank notified the Coast Guard to make future payments on the contract to the bank, not to my friend. This raised a concern with the Coast Guard, who knew that factoring was a high-cost, last-ditch effort to raise capital. The Coast Guard threatened to never do business with my friend again and to rescind its current contract. The Coast Guard didn't want to do business with a company that would not be able to support the product years down the line.

Fortunately, after much negotiating and pleading, my friend was able to save his contract and relationship with the Coast Guard. He watched cash flow like a hawk, and eventually, he and his partners sold the business to a competitor for millions of dollars. My friend is now happily retired and living on the Texas coast fishing.

The moral of this story is that profit and cash are different because of timing. The accrual method of accounting causes transactions to affect profit that won't affect cash for months to come.

The Cash-Flow Statement Is Relatively New but Is Having a Significant Impact on the Look of Future Statements

The cash-flow statement was added to the set of required financial statements because of the savings and loan crisis of the 1980s. The savings and loan banks were recording all these wonderful loans on their income statements and puffing up their bottom-line profits but were not collecting on those loans or realizing the income in cash. Eventually, their lack of cash took them under.

So the Financial Accounting Standards Board (FASB) added the cash-flow statement so that we know whether income actually was ever realized in cash—a very important piece of information in any business.

Unfortunately, the FASB made a big boo-boo (in my opinion) when it finally wrote the rules regarding the cash-flow statement. The FASB gave accountants an option on the way they present the cash-flow statement—and accountants almost always opt for the format that is less user friendly but easier to create.

Until the International Financial Reporting Standards (IFRS) are fully integrated (the date is up in the air as of this 2011 writing), accountants can choose between the direct presentation method and the indirect presentation method. The direct presentation method is akin to our simple model shared at the beginning of this chapter. It simply lists the money that came in and the money that went out. To follow the IFRS, organizations must use the direct method. This is my favorite method—so bravo international accounting community! However, accountants complain that it causes them too much work, so they usually use the indirect method.

As a matter of fact, the basic format of the direct cash-flow statement is replicated in the balance sheet and income statement under the new standards. So, the cash-flow statement was, in essence, ahead of its time and innovative. More about the IFRS later in this chapter.

For those of us still stuck in the 1980s (as am I, with my Stevie Nicks hair and New Wave music tendencies!), the indirect method is still in use. The indirect method reconciles net income to cash. So, instead of listing how much was collected and how much was paid out, it uses reconciling language—such as net increase in payables and net decrease in inventory. Even accountants have a hard time reading and interpreting the indirect method statement, so if it's Greek to you, don't be too hard on yourself.

Figures 4.2 and 4.3 give examples of the direct and indirect methods of cash-flow statements.

The Direct Method Statement of Cash Flows

Cash Flows from Operating Activities
Inflows
Cash from customers
Outflows
Cash paid to suppliers
Other expenses paid

Cash Flows from Investing Activities
Purchase of plant

Cash Flows Provided by Financing Activities
Sale of stock

Change in cash

FIGURE 4.2 • Direct cash-flow statement.

Indirect Method Statement of Cash Flows

Cash Flows from Operating Activities

Net income
Adjustments to reconcile income
Depreciation
(Increase) decrease in A/R
(Increase) decrease in inventory
Increase (decrease) in A/P

Cash Flows from Investing Activities
Purchase of plant

Cash Flows Provided by Financing Activities
Sale of stock
Change in cash

FIGURE 4.3 • Indirect cash-flow statement.

From either of these statements, the user-friendly direct method or the easier-to-create indirect method, you can garner some interesting information about an organization.

Still Struggling

An Increase in Accounts Receivable Is a Negative Cash Flow—Huh?

The operating section of the cash-flow statement either uses direct descriptions of cash flows, such as "cash collected from customers," or more indirect descriptions, such as "increase in accounts receivable." Direct language is used when presenting a direct method cash-flow statement. The other language, "increase in accounts payable," is cloudy and indirect and thus is presented in a style called the *indirect method*. The indirect method of presentation even messes with my head, and I am an accountant!

On the indirect method cash-flow statement

- An increase in accounts receivable will be presented as a negative number. This means that your accounts receivable balance is higher than it was last year at this time. The word *increase* makes you think that this might be a good thing, and it isn't if your sales volume has not increased as well.
- An increase in inventory will be presented as a negative number. This means that your inventory balances are higher than they were last year. Again, if your sales volume is going up, this is reasonable. But if not, it could mean that you are stocking up on cash-draining inventory, which generally is not considered to be a good thing.
- An increase in accounts payable will be presented as a positive number. This means that your accounts payable balance is larger, which means that you are holding onto your money longer and taking longer to pay your vendors. If this corresponds to an increase in sales volume, great. If not, you have to wonder if the company is having a hard time paying its bills or whether it is being cruel to its vendors or both.

I am glad to report that the IFRS favors use of the direct method. As we will discuss in later chapters, though, not everyone will adopt these standards. So you still may see the cloudy, indirect method offered in the statements you read and analyze.

Classifying Cash Flows into Three Categories

What the cash-flow statement does that your bank statement doesn't do is categorize the amounts that you collected and the amounts that you paid. Your bank account statement only lists the check numbers and deposit dates; it doesn't tell you what all those figures were for.

Both the direct and indirect methods divide cash flows into three categories:

- Operations
- Financing
- Investing

Let's talk about each of these in turn.

Operating Activities

The operations section gives us an idea of how much cash the organization generated in its day-to-day delivery of its products and services. This number can and should be compared with the operating income on the income statement. If operating income and operating cash flow are vastly different, you need to start asking some tough questions. It might mean that the organization is recording sales that will never be collected in cash. Ooh.

Cash *inflows* from operating activities include

- Cash receipts for the sale of goods or services
- Cash receipts for the collection or sale of operating receivables (receivables arising from the sale of goods or services)
- Cash interest received
- Cash dividends received
- Other cash receipts not directly identified with financing or investing activities

Cash *outflows* for operating activities include

- Cash payments for trade goods purchased for resale or use in manufacturing
- Cash payments for notes to suppliers or trade goods
- Cash payments to other suppliers and to employees
- Cash paid for taxes, fees, and fines
- Interest paid to creditors
- Other cash payments not directly identified with financing or investing activities

Financing Activities

The financing category tells us how much cash was generated by debt or equity financing. Saying it another way, the financing section details the cash flows between the organization and the folks who help to finance the organization through debt and equity.

An interesting twist here is that interest used to repay debt is not included in the financing category; it is included in the operating category. Remember:

At the very beginning of this book I said that accounting is just a set of rules about how to keep records. Not everything is intuitive or sensible. You are just going to have to accept this one and move on!

Cash *inflows* from financing activities include

- Cash proceeds from the sale of stock
- Cash receipts from borrowing
- Cash receipts from contributions and investment income that donors restricted for endowments or for buying, improving, or constructing long-term assets

Cash *outflows* from financing activities include

- Cash disbursed to repay principal on long- and short-term debt
- Cash paid to reacquire common and preferred equity instruments
- Dividends paid to common and preferred stockholders

Investing Activities

The last category is investing. And, as you might expect, this section of the cash-flow statement details how much cash the entity made and used in making investments in other entities such as the purchase of stocks or bonds of another entity. What you might not expect is that this category includes the purchase and sale of productive assets such as manufacturing equipment. This is, from the profession's perspective, an investment in the company's future and should not be classified under either operations or financing.

Cash *inflows* from investing activities include

- Collections of principal on debt instruments of other entities
- Cash proceeds from the sale of equity investments
- Cash received from the sale of productive assets

Cash *outflows* from investing activities include

- Cash paid to acquire debt instruments of other entities
- Cash payments to buy equity interest in other entities
- Disbursements made to purchase productive assets

In Chapter 17 we examine a cash-flow statement for two competitors.

What Stories Does the Cash-Flow Statement Tell You?

Although the format of the cash-flow statement is nowhere near as straightforward as the formats of the balance sheet and the income statement, you still can glean some important information from it.

One key story you can derive from the cash-flow statement is how the company is generating its cash. Is it from providing goods and services (my favorite method), from selling equity in the company or incurring debt, or from investment activities? I would love to see a company generating plenty of cash from day-to-day operations with minimal reliance on external financing.

The cash-flow statement also gives us a sense of how the organization uses its money. Where do the priorities of the company lie? Is it in growth mode, spending large sums on equipment, or is it selling off its equipment? Does it like to distribute its wealth to owners, or does it use its wealth to spur further growth?

We also can see how liquid the organization is. How much cash does it have at the end of the year, and how does this compare with previous years? Cash-flow statements are usually presented for the current year and two previous years.

The key question the cash-flow statement answers for us is, "Is the net income reported on the income statement ever realized in cash?" If the operating income figure on the income statement and the operating cash figure are miles apart, you need to ask some tough questions. It may be that the entity is inflating income or deflating expenses—or both.

IFRS

As of this writing in 2011, the United States is working to adopt the International Financial Reporting Standards (IFRS) for financial statement presentation. Some major corporations who have an international presence have already adopted the standards. But small business, from my informal survey, is largely unaware that the look and some content of financial statements are changing.

I like the new disclosures the international standards require because I admire transparency in accounting information.

And now that we have seen the format of all three financial statements—the balance sheet, the income statement, and the cash-flow statement—I can tweak them a little bit without frustrating you—I hope!

Please realize that I am working with the same general ledger data, but I am just putting those data in a different outfit—something more chic with an international flare.

The Names Have Been Changed

Two of our core financial statements are getting new names under the IFRS:

- The balance sheet now must be called the *statement of financial position.*
- The income statement now must be called the *statement of comprehensive income.*

The cash-flow statement is still, conveniently called the *cash-flow statement.*

Categories on Each Statement Match

The statements now will be easier to tie together because they will have similar categories of items. The cash-flow statement's three categories—operating, investing, and financing—are used in each statement.

Figure 4.4 shows what the new balance sheet looks like.

BUSINESS	
Operating	
Receivables	13,600
Less: allowance for bad debts	(400)
Inventory	5,200
Prepaid expenses	3,800
Short–term assets	22,000
Property, plant, and equipment	6,800
Less: accumulated depreciation	(1,800)
Goodwill	4,000
Intangibles (net)	12,200
Long–term assets	21,200
Accounts payable	(3,800)
Accrued liabilities	(11,200)
Short–term liabilities	(15,000)
Accrued long–term liabilities	(1,000)
Long–term liabilities	(1,000)
Net operating assets	**27,400**
Investing	
Available for sale assets (short–term)	400
Investments in subsidiaries (long–term)	1,200
Total investing assets	1,600
NET BUSINESS ASSETS	**29,000**
FINANCING	
Financing assets	
Cash	28,600
Total financing assets	28,600
Financing liabilities	
Dividends payable	(600)
Short–term debt	(2,800)
Short–term financing liabilities	(3,400)
Long–term debt	(14,200)
Total financing liabilities	(17,600)
NET FINANCING ASSETS	**11,000**

FIGURE 4.4 • Statement of Financial Position

(Continued)

INCOME TAXES	
Short-term	
Income taxes payable	(1,600)
Long-term	
Deferred income taxes	2,100
NET INCOME TAX ASSET	**500**
DISCONTINUED OPERATIONS	
Assets held for sale	4,000
Liabilities related to assets held for sale	(1,600)
NET ASSETS HELD FOR SALE	**2,400**
NET ASSETS	42,900
EQUITY	
Share Capital	(9,000)
Retained Earnings	(32,050)
Accumulated other comprehensive income	(1,850)
TOTAL EQUITY	**(42,900)**

FIGURE 4.4 · *(Continued)*

Please notice that the balance sheet doesn't balance anymore. Underneath the fancy new outfit are mostly the same old data, and the data do balance if you add liabilities and equity up and compare the sum with assets. I think the standard setters realized, correctly, that whether or not the financial statements add up is a minor concern. What matters is where the organization's resources are tied up; this new format does a much better job answering that question.

Figure 4.5 shows what the new income statement looks like.

BUSINESS	
Operating	
Sales–wholesale	20,000
Sales–retail	**56,800**
Total revenue	76,800
Cost of goods sold	
Materials	(27,000)
Labor	(5,600)
Overhead	(200)
Change in inventory	**1,200**
Total cost of goods sold	(31,600)
Gross profit	45,200

FIGURE 4.5 · Statement of Comprehensive Income   *(Continued)*

Selling expenses	
Commissions	(1,000)
Advertising	(8,800)
Other	**(5,400)**
Total selling expenses	(15,200)
General and administrative expenses	
Compensation	(3,000)
Rent	(1,000)
Depreciation	(1,800)
Other	**(9,200)**
Total G&A	(15,000)
Other operating income (expense)	
Loss on disposal of assets	(3,200)
Other	(1,400)
Total other operating income (expense)	(4,600)
Total operating income	10,400
Investing	
Dividend income	200
Equity in earnings of sub	**400**
Total investing income	600
TOTAL BUSINESS INCOME	**11,000**
FINANCING	
Interest income	2,000
Total financing asset income	2,000
Interest expense	(3,000)
Total financing liability expense	(3,000)
TOTAL NET FINANCING EXPENSE	**(1,000)**
INCOME TAXES	
Income tax expense	(2,600)
Net profit from continuing operations	7,400
DISCONTINUED OPERATIONS	
Loss on discontinued operations, net of tax	(450)
NET INCOME	**6,950**
OTHER COMPREHENSIVE INCOME	
Unrealized loss on securities, net of tax	(150)
TOTAL COMPREHENSIVE INCOME	**6,800**

Please notice that the income statement differentiates between business income and comprehensive income. This is another brilliant move because the user will be less prone to look at just the bottom line and instead be encouraged to verify that the business is healthy and profitable by looking at business income.

As you probably realize, I am simplifying the complexity of this undertaking and the changes that accountants are going to have to make to comply. This is *Accounting Demystified*, not *Accounting Explained in So Much Detail You Lose Interest*, after all. For more information on where this effort is currently and to review the more nuanced aspects of this change, please check out the AICPA's (American Institute of Certified Public Accountants) Web site on the subject: www.ifrs.com.

Summary

The cash-flow statement tells us whether the organization has enough money to stay in business, and it also tells us where the organization got this money.

QUIZ

1. The final balance of cash always matches net income with the accrual method. True or false?

   A. True
   B. False

2. Cash inflows from investing activities include

   A. cash proceeds from the sale of equity investments in other entities.
   B. cash paid to acquire the debt instruments of other entities.
   C. cash proceeds from the sale of stock.

3. A company with good profits does not necessarily have a healthy balance of cash. Why?

   A. Because of double-entry accounting
   B. Because of timing
   C. Because of credit
   D. Because of dividend payments

4. A sale that has not yet been collected in cash is

   A. an accounts receivable.
   B. an accounts payable.
   C. a fixed asset.
   D. a long-term liability.

5. Under IFRS, what method must be used to present the cash-flow statement?

   A. Direct presentation method
   B. Indirect presentation method
   C. Cash method
   D. Accrual method

6. Cash flow is divided into three categories, they are operations, investing, and

   A. credit.
   B. financing.
   C. receipts.
   D. receivables.

7. The cash-flow statement can tell you

   A. how a company is generating its cash.
   B. how the organization uses its cash resources.
   C. how liquid the organization is.
   D. whether the income reported on the income statement is realized as cash.
   E. all the above.

8. **Cash dividends received are classified as**
   A. cash inflow from operating activities.
   B. cash inflow from financing activities.
   C. cash inflow from investing activities.

9. **Cash paid to reacquire common and preferred equity instruments is classified on the cash-flow statement as**
   A. cash outflow from investing activities.
   B. cash outflow for operating activities.
   C. cash outflow from financing activities.

10. **The indirect method cash-flow statement has line items that disclose the increase or decrease in working capital items such as inventory, receivables, and payables. True or false?**
    A. True
    B. False

Chapter **5**

How the Financial Statements Are Related

Remember that the balance sheet is the "mother of all financial statements" and that the income statement and cash-flow statements are babies. A transaction may hit only two statements or it may affect all three.

CHAPTER OBJECTIVE

- Demonstrate how the income statement, cash-flow statement, and balance sheet are related

How the Income Statement Links to the Balance Sheet

The income statement is the detail on how earnings were generated. The basic formula of the income statement is

$$\text{Revenues} - \text{expenses} = \text{profit}$$

Please don't ever forget this formula. If I ever meet you on the street and you tell me that you've read this book, I'll be asking you for this formula!

So all that matters for the income statement are transactions that are considered revenue and expenses. It doesn't matter when cash was affected. It doesn't matter when you buy a fixed asset or incur a long-term debt. Those items belong on the cash-flow statement and the balance sheet, respectively.

The final net income figure on the income statement (the proverbial *bottom line*) is added to retained earnings on the balance sheet. Let me repeat this concept another way. The income statement (Figure 5.1) is linked to the balance sheet (Figure 5.2) through the retained earnings figure.

Income Statement
Sales
Less cost of goods sold
Gross margin
Less operating costs
Operating margin
Less taxes, other
Net income or net profit margin

Balance Sheet	
Assets	**Liabilities**
Cash	Accounts Payable
Investments	Long-Term Debt
Accounts Receivable	
Inventory	**Equity**
Fixed Assets	
Intangibles	Stock
	Retained Earnings

FIGURE 5.1 • Income statement—net income.   **FIGURE 5.2** • Balance sheet—retained earnings.

How the Cash-Flow Statement Links to the Balance Sheet

For the cash-flow statement (Figure 5.3), all that matters is what happened to cash. It is the detail of the item on the balance sheet called *cash*. It doesn't matter whether you made a sale but haven't collected payment in cash yet. It doesn't matter whether you incurred an expense but haven't paid it in cash yet. The income statement accrues for these things; the cash-flow statement ignores transactions until they have an impact on cash.

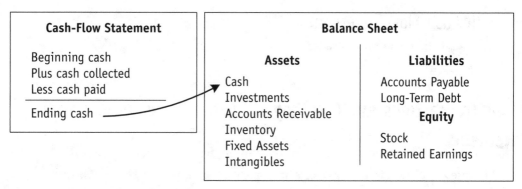

FIGURE 5.3 · Cash-flow statement.

What Each Financial Statement Tracks

Remember, the balance sheet is the "mother of all financial statements." It tracks all the big categories of items.

Balance Sheet

The balance sheet keeps track of all the assets the business holds:

- Cash
- Investments
- Accounts receivable
- Inventory
- Fixed assets
- Intangibles

The balance sheet tracks the amounts the business owes other people:

- Accounts payable
- Long-term debt

The balance sheet tracks the equity the owners have in the business:

- Stock
- Retained earnings

The Income Statement

The income statement tracks only

- Revenues
- Expenses

The Cash-Flow Statement

The cash-flow statement tracks only

- Cash

Simple Transactions and How They Affect the Three Key Financial Statements

Before I get into discussing debits and credits, I want you to get a sense of how simple transactions affect the three key financial statements—a bird's-eye view, if you will.

Let's say that you make cement birdbaths, and you have an inventory of 100 in stock. Each birdbath costs you $20 to make. So your total balance in inventory on the balance sheet is $2,000.

Cash Sale

Today you were lucky enough to sell two birdbaths to a bird enthusiast for $60 cash. What happens to your financial statements?

First, go to the income statement (Figure 5.4) because you made some income. You record revenue of $60 and realize an expense of $40 ($20 per birdbath). This increases your net income by $20.

Income Statement	
Sales	60
Cost of Goods	40
Gross Profit	20
Operating Expenses	0
Operating Profit	20
less Taxes/Other	0
Net Income	20

FIGURE 5.4 • Income statement.

Next, go to the cash-flow statement (Figure 5.5). Cash goes up by $60.

Cash-Flow Statement	
Beginning Cash	
+ Cash Collected	60
–Cash Paid	0
Ending Cash	+60

FIGURE 5.5 • Cash-flow statement.

Now go fill out the balance sheet (Figure 5.6).

Balance Sheet

Assets ☺		Liabilities ☹	
Cash	+60	Accounts Payable	
Accounts Receivable		Long-Term Debt	
Inventory	–40		
Fixed Assets		**Equity ☺ or ☹**	
Intangibles			
		Stock	
		Retained Earnings	+20
	+20		+20

FIGURE 5.6 • Balance sheet.

Cash goes up by $60. Inventory goes down by $40. Retained earnings go up by $20.

Does your little balance sheet balance? Yes, miraculously! This crazy double-entry system works.

On the left side of the balance sheet, the asset side, you increased one asset—cash—by $60 and reduced another asset—inventory—by $40. This leaves you with a total increase on the left side of the balance sheet of $20.

On the other side of the balance sheet, you increased retained earnings by your net income for $20.

Now each side of the balance sheet has gone up by $20. The transaction flowed through the financial statements and altered them appropriately.

Credit Sale: Part One

Now let's make this a bit more complicated. Let's instead say that you made a sale on credit. You don't get to collect the cash right away.

I'm also going to change the numbers a little bit. Let's say that this time you sell 100 birdbaths to a local nursery on credit. The nursery takes the birdbaths and agrees to pay you for them in 30 days.

Now what happens to the financial statements?

First, go to the income statement (Figure 5.7) because you made a sale. Revenues increase by 100 times the $30 selling price, or $3,000. Then you realize an expense for the birdbaths of $20 per birdbath, or $2,000. Revenues of $3,000 less expenses of $2,000 equal an increase in net income of $1,000.

```
                Income Statement

        Sales                    3,000
        Cost of Goods            2,000

        Gross Profit             1,000
        Operating Expenses           0

        Operating Profit         1,000
        less Taxes/Other             0

        Net Income               1,000
```

FIGURE 5.7 · Income statement.

What happens on the cash-flow statement (Figure 5.8)? Nothing! The cost of manufacturing the birdbaths hit the cash-flow statement months ago, so it has already been accounted for. No cash changed hands today, so the cash-flow statement stays dormant.

```
        Cash-Flow Statement

        Beginning Cash
        + Cash Collected
        – Cash Paid

        Ending Cash
```

FIGURE 5.8 · Cash-flow statement.

What happens on the balance sheet (Figure 5.9)?

```
                        Balance Sheet

            Assets    ☺                    Liabilities   ☹

    Cash                             Accounts Payable
    Accounts Receivable    +3,000     Long-Term Debt
    Inventory             – 2,000
    Fixed Assets                      Equity        ☺ or ☹
    Intangibles

                                      Stock
                                      Retained Earnings    +1,000
                         +1,000                            +1,000
```

FIGURE 5.9 · Balance sheet.

You increase accounts receivable by $3,000 for the amount the nursery owes you. You decrease inventory by $2,000 for the birdbaths sold. You increase retained earnings by $1,000.

Same scenario as last time. Assets on the left side of the balance sheet are increased by $1,000 ($3,000 less $2,000), and equity on the right side of the balance sheet is increased by $1,000. Whew! You balance again.

The Drawbacks of Accepting Credit

In early 2011, Target offered me a card that would give me a 5 percent discount on every purchase. It wasn't a credit card but instead allowed Target to extract payment right out of my bank account. Target wants to avoid paying credit card processing fees and collect its cash right away.

I met a CPA who worked for American Express in the 1990s. Her job was to negotiate with Walmart and Sam's to get them to accept American Express cards. Do you remember shopping at Sam's and having to pay by cash or check, period? No credit was accepted. American Express promised Walmart that it would waive any processing fees and eliminate the traditional three-day wait for payment.

Aren't the processing fees how the credit card companies make money? Well, it's not the only way. They also make money when consumers, like me, shop at Walmart and put $150 on our cards and let it ride for a few months. American Express also charges me an annual membership fee and, until I got my act together with automatic bill pay, an occasional late fee.

The only time that you should accept credit is when you fear that you might lose the sale by demanding cash. Cash is best. It is so superior to credit that you might even offer customers a discount for using it, à la Target. Otherwise, you are allowing your customers to get the economic benefit of your products and services without paying for them until later.

Credit Sale: Part Two

In a month's time, you collect payment from the nursery, a $3,000 check. What happens to the financial statements now?

First, you ask if the income statement (Figure 5.10) is affected. No, it is not. You didn't make a new sale or incur a new expense. This is all old, already-recorded revenues and expenses, so you skip the income statement.

FIGURE 5.10 • Income statement.

You go directly to the cash-flow statement (Figure 5.11). Cash is increased by $3,000.

Cash-Flow Statement	
Beginning Cash	
+ Cash Collected	3,000
– Cash Paid	
Ending Cash	+3,000

FIGURE 5.11 • Cash-flow statement.

On the balance sheet (Figure 5.12), you increase cash by $3,000 and decrease accounts receivable by the amount you just collected, $3,000. This gives you a net effect of zero on the left side. Nothing happened on the right side, so you're okay.

Balance Sheet

Assets ☺		**Liabilities** ☹	
Cash	+3,000	Accounts Payable	
Accounts Receivable	– 3,000	Long-Term Debt	
Inventory			
Fixed Assets		**Equity** ☺ or ☹	
Intangibles			
		Stock	
		Retained Earnings	
	0		0

FIGURE 5.12 • Balance sheet.

How are you holding up? If this is just enough detail for you or maybe almost too much detail, I suggest that you skip the next chapter because it goes into debits and credits—the super detail of accounting.

Purchasing a Fixed Asset

Now let's say that you want to purchase a $5,000 color copier to help you create ads and brochures to market your birdbaths. What happens to your financial statements now?

Well, it depends on whether you capitalize the copier or expense it.

Expensing

When you buy a fixed asset, such as a copier, you might have the option of expensing it rather than capitalizing it. Generally, if an asset costs less than $5,000, many large organizations will forgo recording it as a fixed asset and instead just expense it entirely.

So, if you decide to expense a $5,000 copier, it would flow through the financial statements in this way:

Income statement (Figure 5.13): Expenses are increased by $5,000, and net income is reduced by $5,000.

Income statement	
Sales	
Cost of Goods	———
Gross Profit	
Operating Expenses	−5000
Operating Profit	
less taxes/other	———
Net Income	−5000

FIGURE 5.13 · Income statement—expense the copier.

Cash-flow statement (Figure 5.14): Cash is reduced by $5,000.

Cash-Flow Statement	
Beginning Cash	
+ Cash Collected	
– Cash Paid	−5,000
Ending Cash	−5,000

FIGURE 5.14 · Cash-flow statement—expense the copier.

Balance sheet (Figure 5.15): Cash is reduced by $5,000, and retained earnings are reduced by $5,000—you balance!

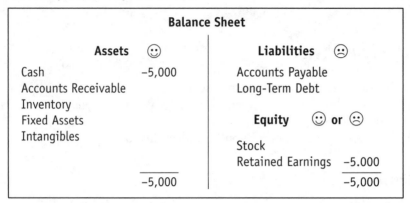

FIGURE 5.15 · Balance sheet—expense the copier.

Capitalizing

If you decide instead to capitalize the copier—or, in simpler terms, record the copier as a fixed asset—here is what would happen to your financial statements on the day of purchase.

Income statement (Figure 5.16): No effect.

Income Statement

Sales
Cost of Goods
_____

Gross Profit
Operating Expenses
_____

Operating Profit
Less taxes/Other
_____

Net Income

FIGURE 5.16 · Income statement—capitalize the copier,
day of purchase.

Cash-flow statement (Figure 5.17): Cash is reduced by $5,000.

FIGURE 5.17 · Cash-flow statement—capitalize the copier,
day of purchase.

Balance sheet (Figure 5-18): Cash is reduced by $5,000, and fixed assets are increased by $5,000.

Balance Sheet

Assets ☺		**Liabilities** ☹
Cash	−5,000	Accounts Payable
Accounts Receivable		Long-Term Debt
Inventory		
Fixed Assets	+5,000	**Equity** ☺ or ☹
Intangibles		
		Stock
		Retained Earnings
	0	0

FIGURE 5.18 • Balance sheet—capitalize the copier, day of purchase.

Later in the year, the income statement is affected because if we capitalize the copier, we necessarily have to depreciate it.

Still Struggling?

What Is Depreciation?

It's a way of accounting for the loss in value of an asset. Depreciation allows businesses to acknowledge two truths about fixed assets.

First, fixed assets, as they age, generally are not worth as much as you paid for them; they lose value. Second, fixed assets are useful to the organization for more than one year. If you expense a fixed asset, you are in essence saying that you have used up its value in the year that you bought it. Most fixed assets are used for several years. A car, a computer, a piece of manufacturing equipment, and a copier all have value longer than a year.

So let's say that you've decided that the copier has a life of five years. If you used straight-line deprecation (the most simplified depreciation method possible: Divide the cost of the asset by its useful life), you would recognize that you used up one-fifth, or $1,000, of its value every year.

So, on your financial statements, at the beginning of the year, cash is down by $5,000, and fixed assets are up by $5,000. Now, at the end of the year, you recognize that part of the asset has been used up, and thus the value of the copier is less. So you record depreciation expense. Key word—*expense*. Go to the income statement (Figure 5.19) and increase expenses by $1,000, thereby reducing net income by $1,000.

Income Statement	
Sales	
Cost of Goods	————
Gross Profit	
Operating Expenses	−1,000
Operating Profit	
less Taxes/Other	————
Net Income	− 1,000

FIGURE 5.19 • Income statement—
capitalize, end of year.

What happens on the cash-flow statement (Figure 5.20)? Nothing. Cash was affected when you paid cash for the copier. Depreciation is what some fancy accountants call a *noncash expense*. It reduces net income without reducing cash in later years—years two through five in our example.

Cash-Flow Statement
Beginning Cash
+ Cash Collected
− Cash Paid
Ending Cash

FIGURE 5.20 • Cash-flow statement—
capitalize, end of year.

On the balance sheet (Figure 5.21), you now need to decrease fixed assets by the $1,000 in depreciation and decrease retained earnings by the $1,000 decrease in net income flowing over from the income statement.

So at the end of year 1, your balance sheet reports

- A decrease in cash of $5,000
- An increase in fixed assets of $4,000 ($5,000 copier less $1,000 depreciation)
- A decrease in retained earnings of $1,000

Assets ☺		Liabilities ☹	
Cash	−5000	Accounts Payable	
Accounts Receivable		Long−Term Debt	
Inventory			
Fixed Assets		**Equity ☺ or ☹**	
copier	5000		
less accumulated depreciation	−1000	Stock	
total fixed assets	4000	Retained Earnings	−1000
Intangibles			
Total Assets	−1000	Total Liabilities and Equity	−1000

FIGURE 5.21 · Balance sheet—capitalize, finalize end of year

So the balance sheet again balances. Assets are decreased by $1,000, and retained earnings are decreased by $1,000. No matter what you do, you check to see that your balance sheet balances.

At the end of year 2, your balance sheet (Figure 5.22) shows

- A decrease in fixed assets of $1,000 for depreciation
- A decrease in retained earnings of $1,000 for depreciation expense

Assets ☺		Liabilities ☹	
Cash		Accounts Payable	
Accounts Receivable		Long−Term Debt	
Inventory			
Fixed Assets	−1000	**Equity ☺ or ☹**	
Intangibles			
		Stock	
		Retained Earnings	−1000
Total Assets	−1000	Total Liabilities and Equity	−1000

FIGURE 5.22 · Balance sheet—end of second year

So, depreciation, in effect, spreads the impact of your purchase on income and retained earnings over a longer time period. When you expense the purchase, it reduces retained earnings (a.k.a. *net income*) by $5,000 in one pop. When you depreciate it, you reduce retained earnings and net income by just a little—$1,000 in our scenario—each year (Figures 5.23 and 5.24).

Income Statement

Sales	
Cost of Goods	
Gross Profit	
Operating Expenses	−1,000
Operating Profit	
less Taxes/Other	
Net Income	− 1,000

FIGURE 5.23 · Income statement—capitalize the copier.

Income Statement

Sales	
Cost of Goods	
Gross Profit	
Operating Expenses	−5000
Operating Profit	
less Taxes/Other	
Net Income	−5000

FIGURE 5.23 · Income statement—expense copier

You really don't have a choice with most purchases.

In our example, we pretended that the organization had a choice between expensing and capitalizing a fixed asset. In most cases, this is not true. The Internal Revenue Service (IRS) has a lot to say about whether an item should be depreciated and for how long.

Many organizations opt to expense small purchases, let's say under $5,000 or $2,500, but when you get up into the tens of thousands of dollars, the IRS frowns on expensing. You see, when you expense a fixed asset purchase, this reduces the taxable income you report to the IRS and the taxes you pay in the year of purchase.

So, for tax reasons, expensing fixed asset purchases is often more attractive. But if you are trying to please the shareholders, capitalizing and then depreciating fixed assets is more attractive because you decrease your income only a little each year.

Now are you ready to talk about debits and credits? Hold onto your hats— Part II is going to get very detailed!

Summary

All transactions affect the balance sheet, but whether they affect the cash-flow statement and/or the income statement depends on their nature and timing. The balance sheet is the super summary of the general ledger and is the mother of the cash-flow and income statements, which are more limited in scope.

QUIZ

1. Net income is linked to the balance sheet through
   A. cash.
   B. accounts receivable.
   C. retained earnings.
   D. stock.

2. In the second year of depreciating an asset, cash is not affected. True or false?
   A. True
   B. False

3. Whether you made a sale or incurred an expense, the cash-flow statement ignores these transactions until they affect cash. Which statement accrues all expenses whether or not they affected cash?
   A. The accounts receivable statement
   B. The cash-flow statement
   C. The income statement
   D. The balance sheet

4. Imagine that you manufacture birdbaths for sale. What kind of sale is represented by the following transaction? Cash goes up, inventory goes down, and retained earnings go up.
   A. Cash sale
   B. Credit sale

5. When you capitalize something, it means that you
   A. record it as an expense.
   B. record it as a liability.
   C. realize it in cash.
   D. record it as a fixed asset.

6. Imagine that you manufacture bird feeders for sale. What kind of sale is this? Net income up, accounts receivable up, inventory down, and retained earnings up.
   A. Cash sale
   B. Credit sale

7. You buy a fixed asset, and the following happens to your financial statements: On the income statement, expenses increase and net income is reduced. On the cash-flow statement, cash is reduced. On the balance sheet, cash is reduced and net income is reduced. Did you capitalize or expense that asset?
   A. Expensed it.
   B. Capitalized it.

8. Fixed assets lose value as they age, and fixed assets are useful to the organization for more than one year. What concept of accounting allows for businesses to acknowledge these two truths about fixed assets?

   A. Expensing
   B. Depreciation
   C. Leasing

9. The cash-flow statement only addresses what happens to

   A. revenues and expenses.
   B. fixed asset purchases.
   C. cash.

10. The balance of accounts payable is reported on which statement?

    A. Balance sheet
    B. Income statement
    C. Cash-flow statement

Part II

An Overview of Common Accounting Reports

Chapter **6**

Different Systems, Different Reports

So far we have been talking about the general ledger and entries into the general ledger. The general ledger system is often called the *financial accounting system*. But the general ledger is not the only system that businesses use for counting. There are several other tools that businesses use to track financial results, including cost accounting systems and budget systems.

CHAPTER OBJECTIVES

- Explore the purpose of cost accounting systems
- Introduce several common types of budgets

These systems may or may not be linked to the general ledger. To get the systems to talk to each other, you have to invest in the technology that lets you do that.

Some organizations are reluctant to take advantage of technology—either because of the cost or because they don't like change. One of those "If it ain't broke, don't fix it" sort of attitudes. In 2004, a city manager of a small East Texas town told me that his bookkeeper is still keeping the city's records by hand! *Whoa!* There are all sorts of levels of financial record-keeping savvy.

Let me introduce you to a few other systems that track financial data that you might run into:

- Cost accounting
- Budgetary accounting
- Tax accounting

Cost Accounting Systems

Cost accounting systems track how much it costs to create, market, sell, and distribute a product or service.

Imagine a cost accounting system for the manufacture of a television set. The system would track how much each component of the TV cost, as well as how many labor hours went into assembling the TV. The system also would track how many labor hours it took to quality-test the TV and how many TVs were rejected and reworked. It would track how much it cost to package the TV and how quickly the TV was shipped out to the customer. I could go on and on.

How It Differs from the General Ledger

This is much more detail than included in the general ledger. The general ledger is kept at a higher level. The general ledger or the financial accounting system will record how much the team made in salaries for the week, but it won't break down that Bob spent 15 hours assembling big-screen TVs and 23 hours on portable TVs or that 8 of Bob's portables were rejected because of poor quality. The general ledger only indicates that Bob was paid (for his shoddy work!).

Some accounting software has modules that allow a company to link the cost accounting data to the general ledger and some do not. Don't be surprised if you have an entirely different team at your company tracking cost accounting data than you have tracking your general ledger transactions.

One of the major criticisms aimed at financial accountants is that their information isn't timely. By the time the information is posted to the general ledger, compiled, reviewed, and reported, the team that needs to make decisions based on that information has moved on. A good cost accounting system will be in real time, giving the frontline team daily or sometimes even hourly information on its progress.

The state of Texas puts every single transaction (except payroll) online in real time. Talk about transparency in government!

Standard Cost and Other Cost Terminology

You may hear the terms *standard cost, indirect cost, direct cost, variable cost,* and *fixed cost* used by a cost accountant. I described what indirect costs, direct costs, variable costs, and fixed costs are in Chapter 3 in our discussion of the income statement.

Standard cost is the cost to which accountants hold the manufacturing team. It's the standard against which actual costs are compared. For instance, the cost accountant may determine that it takes 1.2 hours of manufacturing labor to create a TV. This becomes the standard by which all manufacturing efforts are measured. The cost accountant will track deviations from standard cost and require the manufacturing team to explain the variations.

Cost accountants are the folks who allocate the indirect costs discussed in Chapter 3 to products and services. They also may work with activity-based costing (ABC) (Figure 6.1).

It Costs Time and Money to Be Cool

One key rule to keep in mind in looking at your organization's accounting systems is this:

The frequency and accuracy of information cost time and money.

You have to decide what the information is worth to you.

For instance, I consult with a high-tech manufacturer. A few years ago, the company decided that cost, marketing, and sales information were key to its success and that it needed such information every day, not once a month.

On its internal computer information system, its intranet, the company has a multilayered Excel spreadsheet that contains up-to-the-hour information on hundreds of key metrics.

Any decision maker can access this spreadsheet to find out how many units of each product sold that day and how they were sold—by Internet, by phone, or by third parties. The decision maker can find out how much each unit cost and how much margin was generated on each product line. He or she also can determine whether the company is on track with daily, weekly, and quarterly goals and diagnose what to do if the company misses its targets.

Some of the data are fed into the Excel spreadsheet from the general ledger system, some from the cost accounting system, some from the phone system, and some from the Internet sales tracking system. Creating and updating the spreadsheet was and continues to be a huge investment of time and money on the part of the company. So why does the company do it? Because the up-to-date information lets the company change course and respond to market demands and competitors' actions within a day—not within a month or a quarter. Information is power!

Smith Industries, Bill of Activities					
Part Number: XYZ-123 Planned Volume: 10,000					
			Driver Attributes		
Activities	Drivers	Cost per Driver	Value Added	Nonvalue Added	Total Cost
Unit Level Activities					
Cut to Length	Direct Labor Hours	$11.44	$11.44		$11.44
Rough Turn	Direct Labor Hours	$11.06	$11.06		$11.06
Centerless Grind	Machine Hours	$11.20	$11.20		$11.20
Batch Level Activities Set-Up					
Cut to Length	Set-up Hours	$9.75		$9.75	$9.75
Rough Turn	Set-up Hours	$9.76		$9.76	$9.76
Centerless Grind	Set-up Hours	$10.25		$10.25	$10.25
Inspection					
Cut to Length	No. of Inspections	$0.14		$0.14	$0.14
Rough Turn	No. of Inspections	$0.20		$0.20	$0.20
Centerless Grind	No. of Inspections	$0.25		$0.25	$0.25
Material Movement Receive Material					
Freight in	Pounds	$0.22		$0.22	$0.22
Direct Material	Pounds	$5.20	$5.20		$5.20
Product Level Activities Engineering					
Process Evalution	Engineering Hours	$1.25	$1.25		$1.25
Marketing Direct Product					
Quotation	Proposal Hours	$10.75	$10.75		$10.75
Totals			**$50.90**	**$30.57**	**$61.47**

FIGURE 6.1 · Example of a cost accounting report.

Budgets

A *budget* is a translation of the plans of an entity into financial terms.

Why Have a Budget?

Budgets are simply a management tool that lends focus and accountability to an organization.

Focus

Creation of a budget can focus your organization on what is important. Periodic monitoring of the budget gives an organization feedback on whether it is operating according to plan and *staying* focused on what is important.

For instance, at the beginning of the year, a hospital might decide that in order to improve its services, it needs to renovate the emergency room and buy several key pieces of medical equipment. If by midyear the renovation has not been done and the purchases have not been made, a monthly budget report will highlight the fact and alert management that action needs to be taken.

Accountability

A budget is also useful if you want to hold managers and staff accountable for their decisions and actions. A budget is nothing if it is not monitored, used, and taken seriously.

I once worked for an organization that spent two months creating a budget on several multipage Excel spreadsheets that filled a large binder. At the beginning of the year, every manager was given a copy of the binder—and that was the last anyone ever looked at it!

We spent what we spent, we sold what we sold, and no one was held accountable to it. You can imagine the respect that the managers had for the budget. *None!* In this case, it wasn't even worth having one. If you are using a budget right, you report periodically about whether or not the team is spending or generating revenue according to plan.

You Might Not Need a Budget

Some organizations don't have budgets and don't really need them.

After I had taught a budgeting seminar to CPAs a few years ago, a participant approached me and asked for my help. She was the controller of a rapidly growing Las Vegas business. Her company made the Plexiglas screens that decorate slot machines. (You know how they change every few years—one year the slots are decorated like Monopoly games and the next year it's "Viva Elvis!")

The owner of the company had attended a seminar for entrepreneurs recently. At the seminar, the instructors told him that he needed a budget. He had no idea what he would do with a budget, but he instructed his controller to go figure out how to pull one together for his company.

I stayed overnight in Vegas and met with the controller and her boss the next day. After a long discussion, I recommended that the organization not develop a budget right away. This owner did not want to keep managers informed about what they were spending; in fact, he wanted to keep it secret. He didn't want to create a year-long projection of revenues and expenditures because he was growing so fast that his projections would have been way off.

What he needed and wanted was better cost data. He needed to know how much it cost him to make each screen so that he could be sure to sell it at a high enough price. So the budgeting tool wasn't for him at all. His controller was relieved and promised to compile the cost data the owner was looking for.

A Variety of Budget Types

There are also a variety of budget formats and philosophies. Each organization keeps its budget in its own unique way. I teach budgeting to CPAs and have them draw the format of their budget on flip-chart paper and share it with the rest of the class. The variety of formats and content is striking. There is no right or wrong approach.

Here are three common approaches: line-item budgets, performance-based budgets, and zero-based budgets.

Line-Item Budgets

Many businesses use a line-item budget. The *line-item budget* is simply a list of all the revenue and expenditure categories applicable to the entity. And the categories usually mimic general ledger accounts. So it is the easiest for accountants to generate, use, and tie back to actual transaction results. Figure 6.2 shows an example. Just because the accountants understand how the budget is structured doesn't mean that the managers who use the budget do, however. A line-item budget is designed more for accountants than the leaders of an organization.

Salaries	$300,000
Office Supplies	$5,000
Travel	$24,000
Equipment Maintenance	$2,000
New Equipment Purchases	$3,000
Utilities	$2,000
Phone	$6,000
Other	$1,000
Total	**$343,000**

FIGURE 6.2 · Line-item budget.

Performance-Based Budgets

My favorite type of budgeting is *performance-based budgeting*. It takes more time to create than a line-item budget because it uses the terminology and language of the managers who must follow the budget. It links the manager's strategic plan to the budget. Performance-based budgeting also links performance metrics to dollars. So, instead of just asking a department whether it spent within limits, it also asks whether the department performed its functions well. Figure 6.3 shows an example of a performance-based budget.

Goals/Strategies	1994	1995
A. Goal: INDEPENDENT LIVING: To assist Texans who are blind live as independently as possible consistent with their capabilities.		
A.1. Objective: Increase the number of consumers achieving their independent living goals. **Outcome:** Percent avoiding a dependent living environment	93%	93%
A.1.1. Strategy: To provide a statewide program of development independent living skills. **Outputs:** Number of adults trained	$3,695,823 3,079	$3,439,224 3,184
A.2. Objective: Increase the number of children who achieve their habilitative goals.		
A.2.1. Strategy: To provide habilitative services to blind and visually impaired children. **Outputs:** Number of children receiving services	$2,761,465 8,988	$2,869,277 9,266
B. Goal: MAINTAIN EMPLOYMENT: To assist Texans who are blind or visually impaired to secure or maintain employment in careers consistent with their skills, abilities, and interests.		
B.1. Objective: Increase the number of successfully employed consumers. **Outcome:** Percent of consumers successfully rehabilitated with improved economic self-sufficiency	86.5%	86.5%
B.1.1. Strategy: To provide vocational rehabilitation services to persons who are blind or visually impaired. **Outputs:** Number of consumers served	$28,351,959 12,888	$28,259,959 12,831

FIGURE 6.3 · Performance-based budget.   *(Continued)*

Goals/Strategies	1994	1995
B.1.2. Strategy: To provide translation services leading to successful transition from school to work. **Outputs:** Number of students successfully completing program	$1,311,082 72	$1,781,861 72
B.1.3. Strategy: To provide employment opportunities in the food service industry for persons who are blind or visually impaired. **Outputs:** Number of consumers employed	140	145
B. Goal: Continuation of 1993 salary increase	720,302	
Grand Total, Commission for the Blind	$39,060,851	$38,307,441

FIGURE 6.3 · *(Continued)*

Still Struggling?

A Family of Metrics

Performance metrics tell the user what the organization did with the budget it was allocated. In order to be meaningful, though, performance metrics need to be presented as part of a family of metrics.

For instance, what if I told you that your local county health clinic vaccinated 1,500 low-income children last year? Are you happy with this number? It is hard to tell because it is not presented in context.

What if I told you that there were 90,000 low-income children in the county who were eligible for the vaccinations? Now you aren't very happy.

But what if I went on to describe that the county dedicated only one nurse to the task owing to budget constraints and that she worked only on Tuesday and Thursday mornings? What if I told you that it takes 30 minutes per vaccination and that each vaccination costs $300? Now the 1,500 looks like a miracle number. The 1,500 is what is commonly called an *output metric*, and the constraining metrics are called *input* or *process metrics*.

The real question, however, is whether the program worked and the kids and the community benefited from the vaccinations. For this, we'd find out whether illness in the community was reduced as a result of the vaccinations. This is the Holy Grail of metrics, also known as an *outcome metric*. It is hard to get to but very, very compelling.

Zero-Based Budgets

Zero-based budgeting is also a popular budget philosophy. In *zero-based budgeting*, you assume that you don't exist anymore and must build the budget up from that *zero base*.

For example, let's say you are a copy center inside a large corporation and that the corporation has instituted zero-based budgeting this year. Currently, you have seven employees who process 3,600 copying projects for the company during the year, you take up 800 square feet of space, and you maintain $230,000 worth of equipment.

To implement a zero-based budget, you assume that you don't exist any more. You don't automatically get to keep all those wonderful people and stuff. You must justify every employee you have, every project you take on, every square foot of space you consume, and every piece of equipment you maintain. You don't just get to have the same budget as you did last year and add a new person and 500 new projects.

You propose your output at three levels—maximum, moderate, and minimum. The proposals are documented and put in a stack with every other division's proposals. The leaders of the company rank the proposals in terms of importance. The proposals at the bottom of the stack may not receive funding because they are low priority, and the organization may be out of resources to fund them.

Jimmy Carter popularized this type of budget in his run for the presidency in the 1970s. It was designed to cut government waste—to make all government programs justify their existence and not assume that they would continue along the same path year after year after year.

Personally, I think this kind of deconstruction of a program or department may work once or twice, but you shouldn't make people go through this every year. It might cut the fat out of your organization once, but employees will not take it seriously if they are made to do it every single year. It can be very tedious.

Budgetary Information Is Maintained Apart from the General Ledger

Usually the budgetary information is tracked and reported separately from the general ledger. Many accountants create and maintain the budget using completely different software than the general ledger software. Many accountants use an Excel spreadsheet.

Accountants often keep these systems separate because of the difference between the general ledger and the budget in recognizing a revenue or an expense. The budget might recognize a commitment to spend money even though the general ledger may not have recognized an expenditure yet.

For instance, you might contract with a management consultant in a $3,600 contract. The budget will recognize that $3,600 of the budget for consultants has been consumed, but the general ledger may not pick up the $3,600 as an expense until the consultant bills you.

Some general ledger systems allow you to input the yearly budget figures into the general ledger, and then, as transactions are posted to the system, the budget is updated and reports can be generated. The line items on the budget must match the line items in the general ledger for this to work.

Tax Accounting

How the Internal Revenue Service (IRS) says transactions are to be treated and the way generally accepted accounting principles (GAAP) treat them are often different. In my simple little business, I have a woman who keeps my general ledger and creates my financial reports and another woman who does my taxes. The skills and knowledge to do each are quite different.

GAAP don't change that often. Tax code does. Tax accountants have to keep very fresh on the latest laws that affect their clients' tax returns.

Here is an example: When a company entertains its clients, the entire cost is posted to the general ledger. However, in many instances, the IRS will let the company write off, or recognize, only a percentage of the cost of entertainment. Employee benefits, depreciation, and travel expenses are just a few of the differences between taxes and GAAP accounting, and they are treated differently in the general ledger than they are in the tax records.

My taxable net income in my business never looks the same as the net income my bookkeeper reports on my income statement.

Another factor to add to this complicated situation is state taxes. Some states charge personal income tax; some don't. Almost all states have some sort of corporate income tax, although it might be named something less direct. For instance, in Texas, corporate income tax is called a *franchise tax*. Then there is the issue of sales taxes, estate taxes, and property taxes. Taxes, taxes, taxes!

This is why many major corporations have an entire team of tax specialists who concern themselves only with the tax implications of different decisions. For instance, when a company is looking at whether to lease or buy an asset, the managers look at the effect on the financial statements, but they also look at the short- and long-term effects on taxes. No one likes to pay more taxes than necessary. Because we are all familiar with the beautiful IRS forms, I won't include one here.

Summary

Financial accounting systems are just one aspect of the financial systems necessary to manage an organization. Managers often need cost accounting systems and budgets to stay on track throughout the year.

QUIZ

1. You own Big Mountain Bikes, and you want to know how much all the parts of a bicycle cost, how long it takes to put a bicycle together, and how much it costs to package, ship, and sell a bike. And you want to know this as the bikes are being built, not three months later. Which accounting system would you likely use?
   A. Cost accounting
   B. Financial accounting
   C. Budgetary accounting
   D. Tax accounting

2. At Big Mountain Bikes, you want a budget that links the manager's strategic plan with the budget and that integrates key metrics. What kind of budget will you use?
   A. Line-item budget
   B. Performance-based budget
   C. Zero-based budget

3. Big Mountain Bikes has done well for a few years, but now you want to get the fat out of the organization. You want to create a budget that reevaluates the necessity of every project, product, square foot of space, employee, and piece of equipment. What budget will you use?
   A. Line-item budget
   B. Performance-based budget
   C. Zero-based budget

4. Big Mountain Bikes is now a multimillion-dollar company. You are bigger, the quality is better, but you build the bikes at the same rate as always—one bike every two hours. So you buy an automated welding machine, and you are able to finish bikes in one and one-half hours. Now you expect your workers to build all the bikes this fast. What would an accountant call this new expectation?
   A. Standard cost
   B. Indirect cost
   C. Direct cost
   D. Fixed cost

5. One of the major criticisms aimed at financial accountants is that their information isn't
   A. accurate.
   B. timely.
   C. proper.
   D. added correctly.

6. This budget is simply a list of all the revenue and expenditure categories applicable to the entity?
   A. Line-item budget
   B. Performance-based budget
   C. Zero-based budget

7. The two main benefits of a budget are that budgets enhance
   A. timeliness and responsiveness.
   B. planning and accuracy.
   C. control and accountability.
   D. focus and accountability.

8. A budget helps you to focus on
   A. cost.
   B. what's important.
   C. purchases.
   D. feedback.

9. How the IRS and GAAP treat transactions is often
   A. the same.
   B. different.

10. When a company entertains its clients, only a portion of the cost is posted to the general ledger. True or false?
    A. True
    B. False

Chapter *7*

Quarterly and Annual Financial Reports— A Tour

Every publicly traded company in the United States must publish several financial reports each year and submit them to the Securities and Exchange Commission (SEC). Only public companies are required to create financial statements and submit them to the SEC. A privately or closely held corporation often doesn't have to create financial statements for anyone! Its financials are no one else's business unless the company is seeking a loan or additional equity financing.

CHAPTER OBJECTIVES

- Review the major components of an annual financial report
- Highlight components of financial statements that should be scrutinized

Four of the most commonly used reports are the three 10-Qs—quarterly reports—and the single 10-K—an annual report summarizing the entire fiscal year.

The SEC dictates the disclosures that each section could contain and the title of each section. The SEC even tells corporations what size and type of font to use in the reports. The emphasis is on standardization and comparability of data. The SEC doesn't want any corporation looking any fancier than any other. Creativity is not valued here; all that matters is information.

The 10-K

SEC documents are about as detailed as many corporations get—especially in their disclosures to outsiders. As discussed in Chapter 6 on cost accounting, budgeting, and taxation, there is a wealth of information that companies can generate and use internally to make financial decisions. If you are on the outside of an organization, you can't get your hands on any of these data.

So for this chapter, we are going to explore what we can get our hands on—the SEC 10-K document. (You also can get your hands on the 10-Q, but it covers only a quarter, not a year.) I suggest that you get one of these now so that you have it next to you as we work through this chapter. I will include a few sample pages here and there, but it really would be best if you got one of the forms yourself.

How Do You Get a 10-K?

How do you get a 10-K? Pick one of your favorite publicly traded companies, and go on to its Web site and look for a menu option called "Investor Relations." Usually under this tab you will find a PDF (Adobe) file of the latest 10-K. You can view, download, or print this document and have it handy as you read this chapter.

If you want someone else to print it, you can call or e-mail the investor relations department and ask for a copy. The people there will be happy to mail you one—although this might take a little while. You also can log onto the SEC homepage (www.sec.gov) and find the filings for every company that is traded publicly.

Annual Reports Are Not 10-K's

I need to point out here that an annual report and a 10-K are not the same thing. You may have encountered an annual report as an investor. An annual report is a magazine-style document. It is attractive, colored, and printed on slick paper. A good 70 percent of the document can be dedicated to marketing and giving the reader a warm, fuzzy feeling about the company. The real financial data usually are included near the back of the report and don't last for more than 20 pages. ("No need to bore the investor with financial data" is the philosophy here, I guess.)

I definitely prefer a 10-K to an annual report as a document to analyze the financial results of a company. First of all, the 10-K often provides 40 or more pages of good financial data and information on the company. It doesn't include any marketing hooey (not that I don't like marketing, mind you! I almost majored in it) or pictures of sweet puppies, gorgeous women, or small children to distract you. It is just information, information, information.

So, go ahead and enjoy an annual report, but for real decisions, consult the 10-K or the latest 10-Q.

Subscriptions Will Deliver Financial Info to You

If you have the money to pay for financial data, you can subscribe to any of a number of financial services that will take the financial data published by a company and compile it, analyze it, and sometimes even make conclusions for you. These services will save you a lot of the grunt work. One such company, which is based in Austin, Texas, is Hoover's (www.hoovers.com). For a monthly subscription fee, Hoover's will provide you with a wealth of financial information on a variety of companies.

The Cover of the 10-K

On the cover of your 10-K, make sure to notice the date of the fiscal year end. I have the Dell 10-K in my hands. I read about a quarter of the way down the page that Dell's fiscal year end is January 29, 2010 (Figure 7.1).

This is important for me to know for several reasons. First, I can use this date to gauge how old this information is. As I write, it is June, so this information is already five months old. Dell has published several 10-Qs since then, and if I were doing a serious analysis, I would look at them to modify and update my understanding of what is going on in the business.

Second, I need to be aware that Dell's competitors do not necessarily have the same fiscal year end. While Dell's 10-K is called the 2010 10-K because it is published for the fiscal year ending January 29, 2010, the bulk of the report pertains to calendar year 2009. One of Dell's competitors, Apple, has a September fiscal year end. Apple's 10-K that contains the bulk of its 2009 results is

UNITED STATES
SECURITIES AND EXCHANGE COMMISSION
Washington, D.C. 20549

Form 10-K

(Mark One)

☒   ANNUAL REPORT PURSUANT TO SECTION 13 OR 15(d) OF THE SECURITIES
EXCHANGE ACT OF 1934

For the fiscal year ended: January 29, 2010

or

☐   TRANSITION REPORT PURSUANT TO SECTION 13 OR 15(d) OF THE SECURITIES
EXCHANGE ACT OF 1934

For the transition period from_____ to_____

Commission file number: 0-17017

Dell Inc.

(Exact name of registrant as specified in its charter)

Delaware	**74-2487834**
(State or other jurisdiction of incorporation or organization)	(I.R.S. Employer Identification No.)

One Dell Way, Round Rock, Texas 78682
(Address of principal executive offices) (Zip Code)
Registrant's telephone number, including area code: **1-800-BUY-DELL**

Securities registered pursuant to Section 12(b) of the Act:

Title of each class	Name of each exchange on which registered
Common Stock, par value $.01 per share	The NASDAQ Stock Market LLC (Nasdaq Global Select Market)

Securities Registered Pursuant to Section 12(g) of the Act: None

Indicate by check mark if the registrant is a well-known seasoned issuer, as defined in Rule 405 of the Securities Act. Yes ☒   No ☐

Indicate by check mark if the registrant is not required to file reports pursuant to Section 13 or Section 15(d) of the Act. Yes ☒   No ☐

Indicate by check mark whether the registrant (1) has filed all reports required to be filed by Section 13 or 15(d) of the Securities Exchange Act of 1934 during the preceding 12 months (or for such shorter period that the registrant was required to file such reports), and (2) has been subject to such filing requirements for the past 90 days. Yes ☒   No ☐

Indicate by check mark whether the registrant has submitted electronically and posted on its corporate Web site, if any, every Interactive Data File required to be submitted and posted pursuant to Rule 405 of Regulation S-T during the preceding 12 months (or for such shorter period that the registrant was required to submit and post such files). Yes ☒   No ☐

Indicate by check mark if disclosure of delinquent filers pursuant to Item 405 of Regulation S-K is not contained herein, and will not be contained, to the best of registrant's knowledge, in definitive proxy or information statements incorporated by reference in Part III of this Form 10-K or any amendment to this Form 10-K. ☐

Indicate by check mark whether the registrant is a large accelerated filer, an accelerated filer, a non-accelerated filer, or a smaller reporting company. See the definitions of "large accelerated filer," "accelerated filer," and "smaller reporting company" in Rule 12b-2 of the Exchange Act. (Check One):

Large accelerated filer ☒	Accelerated filer ☐
Non-accelerated filer ☐ (Do not check if smaller reporting company)	Smaller reporting company ☐

Indicate by check mark whether the registrant is a shell company (as defined in Rule 12b-2 of the Act). Yes ☐ No ☒

Approximate aggregate market value of the registrant's common stock held by non-affiliates as of July 31, 2009, based upon the closing price reported for such date on the NASDAQ Global Select Market . . . . $22.7 billion

Number of shares of common stock outstanding as of March 5, 2010 1,957,725,915

FIGURE 7.1 · Dell 10-K, page 1, 2010.

termed the 2009 10-K. So essentially, the Dell 2010 10-K and the Apple 2009 10-K cover the same period.

Also notice on the bottom of this report that the aggregate market value of common stock held by the public is listed. This information allows you to get at the market value of the stock on a particular date—information you can't get anywhere else in the report. (This is the one of the few times that historical value is not used in a disclosure.) If you divide this number by the number of shares outstanding directly below it, you will be able to determine the market price per share as of the last day of the fiscal year. This number is used frequently by shareholders performing an analysis of the financial statements. Dell's aggregate market value is $22.7 billion, and the number of shares is 1,957,725,915. This tells us that the market value of each share on January 29, 2010, is roughly $11.59.

Still Struggling?

What Is This SEC?

The Securities and Exchange Commission (SEC) is a federal agency with a broad mission—to protect investors, maintain fair markets, and facilitate capital formation. One arm of the SEC reviews documents that publicly held companies are required to file, including

- Registration statements for newly offered securities
- Annual and quarterly filings (Forms 10-K and 10-Q)
- Proxy materials sent to shareholders before an annual meeting
- Annual reports to shareholders
- Documents concerning tender offers (a *tender offer* is an offer to buy a large number of shares of a corporation, usually at a premium above the current market price)
- Filings related to mergers and acquisitions

The SEC has created over 150 forms to help those participating in the market stay transparent. The SEC encourages filers to make available all information, whether it is positive or negative, that might be relevant to an investor's decisions.

Part I of the 10-K

The SEC dictates what will be included where in the financial statements. Part I of Dell's 10-K will contain similar information to Part I of Johnson & Johnson's 10-K, for example.

Part I is an overview of the business. It tells what the company is about, what sorts of products it sells, and how it goes about doing business. The subtitles in Dell's Part I are

- General
- Business Strategy
- Operating Business Segments
- Products and Services
- Geographic Operations
- Competition
- Sales and Marketing
- Patents, Trademarks, and Licenses
- Government Regulation and Sustainability
- Backlog
- Trademarks and Service Marks
- Available Information
- Employees
- Executive Officers of Dell
- Risk Factors

Why all this background information? Because it is important to educate the investor. Let's pretend that you are a retired schoolteacher and that you got a tip from your son-in-law that you should invest in a computer company. You know nothing about computer companies, but you know to read the 10-K! This section of the 10-K is very valuable to you. It allows you to compare the operating philosophy of Dell with the operating philosophies of its competitors. You can then decide which computer company you feel more affinity for or have more faith in.

Let's backtrack a bit and talk about a few of these subtitles and sections in Part I.

Business Strategy

Here is an excerpt from Dell's 10-K:

The key tenets of Dell's business strategy are:

Dell built its reputation as a leading technology provider through listening to customers and developing solutions that meet customer needs. We are focused on providing long-term value creation through the delivery of customized solutions that make technology more efficient, more accessible, and easier to use.

This is a great section that allows you to set the company apart from its competitors and is a must-read. It will shape your expectations of financial results.

The fiancial statements are there to tell a story: These statements constitute the "Once upon a time" section of the 10-K. Don't skip them.

Executive Officers

If you are a serious Wall Street investor, reading this list of the folks on the management team is like reading a basketball team's roster. You know who these men and women are, you are aware of their track records, and you have opinions as to whether they can win the game and make a profit.

You might read that the leaders of the company are recent graduates of a prestigious business school with no hands-on experience with business. Nothing against Harvard, but real business experience counts for something. If you had faith in these young leaders and knew them personally, then you could comfortably make the choice to invest. If you did not have this personal faith, a disclosure of their professional experience and credentials, as is detailed in this section, might cause concern.

Item 1A—Risk Factors

This is another must-read section of the 10-K. Once, I succumbed to greed. (Okay, I have succumbed more than once, but I'm only going to tell you about a single instance in this book!) Remember the late 1990s when stock prices were flying high? I have a friend who is an attorney in Dallas, and he and his wife were trading stocks on a daily basis. They'd buy something in the morning and sell it by the afternoon. They had $50,000 or more to play with in the market, and several times I talked with my friend right after he and his wife had doubled their money.

I was thrilled for them and envious. I wasn't getting those fabulous returns on my investments, and I didn't feel like I had the luxury of "playing" with the money I had invested for my retirement.

One day, near the end of the stock market party, I received a gift of $10,000 from a relative. I decided to invest about half of it in the stock market. I called my lawyer friend and asked him where I should put it. "Who is hot, and how can I make a quick buck?" I asked.

He said that if he advised me, I could never complain to him if I lost money. I agreed, and he advised me to invest in a high-tech Internet-related software company. Do you know where this is going? I plunked my money down and watched over the next few weeks as my stock became virtually worthless. The next time that I receive any gift of money, I'm buying a couch!

After I had lost it all, I received the company's 10-K in the mail. As I thumbed through and started to laugh and cry, I read Item 1A, and it was laughably awful. It said such things as

- "We only have one customer, and if this customer does not buy our product, we are toast."
- "We only have one product. We do not have a patent for this product. If a competitor steals our idea, we are toast."
- "We have not finished developing our product and are not sure that it will meet the customers' needs. If it doesn't work, we are toast."

I am paraphrasing, of course, but you get the idea: My investment was toast.

Always read this section of the financial statements. The company is obligated and required to disclose anything it knows that could negatively affect its financial results. You, the investor, have to decide whether the risks that the company discloses in this section are palatable to you. For instance, Dell's 10-K says, "Weak global economic conditions and instability in financial markets may harm our business. . . . "This is the "a rising tide lifts all boats" sort of statement and in my mind is not a cause for alarm about Dell—although it does cause me to be uneasy about the whole world!

What is the moral of this story? Read the 10-K before you invest in a company. If it is a good company, it won't matter that much that you waited a few hours, days, or weeks to invest.

Item 2—Properties

This item tells about the real estate holdings of the company. This will disclose the physical location of the company's operations. Company headquarters may be in the United States, but the company may have manufacturing operations in South America. A shifting or unstable political environment in any country could have serious implications for the company.

Item 3—Legal Proceedings

Here, the company is required to disclose any significant lawsuits in which it is involved. In Dell's case, this item refers the reader to the notes to the financial statements. And in the 2010 10-K, the company discloses that it and its executives are in trouble with the SEC and their investors. If I were investing a significant amount of my portfolio in Dell stock, I would want to know more about these issues and what Dell is doing to make sure that these or similar issues don't happen again.

Part II of the 10-K

Part II is all about money and is the core of the 10-K. Some of the information disclosed in this section is a bit technical—but after reading this book, you should be able to understand a good 80 percent of it with a simple read-through.

Item 5—Market for Registrant's Common Equity, Related Stockholder Matters, and Issuer Purchases of Equity Securities

This section discusses who owns the company, how the equity is structured, and whether the company pays dividends.

Item 6—Selected Financial Data

I love this table. This table gives us five years' worth of financial information for such key items as net revenue, gross margin, operating margin, net income, cash provided by operations, and total assets. This table makes it easy for a person running financial analysis to trend key information. Just by looking at it, you can get a sense of the growth or decline of the business (Figure 7.2).

Item 7—Management's Discussion and Analysis of Financial Condition and Results of Operations

This is hands-down my favorite part of the 10-K—even above the financial statements themselves (which, please notice, we still haven't gotten to). This section, also called the *MD&A*, is a narrative version of the financial information. It tells the story of the financial statements (Figure 7.3).

It's not numbers just sitting there on the balance sheet, income statement, and cash-flow statement; this section tells you how the numbers got there. The MD&A goes on for several pages; it starts with a summary of results of operations and then dissects and examines each component of the income statement.

First, it describes why net revenue—or total sales—has increased or decreased over previous years. Here is an excerpt from Dell's "Results of Operations" section:

> In Fiscal 2010, our overall net revenue decreased year-over-year due primarily to the global economic slowdown that began during the second half of Fiscal 2009. The weakened economy continued to impact the IT [information technology] spending of our Commercial customers, which accounted for 77 percent of our overall revenue for Fiscal 2010.

ITEM 6—SELECTED FINANCIAL DATA

The following selected financial data should be read in conjunction with "Part II—Item 7-Management's Discussion and Analysis of Financial Condition and Results of Operations" and "Part II—Item 8—Financial Statements and Supplementary Data" and are derived from our audited financial statements included in "Part II—Item 8—Financial Statements and Supplementary Data" or in our previously filed Annual Reports on Form 10-K.

	Fiscal Year Ended				
	January 29, 2010	January 30, 2009	February 1, 2008	February 2, 2007	February 3, 2006
	(in millions, except per share data)				
Results of Operations:					
Net revenue	$ 52,902	$ 61,101	$ 61,133	$ 57,420	$ 55,788
Gross margin	$ 9,261	$ 10,957	$ 11,671	$ 9,516	$ 9,891
Operating income	$ 2,172	$ 3,190	$ 3,440	$ 3,070	$ 4,382
Income before income taxes . .	$ 2,024	$ 3,324	$ 3,827	$ 3,345	$ 4,608
Net income	$ 1,433	$ 2,478	$ 2,947	$ 2,583	$ 3,602
Earnings per common share:					
Basic	$ 0.73	$ 1.25	$ 1.33	$ 1.15	$ 1.50
Diluted	$ 0.73	$ 1.25	$ 1.31	$ 1.14	$ 1.47
Number of weighted-average shares outstanding:					
Basic	1,954	1,980	2,223	2,255	2,403
Diluted	1,962	1,986	2,247	2,271	2,449
Cash Flow & Balance Sheet Data:					
Net cash provided by operating activities	$ 3,906	$ 1,894	$ 3,949	$ 3,969	$ 4,751
Cash, cash equivalents and investments	$ 11,789	$ 9,546	$ 9,532	$ 12,445	$ 11,756
Total assets	$ 33,652	$ 26,500	$ 27,561	$ 25,635	$ 23,252
Short-term borrowings.	$ 663	$ 113	$ 225	$ 188	$ 65
Long-term debt	$ 3,417	$ 1,898	$ 362	$ 569	$ 625
Total stockholders' equity . .	$ 5,641	$ 4,271	$ 3,735	$ 4,328	$ 4,047

FIGURE 7.2 · Dell 10-K, 2010, financial data table.

ITEM 7—MANAGEMENT'S DISCUSSION AND ANALYSIS OF FINANCIAL CONDITION AND RESULTS OF OPERATIONS

This section should be read in conjunction with "Part II—Item 8—Financial Statements and Supplementary Data."

OUR COMPANY

We are a leading integrated technology solutions provider in the IT industry. We offer a broad range of products, including mobility products, desktop PCs, software and peripherals, servers and networking, and storage products. Our services offerings include infrastructure technology, consulting and applications, and business process services. We also offer various financing alternatives, asset management services, and other customer financial services for business and consumer customers.

We built our reputation as a leading technology provider through listening to customers and developing solutions that meet customer needs. We are focused on providing long-term value creation through the delivery of customized solutions that make technology more efficient, more accessible, and easy to use. Customer needs are increasingly being defined by how they use technology rather than where they use it, which is why in the first quarter of Fiscal 2010, we transitioned from a global business that is managed regionally to businesses that are globally organized. We reorganized our geographic commercial segments to global business units to reflect the impact of globalization on our customer base. Our four global business segments are Large Enterprise, Public, Small and Medium Business ("SMB"), and Consumer. We also refer to our Large Enterprise, Public, and SMB segments as "Commercial."

We maintain a highly efficient global supply chain, which allows low inventory levels and the efficient use of and return on capital. We have manufacturing locations around the world and relationships with contract manufacturers. This combined structure allows us to optimize our global supply chain to best serve our global customer base. To maintain our competitiveness, we continuously strive to improve our products, services, technology, manufacturing, and logistics.

We are continuing to invest in initiatives that will align our new and existing products and services around customers' needs in order to drive long-term sustainable growth, profitability, and liquidity. During Fiscal 2010, we acquired Perot Systems Corporation ("Perot Systems"), which expands our services business and better positions us for immediate and long-term growth through the sale of additional enterprise solutions. Our business model also includes selling through distribution channels, such as retail, system integrators, value-added resellers, and distributors, which allows us to reach even more end-users around the world. We are investing resources in emerging countries with an emphasis on Brazil, Russia, India, and China ("BRIC"), where, given stable economic conditions, we expect significant growth to occur over the next several years. We are also creating customized products and services to meet the preferences and requirements of our diversified global customer base. We will focus our investments to grow our business organically as well as inorganically through alliances and strategic acquisitions.

RESULTS OF OPERATIONS

Consolidated Operations

The following table summarizes our consolidated results of operations for each of the past three fiscal years:

FIGURE 7.3 · 10-K, Dell, 2010, MD&A.   *(Continued)*

	Fiscal Year Ended							
	January 29, 2010			January 30, 2009			February 1, 2008	
	Dollars	% of Revenue	% Change	Dollars	% of Revenue	% Change	Dollars	% of Revenue
	(in millions, except per share amounts and percentages)							
Net revenue:								
Product	$43,697	82.6%	(17%)	$52,337	85.7%	(3%)	$53,728	87.9%
Services, including software related	9,205	17.4%	5%	8,764	14.3%	18%	7,405	12.1%
Total net revenue	$52,902	100.0%	(13%)	$61,101	100.0%	(0%)	$61,133	100.0%
Gross margin								
Product	$ 6,163	14.1%	(20%)	$ 7,667	14.6%	(11%)	$ 8,579	16.0%
Services, including software related	3,098	33.7%	(6%)	3,290	37.5%	6%	3,092	41.8%
Total gross margin	$ 9,261	17.5%	(15%)	$10,957	17.9%	(6%)	$11,671	19.1%
Operating expenses	$ 7,089	13.4%	(9%)	$ 7,767	12.7%	(6%)	$ 8,231	13.5%
Operating income	$ 2,172	4.1%	(32%)	$ 3,190	5.2%	(7%)	$ 3,440	5.6%
Net income	$ 1,433	2.7%	(42%)	$ 2,478	4.1%	(16%)	$ 2,947	4.8%
Earnings per share—diluted	$ 0.73	N/A	(42%)	$ 1.25	N/A	(5%)	$ 1.31	N/A

In Fiscal 2010, our overall net revenue decreased year-over-year due primarily to the global economic slowdown that began during the second half of Fiscal 2009. The weakened economy continued to impact the IT spending of our Commercial customers, which accounted for 77% of our overall revenue for Fiscal 2010. Our Consumer segment experienced significant unit demand growth year-over-year, but a mix shift to lower-priced products and competitive pricing pressures resulted in a decrease in Consumer revenue and profitability. During the second half of Fiscal 2010, the IT industry started to see signs of economic recovery, and as a result, our unit shipments during the fourth quarter of Fiscal 2010 improved year-over-year for all of our segments. Overall, we have seen indications of strengthening demand in the Commercial segments and continued growth in the Consumer segment, and we believe that, as the global economy continues to recover, our revenue in Fiscal 2011 should improve relative to Fiscal 2010.

During Fiscal 2010, we focused on balancing liquidity, profitability, and growth by emphasizing areas that provided profitable growth opportunities. We also took actions in this challenging demand environment to shift toward a more variable cost manufacturing structure, reduce operating expenses, and improve our working capital management. We are beginning to see the positive impact of these efforts and expect that the benefits of our strategy will carry into Fiscal 2011, with anticipated enhanced operating leverage should revenue growth return. We will continue to work on additional cost reduction and efficiency efforts.

We will continue to focus our efforts on providing best-value solutions to our customers in all areas of enterprise, including servers, storage, services, and software. We believe these solutions are customized to the needs of users, easy to use, and affordable. During the fourth quarter of Fiscal 2010, we acquired Perot Systems, a worldwide provider of information technology and business solutions, and we expect to increase our portfolio of solutions offerings to our customers. Additionally, we will continue our overall strategy of seeking to balance profitability and liquidity with revenue growth.

Revenue

Fiscal 2010 compared to Fiscal 2009

- Product Revenue – Product revenue and unit shipments decreased year-over-year by 17% and 6%, respectively, for Fiscal 2010. Our product revenue performance was primarily attributable to a decrease in customer demand from our Commercial segments and lower average selling prices in our Consumer segment.

FIGURE 7.3 · *(Continued)*

A section on gross margin highlights that gross margin declined owing to "softer demand, change in sales mix, and lower average selling prices." And the section goes on to say that the prices of components are increasing for key components. Not a good combination!

A section on operating expenses breaks out the components of operating expense into two subcategories: (1) selling, general and administrative, and (2) research and development.

The MD&A goes on to discuss many more topics, including the following:

- Segments and revenues by product and service
- Stock-based compensation
- Income and other taxes
- Accounts receivable
- Financing receivables
- Off-balance-sheet arrangements
- Foreign currency hedging
- Liquidity, capital commitments, and contractual cash obligations
- Critical accounting policies

Some of the topics do get a little technical, but it is worth your effort to read them.

Item 8—Financial Statements and Supplementary Data

Here, at last, are the financial statements. This section contains the auditor's opinion, the financial statements, and the notes to the financial statements.

The Auditor's Opinion

The first item is the auditor's opinion. This is an independent third party's appraisal of the forthrightness of the financial statements. Without it, you would just have to take the word of the company.

Auditors may have gotten a bad rap in recent years—some of it deserved—but they are all we have to make sure that the financial statements follow the standards.

I taught a course at a large state agency to help agency employees read the financial reports submitted by small businesses that received state grants. The small businesses had to prove that they were financially stable and meet other financial requirements before this state agency would grant them funds.

The state agency made a weak policy decision because it did not require these small businesses to have their financial statements audited. I couldn't believe the messes that these small businesses were sending in.

Things that never would happen in any world showed up on the financial statements—such things as negative cash of $400,000 plus. Some companies that we knew had to have inventory listed no inventory. Others added personal items such as jewelry to the financial statements and turned in a balance sheet that didn't balance.

Obviously, the state agency could not rely on these financial statements. And looking from a big-picture perspective, it was silly for the state to even ask companies for their financial statements if this was what it accepted.

Types of Opinions

Auditors can express one of three opinions, and the opinion is obvious in the first line of the opinion letter.

An *unqualified* opinion is the best one. It says, in essence, that the financial statements followed generally accepted accounting principles (GAAP). Here is what the Dell opinion letter dated March 18, 2010, by PricewaterhouseCoopers LLP says

> In our opinion, the consolidated financial statements listed in the accompanying index present fairly, in all material respects, the financial position of Dell Inc. and its subsidiaries at January 29, 2010 and January 30, 2009, and the results of their operations and their cash flows for each of the three years in the period ended January 30, 2010 in conformity with accounting principles generally accepted in the United States of America.

This is the best opinion possible.

The second-best opinion is called a *qualified* opinion. It says something similar to the preceding language, except that it lists exceptions. It basically says, "The financial statements follow generally accepted accounting principles except in the following instances . . ." and then goes on to list the exceptions. With this sort of opinion, you, the user of the financial statements, will have to be the judge of whether the exceptions bother you or seem reasonable.

The worst opinion type is the *adverse* opinion. An adverse opinion is bad. It says that the financial statements do not, in all material respects, follow GAAP. This means that the financial statements are not to be relied on to make decisions. An adverse opinion is very serious and will have a negative impact on the reputation of a publicly traded company, and as a result, the company's stock price might plummet.

Because of the serious nature of this opinion, the auditor usually will tell the client what needs to be fixed in order for the auditor to issue an unqualified or qualified opinion and give the client a chance to change the financial statements to comply with GAAP. Most companies will choose to go with the auditor's recommendations rather than suffer an adverse opinion.

Not Everyone Is Audited

I do feel that I need to say here that not everyone is audited. For instance, my records are not audited. I can lie to myself all I like, and no one other than my little family will be affected. Another point is that this has nothing whatsoever to do with an Internal Revenue Service (IRS) audit. The IRS does not express an opinion on the accuracy of the financial statements; it just demands that you cough up what you owe if you have broken the rules.

Financial Statements

Next comes the balance sheet, the "mother of all financial statements." Now accountants like to express themselves creatively, and we don't have much opportunity to do it, so many chief financial officers (CFOs) will alter the name of the three key financial statements to something they like better. So, for instance, Dell calls its balance sheet the "Consolidated Statements of Financial Position."

And even the innards of the statement can contain new and unique terminology. What one company will call "gross margin" on the income statement another will call "contribution margin." I imagine that some of the rules for what to name statements and categories on statements will get more rigid under the International Financial Reporting Standards (IFRS).

Now that you are familiar with the format of the three key financial statements, you will be able to tell which one you are looking at—the balance sheet, the income statement, or the cash-flow statement—no matter what the title is or what the line-item titles are.

The balance sheet is followed by the consolidated statements of income (the income statement) and the consolidated statements of cash flow (the cash-flow statement).

The last statement, which we haven't talked about yet, is the *consolidated statements of stockholders' equity*. This statement gives us detail on the components of stockholders' equity on the balance sheet. It shows how retained earnings have been built up by net income or torn down by net loss. It also shows transactions with treasury stock, stock outstanding, and employee benefit plans and trends it over a three-year period. When looking at your statement of stockholders' equity, pay close attention to the column headers and the row titles.

Notes to the Financial Statements

Finally, we come to the notes to the financial statements. This is the most exciting read in the whole document—*not!* If you ever have insomnia, pull this section of the financial statements out. What? You thought the rest of it was boring? You haven't seen anything yet!

The notes to the financial statements started out as harmless little footnotes at the bottom of the balance sheet or the income statement. Over time, though, users kept asking for more information. Can you tell me about that number?

How about more detail on this number? Now they are so voluminous that they don't fit under the financial statements. Dell's notes go on for 45 pages—and that is not unusually long. And that's for only 16 notes, which tells us that many of the notes are several pages long.

So how do you wade through this stuff? Well, you hit the highlights. Some of the material is so filled with legalese and accountingese that even I have a hard time understanding what is being said. You need a degree in accounting or finance to understand much of the detail the notes provide. However, here are some things that you may want to spend time deciphering:

- *Note: Fair Value Measurements*. This note discloses what Dell's assets and liabilities would be worth if they were sold or cashed in today.

- *Note: Financial Instruments*. This note discloses what sorts of investments the company holds, if any. Are they in bonds, stocks, and foreign corporations? Why would you want to know this? Because you would want to know if the company is investing its excess cash wisely. What's wise? Whatever you think it is! This all depends on whether you are a risk taker or more conservative.

- *Note: Debt*. This note discloses the loans Dell took out during the period and the terms of those loans

- *Note: Acquisitions*. Dell bought another company during 2010 and several in 2009. Important!

- *Note: Commitments, Contingencies, and Certain Concentrations*. This is a good note to read because it is all about risk. A *commitment* is an engagement to assume a financial obligation. For instance, a company might have committed a portion of its cash balance to repay debt. This would not necessarily show up on the cash-flow statement; you have to read about it in the notes. *Contingencies* are things that might happen that could have a material effect on the financial statements; the company is obligated to reveal these items in the notes. *Concentration* is, in essence, another term for risk, so read about any concentrations.

- *Note: Stock-Based Compensation and Benefit Plans*. This is a good section to read if you are an employee of the company.

Some of the notes break down the items on the balance sheet and income statement into more detail. This can be interesting. For instance, the gross account "Inventory" may be broken down into raw materials, work in progress, and finished goods. Another note breaks down financial information into quarterly results.

Certification by the Chairman, CEO, and CFO

As a consequence of the Sarbanes-Oxley Act—the law that sought to plug up some of the loopholes that corporations used to mislead investors (remember Enron and WorldCom?)—corporate executives must sign the financial statements and promise all sorts of things about them. Executives promise that they did not mislead the readers of the reports, that they have reviewed the reports, and that they have put controls in place to help guarantee their accuracy. They also promise that they have disclosed significant fraud to the auditors. Good idea, don't you think?

Summary

The 10-K is a pretty useful document—if not very pretty. After reading this book, you should be able to tackle most of it—except the most technical notes. The more you use it, the better you will be at it.

QUIZ

1. **Where do you get a corporation's 10-K?**
   A. The company's annual report
   B. The company's Web site
   C. A subscription to a financial analysis service
   D. The IRS

2. **Aggregate market value is $28.44 billion, and the number of shares outstanding is 691.55 million. What is the market value per share?**
   A. $4.12
   B. $40.52
   C. $23.23
   D. $41.13

3. **In this part of its 10-K, the company is obligated and required to disclose anything it knows that could negatively affect its financial results.**
   A. Risk factors
   B. Business strategy
   C. Competition
   D. Available information

4. **What is usually the first item in the set of financial statements?**
   A. The balance sheet
   B. The income statement
   C. The auditor's opinion
   D. The cash-flow statement

5. **"The financial statements follow GAAPs except in the following instances. . . ." What kind of auditor's opinion is this?**
   A. Unqualified
   B. Qualified
   C. Adverse

6. **This statement gives us detail on the components of stockholders' equity on the balance sheet. It shows transactions with treasury stock, stock outstanding, and employee benefit plans and trends them over a three-year period.**
   A. Consolidated Statements of Cash Flows
   B. Consolidated Statements of Income
   C. Consolidated Statements of Stockholders' Equity
   D. Consolidated Statements of Balance

7. **The Sarbanes-Oxley Act tried to**

   A. make corporate executives liable for bad financial statements.
   B. plug loopholes that corporations used to mislead investors.
   C. require auditors to pass a minimum of 20 hours of continuing professional education (CPE) a year.
   D. Make auditors liable for misleading statements.

8. **SEC stands for**

   A. Securities Exposure Committee.
   B. Securities and Exchange Commission.
   C. Secret Exchange Commission.

9. **Fiscal year ends are always December 31. True or false?**

   A. True
   B. False

Part III

Debits and Credits Detail—Rules, Rules, Rules

chapter **8**

How to Tell if Something Is a Debit or a Credit

And now for the curriculum covered on the first day of a boring college accounting course—debits and credits. I had to do it to you somewhere!

CHAPTER OBJECTIVES

- List the rules that accounts memorize to be able to properly classify and account for transactions

- Examine an example chart of accounts

When people study accounting, unfortunately, they tend to get confused about debits and credits because of their experience with banks. When banks use the terms *debit* and *credit*, they have it all backward because they talk to you about your account from their perspectives, not from your perspective. So when they say that they are crediting your account, the implication is that it's a good thing. Well, for you, it *is* good, but from their perspectives, it's bad—it means the bank is losing money. If you were a bank and had to credit someone's account, you wouldn't be happy about it.

So, before we can begin a serious discussion of debits and credits, please wipe from your mind the way that banks talk to you about debits and credits. Banks have it all backward.

A Few Key Formulas

From Chapters 2 and 3 we learned a few key formulas that give us the basis of the balance sheet and the income statement. To understand debits and credits, we have to look at those formulas again.

The first formula is the basis of the balance sheet:

$$\text{Assets} = \text{liabilities} + \text{equity}$$

The second formula is the basis of the income statement:

$$\text{Revenues} - \text{expenses} = \text{net income}$$

As usual, the balance sheet is running the show. Remember: It is the "mother of all financial statements." So the balance sheet formula is the root of our double-entry, debit/credit system.

An *increase* in *assets* is always a *debit*. A *decrease* is a *credit*. An *increase* in *liabilities* is always a *credit*; a *decrease* is a *debit* (see Figures 8.1 and 8.2).

Now, how does the income statement formula fit in? The net income from the income statement increases our equity. An increase in our equity necessitates a credit. So when we increase net income, we record a credit.

Looking at the formula for net income, revenues increase net income, so they must be a credit, and expenses reduce net income, so they must be a debit.

To summarize:

Increases in assets = debits.
Increases in liabilities and equity = credits.
Increases in revenues = credits.
Increases in expenses = debits.

This is just something you need to memorize. It is not intuitive. It is just a rule. Write it on the back of your hand or in reverse on your forehead, and look at it several times a day. Just commit it to memory, and the rest will fall into place.

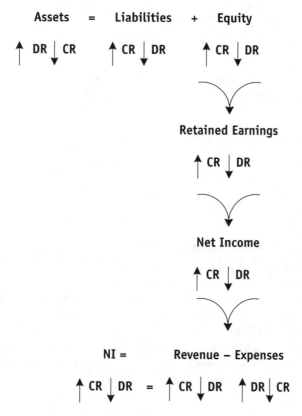

FIGURE 8.1 · Debits and credits flowchart.

	Increase	Decrease
Assets	Debit	Credit
Liabilities	Credit	Debit
Equity	Credit	Debit
Revenue	Credit	Debit
Expense	Debit	Credit

FIGURE 8.2 · Table of debits and credits.

A Special Way of Recording Transactions

Accountants even have a special way that they write down transactions. The debits are flush left, and the credits are indented just a bit. For example, let's say that we bought a new car for $20,000 cash. The entry would be

| Fixed asset | $20,000 | |
| Cash | | $20,000 |

This tells us that the fixed asset was debited and the cash was credited. Just another funny thing to memorize. I'll add the notes *DR* for debit and *CR* for credit (these are standard abbreviations) to future entries, so they will look like this:

| DR fixed asset | $20,000 | |
| CR cash | | $20,000 |

Chart of Accounts

Most companies have a chart of accounts—a listing of all the possible general ledger categories to which the company could post transactions. These accounts usually have simple numerical codes so that the accountant can refer to the account by just the code, the code and the name, or just the name.

Figure 8.3 shows an example of a chart of accounts. In this organization, everything with a code that starts with a 1 is an asset, everything with a code that starts with a 2 is a liability, 3s are for equity, and so on. We will use this chart of accounts for the examples in the remainder of this book.

Still Struggling?

Different Industries, Different Accounts

The chart of accounts can tell you a lot about a company. An airline will have accounts to track fuel, repairs, prepaid tickets, and employee travel expenses, among other things. A jewelry store will have accounts for inventory display cases, insurance, and security. A company that translates books to Spanish will spend most of its resources on personnel and technology. Over time, accountants will tweak the chart of accounts to make the information more meaningful to owners and managers by creating new accounts and using industry-specific terminology.

Summary

Memorize the following formulas: *Assets = liabilities + equity* and *Revenue − expenses = profit*. Get a tattoo if necessary.

Assets		
Cash (111000)		C
1111	General Checking Account	C
1112	Payroll Checking Account	C
1114	Money Market	C
1117	Cash in Registers	C
Accounts Receivable (121000)		D
1219	Accounts Receivable -- Trade	D
1229	In Transit from Credit Card Processors	D
1240	Loans Receivable	D
1200	A/R Miscellaneous	D
Inventory (140000)		E
1400	Raw Materials	E
1420	Work in Process	E
1430	Finished Birdbaths	E
Prepaid Expenses, Deposits, and Other Current Assets (150000)		F
1510	Prepaid Expenses	F
1511	Prepaid Insurance	F
1512	Prepaid Rent	F
1513	Prepaid Interest	F
1519	Prepaid Other	F
1520	Deposits	F
1521	Deposit -- UPS	F
1522	Deposit -- Utilities	F
1523	Deposit -- Rent	F
1529	Deposit -- Other	F
1530	Other Current Assets	F
Total Current Assets (C + D + E + F)		**G**
Land and Buildings (160000)		H
1610	Land	H
1620	Buildings	H
1630	Land Improvements	H
1640	Building Improvements	H
1650	Leasehold Improvements	H

FIGURE 8.3 · Chart of Accounts—Birdbath Company.   (Continued)

Furniture (170000)		H
1710	Furniture, Fixtures, & Equip	H
1720	Data Processing Equipment	H
1730	Data Processing Software	H
1740	Vehicles	H
Accumulated Depreciation (180000)		H
1810	Accumulated Depreciation – Building	H
1820	Accumulated Depreciation – Land Improvements	H
1830	Accumulated Depreciation – Building Improvements	H
1840	Accumulated Depreciation – Leasehold Improvements	H
1850	Accumulated Depreciation – Furniture, Fixtures, & Equip	H
1860	Accumulated Depreciation – Data Processing Equipment	H
1870	Accumulated Depreciation – Data Processing Software	H
1880	Accumulated Depreciation – Vehicles	H
Other Assets (190000)		H
1910	Intangible Assets	H
1911	Covenant Not-to-Compete – Previous Owner	H
1912	Goodwill	H
1913	Customer Lists	H
1918	Other Intangible Assets	H
1919	Accumulated Amortization	H
1920	Cash Surrender Value of Life Insurance	H
1930	Other Assets	H
Total Assets (G + H)		**H**
Liabilities		
Accounts Payable (211000)		K
2110	Accounts Payable – Merchandise	K
2120	Accounts Payable – Operating	K

FIGURE 8.3 · *(Continued)*

2130	Customer Credits		K
Accrued Expenses (222000)			L
2210	Accrued Payroll		L
2220	Payroll Withholding		L
	2221	Federal Withholding	L
	2222	FICA Withholding	L
	2223	Medicare Withholding	L
	2224	State Withholding	L
	2225	Local Withholding	L
	2226	401(k)/Pension Withholding	L
	2227	Miscellaneous Withholding	L
2230	Accrued Payroll Taxes		L
	2231	Accrued Payroll Taxes – FICA Employer's Share	L
	2232	Accrued Payroll Taxes – Medicare Employer's Share	L
	2233	Accrued Payroll Taxes – Federal Unemployment Tax	L
	2234	Accrued Payroll Taxes – State Unemployment Tax	L
2240	Sales Tax Collected		L
2250	Accrued Use Tax		L
2260	Accrued Retirement Plan Expense		L
2290	Other Accrued Expenses		L
Current Notes Payable (230000)			L
2310	Short-Term Obligation		L
2390	Current Portion of Long-Term Debt		L
Total Current Liabilities			
Long-Term Notes Payable (240000)			M
2410	Long-Term Obligation		M
2420	Mortgage Note Payable		M
2430	Loan from Owner/Stockholder		M

FIGURE 8.3 · *(Continued)*

2480	Other Long-Term Obligation	M
<2490>	Current Portion of Long-Term Debt	M
Total Liabilities (K + L + M)		
Owners' Equity/Net Worth		P
For a Sole Proprietor		P
3100	Capital	P
<3100>	Drawings (Close Out into Capital at End of Year)	P
3160	Retained Earnings	P
Total Liabilities and Equity/Net Worth (N + P)		Q
Sales (400000)		1
4010	Birdbath Sales	1
Total Net Sales		1
Cost of Goods Sold (500000)		2
5010	Inventory Expense Birdbaths	2
Cost of Goods Sold		2
Gross Margin (Line 1 minus Line 2)		3
Operating Expenses (600000)		
6010	Wages	4
6020	Vacation Pay	4
6030	Sick Pay	4
6040	FICA Tax	4
6045	Federal/State Unemployment Tax	4
6050	Group Health Insurance	4
6060	Workers' Compensation Insurance	4
6070	Disability Income Insurance	4
6075	Life Insurance	4
6080	Retirement (Pension/Profit Sharing/401(k))	4
6090	Other Benefit Expense	4

FIGURE 8.3 · *(Continued)*

6095	Payroll Processing Expense	4
Occupancy Cost	(610000)	5
6110	Rent Expense	5
6120	Utilities	5
6130	Other Occupancy Costs	5
6131	Customer Parking Subsidy	5
6132	Janitorial and Other Contract Services	5
6133	Other Occupancy Costs	5
Advertising and Promotion	(620000)	6
6210	Advertising	6
Telephone and Other Communication	(630000)	7
6310	Telephone Company Use Charges	7
6320	Network Charges	7
Professional Services	(640000)	8
6410	Legal Fees	8
6420	Accounting Fees	8
6430	Inventory Verification	8
6490	Other Consulting Fees	8
Stationery and Supplies	(650000)	9
6510	Stationery and Supplies – Office Use	9
6540	Janitorial Supplies	9
6590	Other	9
Data Processing Expense	(660000)	10
6610	Data Processing Supplies	10
6620	Data Processing Equipment and Software Rental	10
6630	Outside Computer Services	10
6690	Other Data Processing Expenses	10
Depreciation Expense	(670000)	

FIGURE 8.3 · *(Continued)*

6710	Depreciation – Building		5
6720	Depreciation – Land Improvements		5
6730	Depreciation – Building Improvements		5
6740	Depreciation – Leasehold Improvements		11
6750	Depreciation – Furniture, Fixtures, & Equip		11
	6751	Depreciation – Furniture, Fixtures, & Equip	11
	6752	Depreciation – Data Processing Equipment	10
	6753	Depreciation – Data Processing Software	10
	6754	Depreciation – Vehicles	11
Travel and Entertainment (680000)			12
6810	Business Travel		12
6820	Business Meals and Entertainment (50% Deductible)		12
6830	Food – Staff Meetings, etc. (100% Deduct., De Minimus)		12
Insurance (690000)			
6910	Business Insurance		13
6920	Real Estate Insurance		5
6930	Vehicle Insurance		13
6940	Other Insurance		13
Credit Card and Other Service Charges (700000)			
7010	Credit Card Service Charges		14
	7011	Credit Card Service Charge Master Card/Visa	14
	7012	Credit Card Service Charge Amex	14
	7013	Credit Card Service Charge Discover	14
	7014	Credit Card Service Charge Debit/ATM Card	14
7020	Bank Service Charges		16
7090	Other Service Charges		16
Dues and Subscriptions (710000)			15
7110	Association Membership Fees		15

FIGURE 8.3 · *(Continued)*

7120	Subscription Fees	15
7121	Subscription Fees – Professional Publications	15
Office Expense	(720000)	16
7210	Office Expense	16
Postage	(730000)	16
7310	Postage Expense	16
7311	Customer Package Charges	16
<7312>	Postage and Handling Fees Received	16
Taxes	(740000)	
7410	Inventory and Use Taxes	17
7420	Real Estate Taxes	5
7430	Business Licenses and Fees	17
7490	Other Business Taxes and Fees	17
Education	(750000)	18
7510	Education – Course Fees	18
7520	Education – Travel	18
7530	Education – Meals and Entertainment (50% Deductible)	18
7590	Education – Other	18
Equipment Rent	(760000)	
7610	Office Equipment Rent	16
7620	Store Equipment Rent	18
7690	Other Equipment Rent	18
Repairs and Maintenance	(770000)	
7710	Repairs and Maintenance – Building Equipment	5
7720	Repairs and Maintenance – Furniture, Fixtures, & Equip	18
7730	Repairs and Maintenance – Data Processing Equipment	10
7740	Repairs and Maintenance – Vehicle	18
7790	Repairs and Maintenance – Other	18

FIGURE 8.3 · *(Continued)*

Other Operating Expense (780000)		18
7810	Bad Debts	18
7820	Collection Expense	18
7830	Cash Over/Short	18
7840	Classified Ads – Help Wanted	18
7850	Contributions	18
7860	Vehicle Expense	18
7870	Amortization Expense	18
7880	Penalties	18
7890	Franchise Fee/Royalty	18
7900	Miscellaneous Expense	18
Total Operating Expense (Sum of Lines 4 through 18)		**19**
Operating Income (Lines 3 minus Line 19)		**20**
Other Income (800000)		21
8100	Interest Income – Finance Charges Customers Accounts	21
8110	Interest Income	21
8120	Dividend Income	21
8130	Capital Gains Income	21
8140	Gain on Sale of Fixed Assets	21
8190	Other Income	21
Other Expense (820000)		
8210	Interest Expense	24
8220	Mortgage Interest Expense	5
8230	Loss on Sale of Fixed Assets	22
8240	Uninsured Casualty Loss	22
8290	Other Expenses	22
Net Income Before Taxes (Line 20 plus Line 21 minus Line 22)		**23**

FIGURE 8.3 · *(Continued)*

QUIZ

1. **Assets = liabilities + equity is the formula that rules the**
   A. income statement.
   B. balance sheet.
   C. cash-flow statement.

2. **_____ – _____ = net income.**
   A. Sales; cost of goods
   B. Gross profit; expenses
   C. Revenue; expenses
   D. Sales; expenses

3. **An increase in assets is represented by a**
   A. debit.
   B. credit.

4. **An increase in expenses is recorded as a**
   A. debit.
   B. credit.

5. **Banks talk about debits and credits from their perspective, not the customer's perspective. True or false?**
   A. True
   B. False

6. **The chart of accounts is a listing of the codes assigned to general ledger accounts. True or false?**
   A. True
   B. False

7. **When writing a transaction, credits are justified to the left and debits are indented. True or false?**
   A. True
   B. False

8. **Each organization's chart of accounts will be unique. True or false?**
   A. True
   B. False

9. An increase in liabilities and equity is recorded as a
    A. debit.
    B. credit.

10. An increase in revenue is recorded as a
    A. debit.
    B. credit.

Chapter **9**

A Few Simple Transactions

In this chapter we'll run through a few simple transactions to get used to the double-entry system.

CHAPTER OBJECTIVE

- Apply debits and credits to cash sales, credit sales, and purchase of a fixed asset

First, let's sell a birdbath. We have already gone through this example in Chapter 5, but we didn't consider how it affected the debits and credits.

You make cement birdbaths. You have an inventory of 100 in stock. Each birdbath cost you $20 to make. So your total balance on the balance sheet in inventory is $2,000.

Cash Sale

Today you were lucky enough to sell two birdbaths to a bird enthusiast for $60 cash. What does the entry look like?

First, you get $60 cash. An increase in an asset is a debit. So you put

DR 1111   General checking account (cash) $60

Then you get $60 in revenue. An increase in revenue is a credit. So you put

CR 4010   Sales revenue $60

Although we are all in balance, we are not finished yet. We have to recognize that we have reduced our inventory and incurred an expense in making the sale.

A decrease in inventory is a decrease in an asset, which is a credit. Thus

CR 1430   Inventory $40

We have incurred an expense in order to make this sale of $40. An increase in an expense is a debit. Thus

DR 5010   Inventory expense $40

When it all shakes out, the final, all-inclusive entry looks like this:

DR 1111   General checking account (cash) $60
DR 5010   Inventory expense $40
    CR 4010   Sales revenue $60
    CR 1430   Inventory $40

Yeah! The entry balances: a total $100 debit and a total $100 credit.

From Chapter 5, let's look at what happens to your financial statements as a result of this entry. The income statement records a $60 increase in revenue, a $40 increase in expenses, and a $20 profit or net income (Figure 9.1).

On the cash-flow statement, cash goes up by $60 (Figure 9.2).

On the balance sheet, cash goes up by $60, inventory goes down by $40, and retained earnings (your net income) go up by $20 (Figure 9.3).

Does your little balance sheet balance? Yep. Assets are up by $20, and so is equity.

Income Statement

Sales	60
Cost of Goods	40
Gross Profit	20
Operating Expenses	0
Operating Profit	20
less Taxes/Other	0
Net Income	20

FIGURE 9.1 · Income statement.

Cash-Flow Statement

Beginning Cash	
+ Cash Collected	60
−Cash Paid	0
Ending Cash	+60

FIGURE 9.2 · Cash-flow statement.

Balance Sheet

Assets ☺		Liabilities ☹	
Cash	+60	Accounts Payable	
Accounts Receivable		Long-Term Debt	
Inventory	−40		
Fixed Assets		**Equity ☺ or ☹**	
Intangibles			
		Stock	
		Retained Earnings	+20
	+20		+20

FIGURE 9.3 · Balance sheet.

Credit Sale: Part One

Now let's make this a bit more complicated. Let's instead say that you made a sale on credit. You don't get to collect cash right away.

I'm also going to change the numbers a little bit. Let's say that this time you sell 100 birdbaths to a local nursery on credit. The nursery takes the birdbaths and agrees to pay you for them in 30 days.

Now how do we record this? It is a very similar set of entries, except that we don't collect from the customer right away in cash; we have to recognize an accounts receivable and collect in cash 30 days later. What does the entry look like?

First, we recognize a $3,000 receivable ($30 selling price times 100 birdbaths). An increase in an asset is a debit. So you put

DR 1210   Accounts receivable $3,000

Then we get $3,000 in revenue. An increase in revenue is a credit. So you put

CR 4010   Sales revenue $3,000

Although we are all in balance, we are not finished yet. We have to recognize that we have reduced our inventory by $2,000 and incurred an expense of $2,000 ($20 per birdbath) in making the sale.

A decrease in inventory is a decrease in an asset, which is a credit. Thus

CR 1430   Inventory $2,000

An increase in an expense is a debit. Thus

DR 5010   Inventory expense $2,000

When it all shakes out, the final, all-inclusive entry looks like this:

DR 1210   Accounts receivable $3,000
DR 5010   Inventory expense $2,000
    CR 4010   Sales revenue $3,000
    CR 1430   Inventory $2,000

Yeah! The entry balances—a total $5,000 debit and a total $5,000 credit.

Back from Chapter 5, let's look at what happens to your financial statements as a result of this entry. The income statement records a $3,000 increase in revenue, a $2,000 increase in expenses, and a $1,000 profit or net income (Figure 9.4).

The cash-flow statement (Figure 9.5) is not affected—yet!

On the balance sheet, accounts receivable go up by $3,000, inventory goes down by $2,000, and retained earnings (your net income) go up by $1,000 (Figure 9.6).

Does your little balance sheet balance? Yep. Assets are up by $1,000, and so is equity.

Income Statement

Sales	3,000
Cost of Goods	2,000
Gross Profit	1,000
Operating Expenses	0
Operating Profit	1,000
less Taxes/Other	0
Net Income	1,000

FIGURE 9.4 · Income statement.

Cash-Flow Statement

Beginning Cash
+ Cash Collected
– Cash Paid

Ending Cash

FIGURE 9.5 · Cash-flow statement.

Balance Sheet

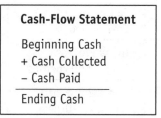

Assets ☺		Liabilities ☹	
Cash		Accounts Payable	
Accounts Receivable	+3,000	Long-Term Debt	
Inventory	– 2,000		
Fixed Assets		**Equity** ☺ **or** ☹	
Intangibles			
		Stock	
		Retained Earnings	+1,000
	+1,000		+1,000

FIGURE 9.6 · Balance sheet.

Credit Sale: Part Two

In a month's time, you collect payment from the nursery, a check for $3,000. Now, what is your entry? You simply have to reverse out your accounts receivable and turn that asset into your favorite asset of all—cash.

DR 1111   General checking account (cash) $3,000
    CR 1210   Accounts receivable $3,000

What happens to the financial statements now? First, you ask if the income statement is affected. No, it is not. You didn't make a new sale or incur a new expense. This is all old, already recorded revenues and expenses, so you skip the income statement (Figure 9.7).

| **Income Statement** |
| Sales |
| Cost of Goods |
| **Gross Profit** |
| Operating Expenses |
| **Operating Profit** |
| less Taxes/Other |
| **Net Income** |

FIGURE 9.7 · Income statement.

Car Dealers—A Study in Creative Revenue Sources

How does a car dealer make money? Like most businesses, car dealers have a variety of ways to bring in profits and cash. And each revenue option has a unique impact on the financial statements. A dealership can, among other revenue-generating activities,

- Sell a car for cash
- Lease a car
- Finance a car
- Sell parts
- Sell repair services
- Sell warranties, insurance, and other coverages

My friend bought a new car a few years ago, and the salesperson asked her what she could pay each month for her car. She told the salesperson that her maximum payment was $300 a month. Notice how the salesperson didn't ask her about the total purchase price of the car—but instead asked her how much she could pay per month.

It turned out that the salesperson could get her into a pretty sweet ride with leather seats for $300 a month. The only problem was that it would take my friend seven years to pay it off! The salesperson also discussed some complicated lease options with my friend.

After all the warranties, options, and fees were added in, my friend's payment was up to $340 a month. She walked out and bought a used car off of Craig's list with bank financing for $230 a month. Go girlfriend!

Being a wise consumer means understanding what motivates the dealer and how the dealer is making his or her money. Is the dealer making money by taking your car back and selling it or re-leasing it at the end of the lease term? The car still remains on the dealer's balance sheet as an asset, but it is actually riding the highways earning the dealer (or, in this case, the lessor) cash!

Is the dealer making money off of interest because you have stretched a simple purchase out seven years? Here, the car is no longer on the dealer's balance sheet. And depending on how it is financed, the dealer may get cash plus interest today from a financing company that collects payments through the years, or the dealer may be collecting interest and principal himself or herself for seven years.

Is the dealer making money by selling you a warranty that you don't need? (Warranties are a corporation's way of earning extra money off of you in case the product it just sold you is defective—sounds like a real rip-off when I put it this way, doesn't it?) A relatively small percentage of warranties are used, and the dealer knows this. Dealers cash in most of the warranty payment and hold a little in reserve for the occasional lemon.

Dealers might forgo the profit that shows that you are paying the dealer's cost for the car if the salesperson can get you to stretch payments or buy extras and warranties. Always know how dealers are making their money so that you can bargain accordingly.

Cash-Flow Statement	
Beginning Cash	
+ Cash Collected	3,000
− Cash Paid	
Ending Cash	+3,000

FIGURE 9.8 · Cash-flow statement.

You go directly to the cash-flow statement (Figure 9.8). Cash is increased by $3,000.

On the balance sheet, you increase cash by $3,000 and decrease accounts receivable by the amount you just collected, $3,000. This gives you a net effect of zero on the left side. Nothing happened on the right side, so you're okay (Figure 9.9).

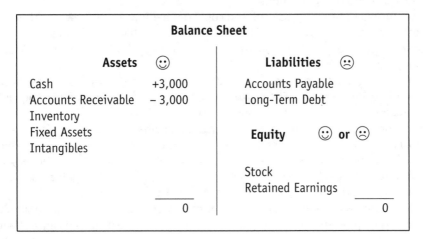

FIGURE 9.9 · Balance sheet.

Purchasing a Fixed Asset

Now let's say that you want to purchase a $5,000 color copier to help you create ads and brochures to market your birdbaths. How do we record this?

Back from Chapter 5, you might remember that how we record it depends on whether we capitalize the asset or expense it. You are going to capitalize this copier—to record it as a fixed asset. And I am going to keep it simple and say that we paid cash for it.

So the entry must record an increase in fixed assets of $5,000 and a decrease in cash of $5,000.

DR 1710   Furniture, fixtures, and equipment (FF&E) $5,000
  CR 1111   General checking account (cash) $5,000

At the end of the period, we need to depreciate this copier. Using the simple straight-line method of depreciation and a life of five years, we can say that we get $1,000 of use out of the copier every year. We will recognize this depreciation as an expense. An increase in expenses is a debit. Thus

DR 6751   Depreciation expense, FF&E $1,000
  CR 1850   Accumulated depreciation, FF&E $1,000

"Hey!" you might be saying. "What kind of curve ball is this, accumulated depreciation?"

Sorry, it is a bit strange. Accumulated depreciation is what we fun, terminology-happy accountants call a *contra account*. It always is disclosed in the financial statements right underneath fixed assets, showing how much depreciation has been accumulated against (or *contra*) the fixed assets.

For example, you might have a balance sheet that looks like this:

Fixed assets	$100,000
Less accumulated depreciation	$ 90,000
Net fixed assets	$ 10,000

This would tell you that the fixed assets are old and used up, would it not? If the net fixed assets were $95,000, you would know that this was some new stuff that you are looking at here.

So in a review of what we covered in Chapter 5, what is the effect on the financial statements?

On the day you purchase the copier, here is what happens to your financial statements:

Income statement: No effect (Figure 9.10).

Cash-flow statement: Cash is reduced by $5,000 (Figure 9.11).

Balance sheet: Cash is reduced by $5,000, and fixed assets are increased by $5,000 (Figure 9.12).

Income Statement

Sales
Cost of Goods
_____

Gross Profit
Operating Expenses
_____

Operating Profit
less Taxes/Other
_____

Net Income

FIGURE 9.10 · Income statement.

Cash-Flow Statement

Beginning Cash	
+ Cash Collected	
– Cash Paid	–5,000
Ending Cash	–5,000

FIGURE 9.11 · Cash-flow statement.

Balance Sheet

Assets ☺		Liabilities ☹	
Cash	−5,000	Accounts Payable	
Accounts Receivable		Long-Term Debt	
Inventory			
Fixed Assets	+5,000	**Equity** ☺ or ☹	
Intangibles			
		Stock	
		Retained Earnings	
	────		────
	0		0

FIGURE 9.12 · Balance sheet.

At the end of the year, when you depreciate the copier, the income statement is affected. So you record depreciation expense. Key word—*expense*. Go to the income statement (Figure 9.13) and increase expenses by $1,000, thereby reducing net income by $1,000.

What happens on the cash-flow statement (Figure 9.14)? Nothing. Cash was affected when you paid cash for the copier. Depreciation is what some fancy accountants call a *noncash expense*. It reduces net income without reducing cash in later years—years 2 to 5 in our example.

On the balance sheet, you now need to decrease fixed assets by the $1,000 in depreciation and decrease retained earnings by the $1,000 decrease in net income flowing over from the income statement.

Income Statement

Sales	
Cost of Goods	────
Gross Profit	
Operating Expenses	−1,000
Operating Profit	
less Taxes/Other	────
Net Income	− 1,000

FIGURE 9.13 · Income statement.

The final effect of all these transactions on the balance sheet at the end of the first year is

- A decrease in cash of $5,000
- An increase in fixed assets of $4,000 ($5,000 copier less $1,000 depreciation)
- A decrease in retained earnings of $1,000 (Figure 9.15)

So the balance sheet again balances. Assets are decreased by $1,000, and retained earnings are decreased by $1,000.

No matter what you do, you check to see that your balance sheet balances.

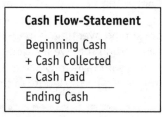

Cash Flow-Statement

Beginning Cash
+ Cash Collected
– Cash Paid
_____
Ending Cash

FIGURE 9.14 · Cash-flow statement.

Balance Sheet				
Assets ☺			**Liabilities** ☹	
Cash	−5,000		Accounts Payable	
Accounts Receivable			Long–Term Debt	
Inventory				
Fixed Assets			**Equity** ☺ **or** ☹	
Copier	5,000			
Less Accumulated Depreciation	−1,000		Stock	
Total Fixed Assets	4,000		Retained Earnings	−1,000
Intangibles				
Total Assets	−1,000		Total Liabilities and Equity	−1,000

FIGURE 9.15 · Balance sheet.

Still Struggling?

Depreciation and Amortization

Amortization is the same thing as depreciation, only for intangibles.

The reason we depreciate something is twofold: to recognize that the value of the fixed asset decreases over time and to recognize that we are getting the benefit of the fixed asset over a period of years. The purchase doesn't benefit us just in the year in which we bought the fixed asset.

Amortization is the same concept as depreciation, except that depreciation is applied to fixed assets and amortization is applied to intangibles. Intangibles would include patents, brand names, and other intellectual property.

Another thing we amortize, or spread over time, is long-lived expenses such as warranty expense. Instead of pretending that we are going to incur all the warranty expense for a product in the year in which we create and sell the product, we amortize that cost, spreading it out over the length of the warranty.

Lease versus Buy Decision

Should you lease that fixed asset or buy it? There are many factors to consider, and whole books have been written on the subject. Moreover, several software programs also can help you to make the decision. Your lender and/or the company from which you are leasing equipment or fixed assets should be able to help you in the analysis.

A lease is treated as an expense; it flows through the income statement and hence reduces retained earnings on the balance sheet. So you realize an expense each time you make a lease payment.

If you purchase an item, it is recorded as a fixed asset on the balance sheet and is depreciated over the useful life of the asset. Depending on that useful life of the asset, you may be expensing the cost of the asset more slowly if you capitalize it than if you lease and expense it.

Here are some questions you need to ask before you can decide whether to lease or buy:

- What effect will a lease or a purchase have on cash flow?
  - Is a down payment required? Generally leases don't require a down payment; purchases do.
  - At the end of the lease, do you have the right to sell the asset and earn some cash? In general, at the end of a lease, you don't own the fixed asset; it reverts to the lessor. If you purchased the fixed asset, you might

be able to realize a nice chunk of cash flow somewhere down the line when you sell it. Some leases allow the lessee to pay a chunk of cash at the end of the lease to own it outright. (Be careful with these arrangements because accounting standards and Internal Revenue Service (IRS) rules may consider such arrangements to be substantially a purchase and not a lease.)

o Are you going to pay cash for the fixed asset now or finance it over time?

o What is the effect on cash flow for each monthly payment, whether on the loan you used to purchase the fixed asset or on the lease?

• What effect will the lease or purchase have on income?

o How fast will expenses be realized on each option? Under a lease, the entire payment is recorded on the income statement and reduces income. If you decide to purchase it outright (not lease it), the only expense realized is depreciation expense. How long is the useful life, and how quickly will you realize the depreciation expense on the income statement?

o What effect will each option have on taxes? Congress often weighs in on this question because some leases receive preferential tax treatment. And even without preferential treatment, the effect on income is different in each option, and that affects income taxes.

• What effect will the lease or purchase have on the balance sheet?

o Will putting the asset on the balance sheet "bust the covenants" of a loan or skew key financial metrics? Do you have an outstanding loan that has restrictions on how much more debt you can incur or how much you can have recorded as fixed assets? Do your investors have expectations about your fixed asset balance and accumulated depreciation balance that would be negatively affected by a purchase?

o Will leasing the item be misleading to investors? Would disclosing it on the balance sheet as something the business needs to operate be a more realistic and reasonable representation of reality?

Don't forget the time value of money. This concept reminds us that $1 today is worth more than $1 in five years because we could have invested the $1 and made some interest income from it. So the timing of cash inflows and outflows will have an impact on your decision. (For a metric that helps you to examine cash flows, see Internal Rate of Return in Chapter 15.)

Summary

Transactions are multifaceted but always must balance. The trick is in recognizing which accounts are affected when. Begin by deciding if the transaction affects cash, other assets, liabilities, equity, revenue, or the expense account.

QUIZ

1. **The sale of two birdbaths for cash will not affect the income statement. True or false?**
    A. True
    B. False

2. **You sell 100 birdbaths on credit to a nursery. What two accounts do you debit?**
    A. Cash and sales revenue
    B. Accounts receivable and inventory expense
    C. Sales revenue and inventory
    D. Cash and inventory expenses

3. **The time value of money concept says that $1 today is worth more than $1 in five years. True or false?**
    A. True
    B. False

4. **You sell 100 birdbaths on credit to a nursery. What two accounts do you credit?**
    A. Cash and sales revenue
    B. Accounts receivable and inventory expense
    C. Sales revenue and inventory
    D. Cash and inventory expenses

5. **The sale of those 100 birdbaths on credit will not affect the cash-flow statement. True or false?**
    A. True
    B. False

6. **Accumulated depreciation is a _____ account and is disclosed in the financial statements right underneath _____.**
    A. sales; cost of goods
    B. contra; intangible assets
    C. contra; fixed assets
    D. current asset; land and buildings

7. **The purchase of the copier for cash will not affect the cash-flow statement. True or false?**
    A. True
    B. False

8. **Depreciation is applied to fixed assets, amortization is applied to what?**
   A. Land
   B. Intangibles
   C. Building improvements
   D. Furniture

9. **A lease is an expense and flows through the fixed asset account on the balance sheet. True or false?**
   A. True
   B. False

10. **A lease is treated like an expense; it flows through the income statement and hence reduces what on the balance sheet?**
    A. Accounts payable
    B. Fixed assets
    C. Retained earnings
    D. Accounts receivable

Chapter **10**

Inventory Valuation

Let's talk about another common transaction in business—the purchase, manufacture, and sale of inventory.

CHAPTER OBJECTIVE

- Review how to account for raw materials inventory and finished goods inventory

Manufacturing Business: Inventory, Inventory, Inventory

A manufacturing business has several types of inventories. Let's go back to our birdbath business example.

As a birdbath manufacturer, you have a certain amount of stuff on hand for building the birdbaths—bags of cement, wire, and metal supports. Such stuff is commonly called *raw materials*.

You also will have some birdbaths that are in the works but are not finished. Maybe they are still drying, or maybe on Tuesday you made 100 bowls and on Wednesday you started work on 100 bases and haven't assembled them yet. This is called *work-in-process inventory* or *work-in-progress inventory*.

Still Struggling?

How to Reduce Inventory

When your resources are tied up in inventory, they aren't in your favorite spot—cash! What can you do about it? You could

- Make the vendors keep the inventory and ship it from their locations.
- Outsource components so that you don't have to keep the inventory to build those components.
- Order inventory "just in time," or only when you absolutely must have it.
- Pay vendors only as you use the inventory on hand.
- Ask vendors to install vending machines so that you pay only as you need the inventory.
- Allow the vendors to be part of your ordering system so that you order inventory in real time.
- Apply *kaizen*/Six Sigma principles to garner purchase, storage, manufacturing, and shipping efficiencies.
- Improve the quality of your product so that you minimize the need for repairs or replacement parts.
- Reward employees for keeping inventory low.
- Make products to order rather than to sit on a shelf for later sale.
- Limit employee access to inventory to reduce shrinkage.
- Use the same inexpensive core inventory to create multiple products.
- Reduce models and options.
- Stock only items that have a quick turnaround.
- Manage customer expectations.

- Tear down the warehouse.
- Quit doing business with clients that make you hold excess inventory.
- Get rid of obsolete inventory.
- Increase the accuracy of your inventory forecasts.
- Limit or forbid returns.
- Reduce try-before-you-buy and rental programs.

At some point you have manufactured and assembled the birdbaths, and they are ready for sale. This inventory is called *finished goods inventory*.

Some businesses spend a lot of effort and time tracking the balances in each of these categories. They may have a separate account for each of these categories on their books—one for raw materials, one for work in progress, and one for finished goods.

The way that inventory is valued is also of concern to manufacturing operations. Have you ever heard of LIFO and FIFO? They are not cute names for poodles; they are acronyms for methods of valuating inventory.

LIFO stands for "last in, first out." This method of valuing inventory assumes that any inventory that a manufacturer sells or uses is from the last inventory purchased. So looking at raw materials only for this example, we assume that the last bag of cement you bought is the first bag used to make the birdbaths. This may not be true in reality, but it is the way the bag of cement is accounted for. This results in a difference in the cost incurred in making a birdbath. If the cost of cement is going up each time you buy a bag, then the LIFO method will cause the cement price to be at its highest and thus the cost of making the birdbaths to be at its highest.

FIFO stands for "first in, first out." This method of valuing inventory assumes that any inventory that a manufacturer sells or uses is from the first inventory purchased. In our example, accounting pretends that the oldest bag of cement is used in the manufacturing process. So, if the price of cement is going up, the FIFO method would cause the cost of each birdbath to be the lowest cost possible.

There is a third method for computing the value of inventory. It is called the *weighted-average method*. Here the manufacturer takes the total cost of all items in inventory and divides it by the total number of units in inventory:

Total cost of goods for sale at cost + total number of units available for sale
$$= \text{weighted-average cost per unit}$$

This method tends to even out price fluctuations.

Here's an example: Suppose that you purchase five bales of wire at $10 apiece and five bales of wire at $20 apiece. Then you sell five birdbaths.

Five bales at $10 each = $50

Five bales at $20 each = $100

Total number of bales = 10

Weighted average   = ($50 + $100)/10 = $15

$15 is the average cost of the 10 bales.

So which method should you use? It is surprisingly a very complex decision. Several factors come into play. For one, if prices are going up and you use the FIFO method, your profit will be maximized on the sale of birdbaths (assuming low cost and stable pricing). This also means, because you are taxed on your profits, that your taxes are maximized as well.

Service Business: Minimal or No Inventory

Before we dig into our discussion of inventory, I want to distinguish between a service business and a manufacturing business in terms of inventory. A service business has minimal or no inventory. Take my business, for example. I am an author, course developer, and speaker. All I have is intellectual property: the 20-plus courses I have developed plus about a dozen books that I send to my customers in PDF form. When I make a sale, I am selling myself—I am selling myself going into an organization and teaching a class using the course material I have developed and to which I retain the rights. The only inventory I have are the books and manuals that I have written. In Chapter 16, I talk about metrics to help you track your success in managing your working capital in a service business. Pay close attention to "Days to bill."

Another factor that comes into play is your assumptions about the future. Do you believe that prices are going to continue to go up or go down? Predicting the future is impossible, but you might think that you have a firm handle on it for the near term.

Unfortunately, you can't change between one method and the other as it suits your purposes. Once you pick a method, you are stuck with it. You can change it, but the accounting and paperwork nightmare the change causes is prohibitive. The Internal Revenue Service (IRS) also may have something to say about your choice.

So let's run through a simple example showing how inventory moves through a birdbath manufacturer and the effect on the financial statements.

Moving Inventory through Raw Materials, Work in Process, and Finished Goods

This is like one of those crazy word problems you had to do in eighth-grade algebra, so if you didn't get into that, you won't get into this. I drew some pictures to help out.

On Monday, you have 10 bags of cement and 2 rolls of wire netting delivered by a local supplier (Figure 10.1). The supplier demands cash on delivery. A bag of cement costs $2.50, and a roll of wire costs $10.

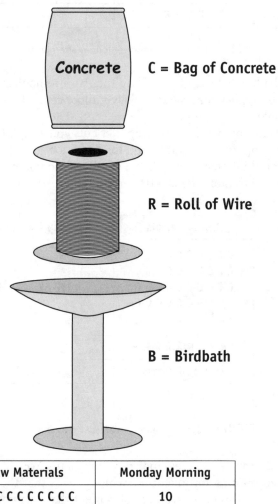

Concrete   C = Bag of Concrete

R = Roll of Wire

B = Birdbath

Raw Materials	Monday Morning
C C C C C C C C C C	10
R R	2

FIGURE 10.1 · Inventory—Monday morning.

Monday afternoon, the crew gets busy making birdbaths and goes through eight bags of cement—$20—and both rolls of wire—$20—to make four birdbaths (Figure 10.2). (As a rule, each birdbath takes a half roll of wire and two bags of cement to manufacture.) So each birdbath costs $10 ($5 for two bags plus $5 for a half roll of wire).

Raw Materials	Monday Afternoon
C C	2
Work in Process	
B B B B	4

FIGURE 10.2 · Inventory—Monday afternoon.

The birdbaths will be ready to sell by Tuesday afternoon at the earliest. Tuesday morning, the supplier comes out to deliver more cement and wire. However, the supplier would prefer that you buy more cement all at one time rather than have several deliveries per week, so the supplier cuts you a deal. If you buy 40 bags of cement, the supplier will sell it to you for $2.25 a bag. The cost of the wire stays the same. You think that sounds like a good deal, so you buy 40 bags of cement. You also buy 10 rolls of wire at $10 per roll (Figure 10.3).

Raw Materials	Tuesday Morning
C C C C C C C C C C C C C C C C C C C C C C C C C C C C C C C C C C C C C C C C C C	42
R R R R R R R R R R	10
Work in Process	
B B B B	4

FIGURE 10.3 · Inventory—Tuesday morning.

Tuesday afternoon, the crew makes six birdbaths. You decide to use the FIFO method of accounting for inventory, which means that the first inventory in is the first used. So you have two bags of cement that cost you $2.50 and 10 bags of cement that cost you $2.25. You also use up three rolls of wire. So one of your birdbaths cost $10 (using the original costing) and five of your birdbaths cost $9.50 each ($2.25 × 2 = $4.50 plus $5).

Tuesday afternoon, you acknowledge that the birdbaths you made on Monday afternoon are ready to sell and you put them out on the floor. In other words, you move the work-in-process inventory of birdbaths to finished goods inventory (Figure 10–4).

Raw Materials	Tuesday Afternoon
C C C C C C C C C C C C C C C C C C C C C C C C C C C C C C	30
R R R R R R R	7
Work in Process	
B B B B B B	6
Finished	
B B B B	4

FIGURE 10.4 · Inventory—Tuesday afternoon.

Wednesday morning, a customer comes in to buy two birdbaths for cash. You sell each birdbath for $20.

What is the profit, then, on each birdbath sold on Wednesday morning? $20 per bath less $10. Later in the week, when you sell the birdbaths that used the cheaper cement, the profit would be $10.50—$20 per bath less $9.50 (Figure 10.5).

Raw Materials	Wednesday Morning
C C C C C C C C C C C C C C C C C C C C C C C C C C C C C C	30
R R R R R R R	7
Work in Process	
B B B B B B	6
Finished Goods	
B B	2

FIGURE 10.5 · Inventory—Wednesday morning.

Wow! This is a lot of record keeping! You can imagine that most folks wouldn't bother keeping track of their inventory in such great detail, especially if the turnaround is just in a matter of days. But you can see how the cost of the materials and the assumptions you make about which raw materials are used first in the process can make a difference to the proverbial bottom line (profit).

Summary

Because of the nature of inventory, a series of accounts is created to track whether it is finished and ready to sell or has yet to be converted into a product. The movement of inventory through the manufacturing process creates a lot of entries for the accountant!

QUIZ

1. **A personal trainer would have large amounts of inventory. True or false?**
   A. True
   B. False

2. **You are still making birdbaths, and you have 20 bowls completed and 20 stands drying, and they will be assembled in a couple of days. What kind of inventory are these 40 pieces?**
   A. Raw materials
   B. Work in progress
   C. Finished goods

3. **If you are making birdbaths, the bags of concrete and wire are what kind of inventory?**
   A. Raw materials
   B. Work in progress
   C. Finished goods

4. **I need to find a value for my inventory, so I decide that the oldest bag of cement is the next bag of cement I use. Which method of inventory valuation am I using?**
   A. LIFO
   B. FIFO
   C. Weighted average

5. **After you decide on the inventory valuation method you are going to use, you can change whenever you want to minimize taxes. True or false?**
   A. True
   B. False

6. **FIFO pretends that the newest raw material item is used first in manufacturing products. True or false?**
   A. True
   B. False

7. **The weighted-average method of inventory valuation tends to even out price fluctuations in the accounting records. True or false?**
   A. True
   B. False

8. **A service business usually has minimal amounts of inventory. True or false?**
   A. True
   B. False

9. Work-in-process inventory is inventory that is finished and waiting for customers to pick it up. True or false?
   A. True
   B. False

10. LIFO stands for
    A. last in freaks out.
    B. last in, first out.
    C. last included, finds others.

Chapter **11**

Guiding Principles of Accounting and Adjusting Entries

In accounting, we have experts who spend large amounts of time theorizing about why we do what we do. Many of them are professors, some are partners in accounting firms, and others work for a standards-setting board. And these reasons for doing what we do have become what we call *accounting principles*.

CHAPTER OBJECTIVES

- Discuss guiding principles that accountants use to make decisions
- Explain end-of-year transactions and entries

I like to think of accounting principles as guides that help us to make good choices in creating financial information. When in doubt about how to treat a transaction, you can consult these principles and concepts. If it is a very technical issue, you may have to consult with one of those thoughtful "experts"—a certified public accountant (CPA) or the Financial Accounting Standards Board (FASB) and the Governmental Accounting Standards Board (GASB).

Guiding Principles of Accounting

These are the basic accounting principles, concepts, and assumptions that we will cover in this chapter:

- Business entity
- Continuing concern
- Conservatism
- Objectivity
- Time period
- Revenue recognition
- Cost
- Consistency
- Materiality
- Full disclosure
- Matching

Business Entity

A business—whether it is a sole proprietorship, a partnership, or a corporation—is a separate and distinct entity. The records of the business are not to mingle with those of other entities, including the owner of the entity. For example, if the owner of a partnership buys a house for his family, it does not go on the books of the partnership.

Continuing Concern

A business is assumed to live on and on unless expressly stated otherwise. This is known as the *continuing-* or *going-concern concept*, and the financial records are maintained on the assumption that the business will continue forever. When an auditor has doubt that the business will live much longer, he or she will report in the auditor's opinion that the business is a "going concern" and detail why the business is likely to fail or cease business.

Conservatism

This is also known as the *prudence principle*. Dear Prudence, won't you come out to play. Until the Enron fiasco, I mistakenly believed that all accountants were trained to be conservative. (I know that we were definitely trained to dress conservatively. When I graduated from college, white shirts, blue suits, and those little red ties that looked like whipped cream flowers were all the rage for female accountants.)

I was trained to record transactions only if they definitely had happened or were going to happen. And I was trained to record, when in doubt, the most conservative number—the worst-case scenario, if you will. If there was a choice between a high revenue number and a low revenue number, you were to go with the low revenue number. In that way, if things turned out for the better, you could adjust upward and make everyone happy. If things went bad, you'd have already faced it.

Conservatism asks that you don't overstate revenues or understate expenses. It also asks that what you record be fair and reasonable. Or another way to look at it is that it asks you not to anticipate any profit unless realized but to provide for all probable losses.

Objectivity

All transactions entered into the accounting records of a business should be based on evidence—not opinion. Instead of guessing how much a vendor is going to request as payment, you wait until you get the invoice and enter the bill amount. You don't just pull numbers out of the sky. If you are forced to do this for some reason, you disclose your method for guessing in the notes to the financial statements.

This is one of the reasons that accountants don't bother putting a value on a brand name, such as the Coca-Cola brand. It is impossible to figure out with any great accuracy how much that would be worth. The brand is worth millions, maybe billions, but until someone pays actual cash for it, you would just be guessing at its worth. Guessing makes us accountants uncomfortable, so we try to avoid it

Who Comes Up with All This Stuff Anyway?

Congress created the Securities and Exchange Commission (SEC) in 1934 as a reaction to the stock market crash that led to the Great Depression. Before 1934, corporations were unregulated, and insider trading and other funny business practices were common and legal.

The Securities Exchange Act of 1934 both created the SEC and directed corporations to present registration statements for new issuances of stock and to make a "full and fair" disclosure of financial information. Congress gave the SEC the power to regulate the accounting profession. The SEC handed this job off to the profession, which promptly formed a self-regulating body. This body has had many names but is now called the *American Institute of Certified Public Accountants* (AICPA).

The AICPA then turned around and created several rule-making boards. The first board is the Financial Accounting Standards Board (FASB). The FASB was formed in 1973, has seven full-time members, and has issued 140 pronouncements that make up the bulk of generally accepted accounting principles (GAAP). The FASB's mission is to "establish and improve standards of financial accounting and reporting for the guidance and education of the public." In 1984, the AICPA created the GASB, which is similar to the FASB except that it issues GAAP for governmental entities.

After the Enron debacle, the federal government again intervened and criticized the accounting and auditing profession for doing a poor job with financial statements. The federal government created another standard setter, the Public Company Accounting Oversight Board (PCAOB) in 2002. You may have heard of the Sarbanes-Oxley Act, or "Sarbox"?

Sarbox refers to the law that created the PCAOB and a litany of audit and accounting requirements. One of them is the letter that executives must sign in the back of the financial statements that promises that the statements are free of material error and that internal controls are in place and working. I talked about that briefly in Chapter 7.

And as I mentioned in Chapter 4, the United States is doing its best to put aside its narcissistic tendencies and go international. The International Financial Reporting Standards (IFRS) likely will be implemented by publicly traded U.S. corporations by 2013.

So, if you are wondering whose rules to follow in case of an accounting question, here is the list of the rule makers, with the most influential being at the top:

- Securities and Exchange Commission (SEC)
- American Institute of Certified Public Accountants (AICPA)
- Financial Accounting Standards Board (FASB)
- Governmental Accounting Standards Board (GASB)
- Public Company Accounting Oversite Board (PCAOB)

Time Period

Have you ever heard of a *fiscal year*? This accounting principle says that all accounting periods should be of similar length. Many fiscal years will begin on January 1 and end on December 31, but a business can choose any time period.

Many companies choose a fiscal year that ends when sales are at their peak so that the cash balance and other balances will look as attractive as possible. For instance, a school textbook publisher I worked with made the majority of its sales in August, when the school districts purchased their books, so its fiscal year end was in September.

Some companies choose a fiscal year to end during a time that is not so busy for the accountants so that the accountants will have time to prepare the financial statements. Whatever you choose, you have to stick with it because of the consistency concept (discussed later).

Revenue Recognition

Revenue should be recorded when the transaction actually occurs. Generally, revenue is recognized when the customer is billed or cash is received.

Sometimes, deciding when to recognize revenue is more complicated, such as when a service firm, say, a consultant, is working on a long-term project. Remember that conservatism asks that we not overstate revenues. One of the major sticking points of changing from U.S. GAAP to IFRS regards revenue recognition. U.S. GAAP are written to be industry-specific, and IFRS rely on a set of more simple principles. As of this writing, the jury is still out on what the FASB and AICPA will do to guide the creators of financial statements.

In other words, if you have a question on this, it can get very technical. You may have to wade through the FASB's accounting pronouncements.

Cost

We don't work with *market value* much in accounting. Whatever was paid to purchase a fixed asset remains that asset's value until it is sold or disposed of. This makes things easier for accountants—but not necessarily more accurate. For example, if your business purchased a warehouse in 1982 for $180,000, then the book value would remain at $180,000 less depreciation until you sold it or it burned down. Even if the warehouse is worth $500,000 in 2011, its value remains at $180,000.

This is one of the biggest drawbacks of the accounting model. If assets are valued at historical value, this might understate or sometimes overstate the value of the assets. But given our principle of objectivity, you can see the theoretical and practical dilemma. What evidence would we have of the market value of the warehouse?

In 2006, the profession decided that marketable securities (e.g., stocks, bonds, and derivatives) should be valued not at historical cost but rather at fair value. *Fair value* is described in IFRS as "the amount for which an asset could be exchanged between knowledgeable, willing parties in an arm's-length transaction." Is that vague enough for you? CPAs have to get 40 hours of education each year to keep their license, and CPAs can opt to attend two-day courses on this very topic. I've even been invited to attend fair-value conferences taught by experts in the field. Obviously, fair-value determination gets very granular and requires the application of plenty of professional judgment. It is so much easier to go with historical cost!

Although most financial statements still are based on historical cost, you should know that if you are selling your business, the purchaser won't care what you paid, but he will care what it is worth. You will have to come up with a market value for all your assets. And whatever the buyer pays you over book value (historic value on your books) for your business becomes my least favorite concept in accounting—goodwill. Don't make me talk about it; it is a very silly concept, and to make it even sillier, goodwill must be amortized. The books have to balance, after all!

Consistency

Changing your mind about how a transaction is treated from period to period is frowned on in accounting. Once you make up your mind about something, you should stick with it. Otherwise, the financial statements won't be comparable, and users of the financial information won't know what's going on from year to year. If you do change your mind, you must disclose the change in the financial statements.

The principle of consistency also means that the same accounting treatment is applied to similar events from period to period. Once you choose a fiscal year and a method for valuing inventory, for instance, you are stuck with those choices.

Are you getting a sense of what sort of personalities would be attracted to the accounting profession? Folks who don't mind doing the same thing every time, who want to record things only once, and who take the most conservative or pessimistic view are well suited to financial accounting. (I am going to get a lot of letters on this one.)

Internal Controls Aren't Vitamins

Internal controls are policies and procedures that help you to get things accomplished. Thinking of this from a personal perspective, consider this question: How do you make sure that you get to work on time every day?

I have controls in place to make sure I am not late to teach my classes. One of my recurring nightmares when I am stressed out is that I show up for class three or four hours late. I then have to face hostile participants who are ready to go to lunch. To make sure that this nightmare does not become a reality, I pick out and press my clothes the night before. I write down an estimate of how long it will take me to get ready in the morning and to travel to the site. I factor in how long it will take me to set up the room. (Some of my classes require more setup than others.) I also pack my supplies, such as my laptop, my pens, my toys, etc., and put them by the front door. I set two alarm clocks, one battery-operated and the other electric; in this way, even if one doesn't work, I have another. If I am at home, I tell my husband what time I need to be up; if he wakes up and I'm not up yet, he can get me up. If I am on the road, I call for a wake-up call from the hotel. And I could keep going with this—My controls reduce my anxiety.

Organizations also have anxieties. They worry about whether their products or services will be delivered to the customer in good condition and on time. They worry about whether their financial statements will be accurate. They worry about whether their employees will get sent a payroll check each week. In order to get where they want to go and do what they need to do, they have to put controls in place. Controls are little procedures that ensure that goals are met.

The Sarbanes-Oxley Act (also known as "Sarbox") requires auditors to evaluate the internal controls that contribute to the creation of accurate financial statements. The hope is that these controls will keep shyster accountants from lying about financial results in the financial statements.

Materiality

Here we accountants cut ourselves a little slack; we get a little rebellious. (Get out the Harley!) If you hear an accountant say that something is *not material* this means that it has no significant impact on the financial statements. This allows us to sometimes bypass GAAP rules, especially when the cost of complying with GAAP is prohibitive.

Auditors love to use the phrase *not material* in conducting their audits. Auditors can't examine every single transaction, so the purchase of a stapler in a multibillion-dollar corporation usually will not come under scrutiny. Even if the stapler were accounted for improperly, who would really care? It isn't *material*. Next time your significant other gives you a hard time about buying an expensive pair of shoes, tell him or her that the purchase was not material and to focus on the big picture.

Still Struggling?

Materiality

If you work with auditors frequently, you will hear them say "not material" over and over and over. Auditors are responsible for designing their audits of financial statements to determine whether they are materially misstated. In other words, they are looking for big, misleading mistakes in the financials. Not the small stuff. If they were looking for absolute accuracy in the financial statements, they'd be camped out at the client's offices forever!

So, when I audited a $23 billion teacher's pension fund, I designed my audit to catch errors bigger than $500,000. Anything less than that was "immaterial." Yes. You read that right. Later, when I audited a small not-for-profit business, my materiality level was $350. Materiality, good looks, and smarts are relative. When auditors do find a material error, they ask the client to make journal entries to the books to correct the mistake.

Full Disclosure

This reminds accountants that all disclosures in the financial statements are considered complete unless stated otherwise. Information that may affect a user's understanding of the financial statements must be disclosed. A knowledgeable user should be able to make an informed judgment about the financial condition of the business given the information provided.

Matching

This principle says that the expenses incurred in generating revenue should be matched with the revenues they generate. Here is an example: Let's say that you use a software program to design custom birdbaths for your customers. The software may have been purchased several years before, but you are using it now to generate income. In accounting, we like to match the software expense to the revenue it helped generate. It is only fair. Why should the first year be the only year burdened with the cost of the software?

The matching principle is one of the main reasons we bother with depreciating things. A depreciation expense is recorded every year that an asset is used. In this way, the cost of purchasing the software is not recorded in a way that artificially reduces profit in the year of purchase and then artificially inflates revenues in future years. Matching evens out the resulting profit (revenues less expenses).

The matching principle also causes us to make adjusting entries at the end of the year to make sure that we are stating all accounts fairly.

Adjusting Entries

Adjustments to the General Ledger at the End of the Period

Accountants make what are called *adjusting entries* for three reasons:

1. To bring balances up or down to where they should be
2. To match expenses to the revenues that generated them and vice versa
3. To give the accountants a chance to rest

Adjustments to Ensure Accuracy

At the end of a period, the accountant often has to make adjusting entries to several accounts to better represent what the balance in these accounts really should be.

Here's an example: Let's say that it's December 31, the last day of your fiscal year. The electric company usually bills you on the twentieth of every month for the previous month. So the last bill you got was for November electricity. You don't know how much the company is going to charge you for December electricity, but you should record an expense for the electricity at the end of the year so that the expense isn't understated for the fiscal year.

Now you have to do some estimating and make an adjusting entry. If your bill from November was $2,700, then you might assume that the bill for December would be similar.

At the end of the year, you would make an adjusting entry as follows:

DR Electricity expense	$2,700	
CR Utilities payable		$2,700

In this way, the revenues for the year are matched accurately to the expenses that helped to create them. When the real bill arrives during the next fiscal year, the accounts can be adjusted to the proper amounts.

Think about the concepts of materiality and objectivity discussed earlier in this chapter. You do not have objective evidence on December 31 of exactly what the electric company is going to bill. But you can "guesstimate" it based on previous December bills or assume that it will be similar to November's bill. This is pretty objective. An estimate will be just fine, and you arrived at it in a fair, objective manner. The amount that your estimate is different than the actual electricity expense for December is not material to the overall financial statements of the entity.

Adjustments to Match Expenses to Revenues

Accrual accounting minimizes profit distortions. The matching principle requires that expenses be recognized along with the revenue they help to generate. You cannot falsely reduce profits by paying a bunch of expenses in advance or artificially inflate revenue by having clients prepay for services or products.

Using the same example as earlier, you made sales and created your product or service using the electricity in December, and you must recognize that fact by estimating electricity expense.

Adjusting Entries—Let the Accountant Rest

Another reason for adjusting entries is that accountants don't want to have to keep track of every little detail on a monthly basis. It is just easier to make year-end entries for some items instead of doing it every day, every week, or every month.

For instance, let's say that you have 100 printers in your office, and they all use toner cartridges. When you buy the cartridges, they go into office supply inventory as an asset. At the end of the year, an inventory is taken to determine how many toner cartridges are left. What is used during the year is recorded as an expense. An adjusting entry is made to reduce the inventory balance.

The toner cartridges are no longer a happy asset that you own; they are gone. You used them up, so the cost needs to be recognized as a cost of doing business, an expense. We wait until the end of the year to do this inventory and to adjust the expense because it would be tedious and time consuming for the accountant to make an entry recording toner cartridge expense every time a toner cartridge is retrieved from the office supply cabinet.

Usually, low-dollar—or immaterial—items are not tracked daily. If we were instead talking about an inventory of $300 printers, you would make entries to account for them every month or every time one is taken out of the supply room.

Each Organization's Situation Is Unique

The information that follows about adjusting entries is not exhaustive. There are items that will be unique to your situation that you need to take into account. Remember, the goal is to update the accounts for all items that have been used within the fiscal year.

Common Adjusting Entries

Here are some items that usually require an adjusting entry:

- Wages earned by employees but not yet paid
- Payroll taxes due but not yet paid

- Property taxes
- Interest expense and principal payments on a loan
- Prepaid insurance
- Inventory on hand at the end of a period
- Supplies expense or supplies consumed
- Interest income earned but not yet received
- Depreciation expense
- Bad debts
- Dividends payable
- Income taxes payable
- Income receivable
- Expenses payable

Some Sample Entries

Supplies

Let's go back to the toner cartridge example. Assuming that earlier in the year you recorded the purchase of the toner cartridges as an asset. You now need to recognize an expense for the toner cartridges that were used. So you reverse out or reduce the asset and record an expense. Because happy assets are recorded as debits, you credit the asset account and debit expenses. This works out well because increases to expenses are always debits.

DR Office supplies expense—toner cartridges $700
    CR Office supplies—toner cartridges $700

See how close these accounts sound? Office supplies expense and office supplies. This can get a little confusing. One is an expense, and one is an asset. If you think this similar naming will cause problems in the future, you may want to come up with a more unique name for one or both of them.

Prepaid Insurance

You might, like I do, pay insurance for months at a time, in advance so that you don't have to keep writing a check every month. Let's say that you pay six months in advance in October. Each month costs $200, for a total of $1,200 in insurance expense.

When you initially purchase the insurance, you record it as an asset. It is a happy thing that you will have the benefit of in the future. Here is what you do when you first buy the insurance.

DR Prepaid insurance $1,200
    CR Cash $1,200

At the end of the year, you recognize that half the happy asset has been used up and recognize an insurance expense. You enter

DR Insurance expense $600
    CR Prepaid insurance $600

Wages Expense

Rarely will the end of the year fall conveniently on the same day that you pay payroll. So it is likely that your employees have worked hours that they have not been paid for. Here is the entry:

DR Wages expense $5,704
    CR Wages payable $5,704

You also may want to recognize all applicable payroll taxes and payroll deductions.

Depreciation Expense

Depreciation is one of those weird entries that never affects cash. We in accounting call it a *noncash* transaction. Depreciation is realized as you use up an asset. As the asset ages, its value is diminished, and an expense for it should be recognized. This is similar in concept to the previously discussed examples of supplies expense and prepaid insurance expense.

For example, when you buy a copier in January, you make the following entry:

DR Copier $10,000
    CR Cash $10,000

So it is now recorded as a happy asset. By the end of the year, though, you have used up some of the copier's useful life. Copiers last only so long before they have to be replaced. So let's say that we think that the copier will last five years. At the end of the first fiscal year, in December, you recognize that one-fifth of the life of the copier has been used. Thus $2,000 of value has been consumed (using the *straight-line depreciation* method). So you make this entry:

DR Depreciation expense $2,000
    CR Accumulated depreciation $2,000

Whoa! Were you expecting that I would credit "copier"? This makes perfect intuitive sense. However, it is not the way we do it. This is a strange rule—for which we have a good explanation.

Remember from Chapter 9 that the account "Accumulated depreciation" is a contra account. A contra account is listed next to another account in the financial statements. In other words, it is mated with another account.

For example, accumulated depreciation is mated with the equipment asset and would be disclosed on the balance sheet like this:

Equipment	$10,000
Less accumulated depreciation	$ 2,000
Net equipment	$8,000

Why do we bother with this contra account thing? Because we want to show the original value of the asset. The contra account helps to indicate the age of an asset. If the contra account were $10,000, we would know that this copier was at the end of its useful life and soon would have to be replaced.

The net equipment number is also called the *book value* of the asset. This is not necessarily the asset's real market value; it is simply the historical cost of the asset less accumulated depreciation. We might be able to sell that copier for $9,000 at the end of the first fiscal year, but on the books, we stick with $8,000. Remember the principle of historical cost from earlier in this chapter? We accountants don't like to mess with market value—it fluctuates too wildly.

Still Struggling?

Depreciation Types

Accounting standards give you a choice of how to depreciate or amortize an item—not many choices, but a choice nonetheless.
These methods are your choices:

Straight line (SL). Here, you take the total value of the asset and divide it by the number of years of useful life. This results in the same depreciation charge each year. For example, we have a $10,000 van that has a five-year life. Each year, we realize $2,000 ($10,000/5) in depreciation.

Sum of the years' digits (SYD). This one is a little more fun for those who like math. This method results in a higher amount of depreciation in earlier years.

Take our van again, with its five-year life. If we sum all the years' digits (1 + 2 + 3 + 4 + 5), we get 15, which becomes our denominator. Then, in the first year, we say that the van has five years of life left. So our numerator that year is 5, and our depreciation rate is 5/15. Thus $10,000 × 5/15 = $3,333 in depreciation for year one. In year two, we have four years left, so 4 becomes our numerator, and our rate of depreciation is 4/15. Figure 11.1 shows the way the whole thing shakes out.

Year	Depreciable Cost Rate	Depreciable Expense	Accumulated Depreciation	Book Value
1	10,000 x 5/15	$3,333	$3,333	$6,667
2	10,000 x 4/15	$2,667	$6,000	$4,000
3	10,000 x 3/15	$2,000	$8,000	$2,000
4	10,000 x 2/15	$1,333	$9,333	$667
5	10,000 x 1/15	$667	$10,000	$0

FIGURE 11.1 · Sum-of-digits balance method depreciation.

Double-declining balance (DDB). Under this method, the remaining book value (not the total original book value) is multiplied by double the straight-line percentage rate. In our example, the straight-line rate was 20 percent each year (100 percent/5); double that is 40 percent. It is a method that leaves a residual value on the asset: The entire amount is not depreciated over the life of the asset. It is not a very popular method.

In the first year, we multiply the value of $10,000 by 40 percent and get a $4,000 depreciation and a remaining book value of $6,000. In year two, we take the remaining $6,000 book value and multiply it by 40 percent; we get $2,400 of depreciation and have a $3,600 book value left. And we repeat it and repeat it through year 5 (Figure 11.2).

Year	Depreciable Cost Rate	Depreciable Expense	Accumulated Depreciation	Book Value
1	10,000 (20% x 2)	$4,000	$4,000	$6,000
2	6,000 (20% x 2)	$2,400	$6,400	$3,600
3	3,600 (20% x 2)	$1,440	$7,840	$2,160
4	2,160 (20% x 2)	$864	$8,704	$1,296
5	1,296 (20% x 2)	$518	$9,444	$778

FIGURE 11.2 · Double-declining balance method of depreciation.

Units of production. Instead of using time to calculate depreciation, this method uses units. For example, we estimate that a manufacturing machine will produce 200,000 units over its life. In the first year, it produces 50,000 units, so we depreciate a quarter of its value in the first year (50,000 units/200,000 units per life = 25 percent).

Modified accelerated cost recovery system (MACRS). This is the Internal Revenue Service (IRS) system for depreciating assets. It is a two-step process. First, figure out how long the IRS says that your asset will live. Second, use a handy-dandy table to get your rate. For example, assets that can be depreciated over three years include tractors and race horses over two years old. No, really! Five-year property includes autos, trucks, computers, and dairy cattle. And the list goes on.

Once you decide what the useful life of your property is based on the IRS list, then you refer to a MACRS table that tells you what the depreciation rate is in each year.

MACRS is an accelerated depreciation method, which means that more depreciation is taken in the first years than in the later years. This differs from straight-line depreciation, in which the same amount is taken every year regardless of the age of the asset.

Unearned Revenue

In a lovely, perfect world, your clients pay you in advance for all the work you do for them. Many businesses actually do work this way, advertising firms, for example. Let's say that I take on a three-month project to develop a finance training curriculum for a client that is due at the end of February, and I accept a payment in advance of $9,000 in November. In November, I make this entry:

DR Cash	$9,000
CR Unearned consulting revenue	$9,000

Unearned consulting revenue is a liability account. Interesting, eh? It acknowledges that I owe the client services and that I have not yet delivered.

At the end of the year, I should acknowledge that I have completed a third of the project. I do this so that the revenues are matched to expenses. In December, I make this entry:

DR Unearned consulting revenue	$3,000
CR Consulting revenue	$3,000

In February, when I finish the project, the entry is

DR Unearned consulting revenue	$6,000
CR Consulting revenue	$6,000

Revenue Earned but Not Received

The opposite of the preceding scenario also could happen. Let's say that the client has not paid me in advance but instead will give me a check the day

I finish the project in February. I am still making an effort to complete the project and incurring expenses related to the project in the current fiscal year. So, in December, I need to recognize some consulting revenue receivable. Because receivables are assets, I debit the account to increase it:

> DR Consulting revenue receivable $3,000
>   CR Consulting revenue $3,000

The next year, in February, I will make the following entry:

> DR Cash $9,000
>   CR Consulting revenue $6,000
>   CR Consulting revenue receivable $3,000

This one was a little complex. It has three legs. I had to increase cash because the client paid me with a nice check for $9,000. Then I had to reverse the receivable of $3,000 because the bill is all paid up—it is no longer receivable. Finally, I had to recognize the remaining revenue of $6,000. Whew!

Closing the Books

Each of the financial statements acts differently at the end of the year. The income statement is refreshed, the balance sheet is tweaked, and the cash-flow statement is flipped. (This sounds like a good day at the spa to me!)

The income statement is refreshed every year. It is zeroed out. We start each year with zero revenue and zero expenses. Throughout the year, we build up the balances in the revenue and expense accounts and calculate the resulting profit (revenues less expense). The resulting profit is posted to the balance sheet in the retained earnings account. For this reason, revenues and expenses are sometimes called *temporary accounts*.

All the balance-sheet accounts, in contrast, are called *permanent accounts*. The balance sheet is not wiped clean every year; it is tweaked. The accounts on the balance sheet are just adjusted—either increased or decreased—throughout the year. The asset, liability, and equity accounts always have a balance.

The cash-flow statement is, in effect, flipped every year. The ending balance of cash for this period is used as the beginning balance of cash for the next period.

Now, why does all this matter? Because you should understand what the term *closing the books* means. It's the process of closing out the temporary accounts—revenues and expenses—and posting the results to the balance sheet.

Many software programs will do this whole process automatically for you. The program will automatically adjust the retained earnings each time you make an entry for a revenue or an expense. In this way, the balance sheet is always up to date.

When, at the end of the year, you command the software to "close the books," it will wipe out the revenue and expense accounts and may make it impossible to enter any more revenue or expense transactions for the year on which you are working. So be *very* careful to push this button only after you have recorded everything that you want to for the period. Otherwise, you will have to make *adjusting journal entries*—not a huge deal but not as easy as just entering expenses or revenues.

Trial Balance

A *trial balance* is a list of all the accounts in your chart of accounts with their respective balances listed in a debit or credit column. The debit and credit columns are totaled at the bottom of the report.

The reason it is called a *trial balance* is that it is used to prove that your debits do indeed equal your credits. If they do not, your trial did not work, and you have some investigating and adjusting of accounts to do.

You might have heard stories of accountants spending days trying to track down 84 cents that was throwing their books off balance. One cool thing about the latest accounting software is that it will not allow you to make any unbalanced entries. Your debits must equal your credits each time, so the ending balances are sure to work, and your accountant doesn't have to waste his or her time tracking down trivial amounts.

Summary

An accountant's mettle is tested when he or she ventures beyond the day-to-day transactions covered in earlier chapters. The accountant has to use creativity and professional judgment in accounting for unusual transactions and in closing the books at the end of the year. The accounting principles help accountants to think through the impact of their treatment of a transaction.

QUIZ

1. When the auditor doubts that the business will live much longer, the auditor calls the business a
    A. continuation disclosure.
    B. contingency.
    C. full disclosure.
    D. going concern.

2. This concept asks that you don't overstate revenues or understate expenses.
    A. Revenue recognition
    B. Objectivity
    C. Conservatism
    D. Cost

3. "Establish and improve standards of financial accounting and reporting for the guidance and education of the public" is the mission statement of which of the following entities?
    A. SEC
    B. AICPA
    C. FASB
    D. GAAP

4. A fiscal year can start and end when you decide as long as it equals a full year. True or false?
    A. True
    B. False

5. The IFRS rely on broad principles. However, the GAAP are
    A. specific to a country.
    B. specific to the industry.
    C. specific to a government.
    D. specific to nonprofits.

6. Your business buys a storefront for $100,000. The book value remains $100,000 until three years later, when someone buys an almost identical storefront next to yours for $400,000. Then the historical book value must change because obviously someone will pay you more than $100,000 for your storefront. True or false?
    A. True
    B. False

7. **Internal controls are policies and procedures that do what?**
   A. Ensure that all employees have fun
   B. Make life miserable for employees
   C. Ensure that your company goals are met

8. **Auditors love the phrase *not material* when they conduct audits because**
   A. they can't audit every possible transaction.
   B. they want to audit everything.
   C. they want to focus on the little things.
   D. the big picture is not important.

9. **Depreciation is a noncash transaction. True or false?**
   A. True
   B. False

10. **The only depreciation method that does not take higher depreciation in the earlier years is**
    A. straight line.
    B. sum of years' digits.
    C. double-declining balance.
    D. modified accelerated cost recovery system.

Chapter 12

Governmental and Not-for-Profit Accounting

Now that you know the basics and before we get into applying them, I should say a few things about two aberrant types of accounting—government and not-for-profit accounting. Governments and not-for-profits have different operating objectives than for-profit entities, and their financial statements reflect those differences.

CHAPTER OBJECTIVES

- Compare government and not-for-profit financial statements with for-profit financial statements
- Review government and not-for-profit accounting terminology

For-profit—or proprietary—entities are in it for the money. They want to earn profit and cash so that they can distribute it to the owners so that the owners can live well. Governments take money from their owners (the citizens) to provide services to their owners. Governments build and maintain roads, provide fire and police protection, educate our children, and so on. To pay for all of this, governments collect taxes. The government is not supposed to make a profit from its collections! Every dime collected is supposed to be used for the benefit of the citizens.

Not-for-profits are not governments: They do not collect taxes, and they do not exist to benefit any owners. Not-for-profits are designed to use their resources to help specific people or groups. For instance, a not-for-profit might collect donations to run a home for troubled teenagers. All donations collected are to be used for the benefit of the troubled teenagers—not distributed to any owners or accumulated in a Swiss bank account.

In this chapter, I want to highlight some of the key differences between proprietary (or commercial) accounting and governmental and not-for-profit accounting. Because of their different operating objectives, they also have different financial reports and financial terminology. So far we have been talking about proprietary or for-profit accounting. Again, I am not going to drill down into a lot of detail. I am going to give you a big-picture view.

Key Differences between Proprietary and Governmental and Not-for-Profit Accounting

Governmental and not-for-profit accounting is different from proprietary accounting in several key ways:

- Both avoid the word *profit*.
- Both pool resources into categories, programs, or funds.
- Both require retitled and re-formatted financial statements.

GAAP for Government and Not-for-Profits

Governmental accounting and not-for-profit accounting also differ in who sets their standards. Governmental entities, such as municipalities, counties, and states, use generally accepted accounting principles (GAAP) promulgated by the Governmental Accounting Standards Board (GASB). Many not-for-profits follow GAAP promulgated by the Financial Accounting Standards Board (FASB). Some that operate like government entities may choose to use GASB standards.

With that said, let's start with an overview of governmental accounting.

Governmental Accounting

The Funds

One of the unique features of governmental financial statements is that governments use pools or funds to track and report on their resources. When you look at a huge proprietary conglomerate, such as IBM, you will see all the revenues and expenditures consolidated into one huge category. As far as the readers of the financial statements can tell, all the money is flowing in and out of one big purse.

Governments, on the other hand, keep track of their money in distinct pockets in the one big purse. (Think back to those huge, multipocket granny purses they used to sell on late-night TV in the 1970s.) Governments keep their funds separate so that they can track the revenues and expenditures for different programs and functions.

Governments hate to commingle the resources of one fund with those of another fund. *Commingling* means that money from one fund is being used to pay for another fund's program or project. For example, commingling occurs when you use money set aside to pay for school lunches to pay for the football team's new equipment. The federal government especially forbids commingling its funds with other funds because it wants federal grants to be used only for the purposes intended by Congress.

Examples of Funds

For example, let's say that you run a county government, and the new First Lady of the United States has a pet project that Congress is backing her on. She wants to build one new library per 200,000 children across the country. These funds will be funneled down to the local level through the counties. So you've received funding for three new libraries in your county from the feds.

The feds want to be sure that you don't use their money for any other purpose except to build libraries. If you do—if you use the library funds to fix a sewer line, for example—the feds will pull the plug on the program and take their money back plus a penalty.

So you create a separate fund to track this library grant until the libraries are finished. You do not commingle the feds' money with any other money. Each year that it takes you to build the library, you are able to report to the feds how much of their money was spent and on what items.

Here's another example: A highway near my house has taken literally 10 years to complete. This is so because the city leaders did not specifically set aside money in their budgets or in a special fund to pay for the construction. Each year, they just use any surplus money out of sales tax revenues to work on the road. Therefore, in essence, the road construction funds are commingled with other funds the city uses to operate. When an emergency comes up, as it always does, the city must use the money it planned to spend on the road to handle the emergency, such as to renovate a school or buy new vehicles for the police department.

If, instead, the city had issued bonds or debt to build the road and put the money aside in a special fund for the road, city leaders less likely would have been tempted to sacrifice the road construction for other immediately pressing needs.

Where the Government Gets Its Resources

In a commercial entity, the owners of the company have a handful of options to bring in resources: They can earn profit, take out a loan, sell a share of their company to others, get government funding, or chip in their own resources. Governments have similar options—but each has a political cost:

- *Collect taxes.* Taxes are so popular with the citizenry! Citizens absolutely adore it when you raise their taxes, and to show their gratitude, they often help the politician who proposes tax increases to move on to another career.

- *Charge fees and penalties.* Did you want to park there? Well, that is going to cost you. How about owning a pet, entering a park, or starting a business? My phone bill has almost a dozen fees and taxes on it because so many governments are enjoying a piece of the telecommunication action.

- *Pursue grants and gifts.* Grants come with plenty of strings attached. And usually, grantors require that you match their grant with your own funds— so the grants aren't free, just supplemental. The extra paperwork and audit requirements alone might turn you off from taking the money.

- *Issue debt.* By issuing debt, the government can get something done today that can be paid for by future citizens. Debt payments must be made on time, with interest, much like a mortgage. Long-term debt goes against a conservative governing principle called *interperiod equity*, which is a fancy way of saying that current resources should pay for current services, and our children shouldn't have to pay for us later. The federal government isn't doing well with this concept—because our huge federal deficit means that each citizen is $487,000 in debt as of September 2008 (according to ex–Controller General of the United States David Walker).

- *Sell something the government owns.* I enjoyed a ridiculous but true story on the *Daily Show* about the State of New Mexico selling the state capital to an investor and then leasing it back in 2010. This allowed the state to balance its 2010 budget. Of course, you could be sensible and simply sell unneeded facilities, equipment, or land.

- *Sell equity in the government.* Until Texas got creative with its road-building projects, I didn't think that government could use equity to raise funds.

But I wasn't confronted with the dilemma our state leaders faced in 2002. The citizens in Austin were demanding new roads because our population grew nearly 50 percent in the 1990s, and it was getting harder and harder to get around. "May we raise your taxes to pay for it?" asked our government leaders. "No!" said the citizens. "May we charge you a toll for driving on the roads?" "No!" "May we issue debt to build the roads?" Again, the citizens said, "No!" Yet the citizens still were demanding roads. A Spanish engineering conglomerate solved the problem. The company offered the state an upfront payment and promised to build plenty of roads in short order. And it did; it only took a few years to cover my area of town with brand new roads. But there is always a catch! The state has to maintain and improve the roads and allow the Spanish company to collect the tolls for decades. So the state sold part of itself to the Spanish! I feel so violated. But I must admit to loving those roads when I have to get to the airport during rush hour.

Types of Funds

So now that we understand the purpose of the government having funds, let's talk about the different types of funds. There are three supercategories of funds:

- Fiduciary funds
- Proprietary funds
- Governmental funds

Each of these general categories has several fund types, and each fund type can have several fund titles. For example, the governmental fund supercategory contains several fund types—one being special revenue funds. A government may have as many special revenue funds as it likes, lumped under special revenue fund type. Here's an example:

- Government funds—supercategory
  - Special revenue fund—fund type
    - Federal Highway Construction Grant—fund title

Fiduciary Funds	Proprietary Funds	Governmental Funds
• agency funds	• enterprise funds	• general fund
• pension trust funds	• internal service funds	• special revenue funds
• investment trust funds		• capital projects funds
• private purpose trust funds		debt service funds
		• permanent funds

Fiduciary Fund Supercategory

You have heard a bank referred to as a *fiduciary institution*, right? This means that the bank is entrusted with protecting your money. When you decide you want your money back, the bank has to give it to you.

This superfund category accounts for monies that the government is holding in trust on behalf of others. These monies are not to be spent by the government—ever.

Agency Funds

When you are an *agent* for someone else, you are acting on behalf of that person. A real estate agent acts on the seller's behalf. A sports agent acts on a baseball player's behalf.

Agency funds are simply monies held on someone else's behalf. The account eventually will be emptied out and distributed to the true owners. For instance, when a county collects property taxes, not all the taxes belong to the county. Some of the taxes are collected on behalf of the school district. When the county collects these funds on behalf of the school district, it deposits them in an agency fund and eventually gives the entire amount in the agency fund to the school district.

Pension Trust Funds

Pension trust funds are monies that employees set aside for their retirement. The monies are not to be spent by the government on roads, buildings, salaries, or anything else.

In Texas, we have two major retirement systems that are affiliated with the state: the Employees Retirement System and the Teacher Retirement System. Each has more than $20 billion in investments ready to fund its members' retirement. Every time we get a new legislative group in office, the question inevitably comes up as to whether state leaders can borrow from these pension trust funds just to get them through the latest budget crisis. Do you see any danger here?

Some poor accountant from the comptroller's office has to go to the capitol every few years and meet with the new legislators and explain that the money is being held in a fiduciary capacity and cannot be spent.

Investment Trust Funds

Investment trust funds are created when one government makes investments on behalf of another government. Often governments will have excess cash for a few months of the year. As you can imagine, a county will be cash rich right after property taxes are assessed each year but may be running low on cash several months later. Instead of letting that extra cash sit in the local bank making a puny return, the government might put it into higher-yield investments.

But wise investing is a skill that not all government managers have. So governments pool their investments and hand them over to one financially savvier manager who chooses the investments. In this way, they are getting a higher yield, but they don't have to worry about what to invest in.

The entity that is taking care of the pool cannot spend the pool. When the contributing government wants its money back, the investing entity must produce it immediately.

Private-Purpose Trust Funds   Private-purpose trust funds are funds that are set aside for specific uses for the benefit of specified individuals and organizations. For instance, let's say a rich widow dies and leaves her downtown Victorian mansion to the city. In her will, she stipulates that the house must be used as a home for unwed mothers. Her house cannot be used for any other purpose but to house unwed mothers. The city cannot sell it and use the proceeds to renovate city hall or use it as offices for city employees.

Proprietary Funds

The proprietary funds supercategory accounts for activities that the government is involved in that mimic the commercial world. The term *proprietary* means "owned."

Oddly enough, these funds are accounted for using commercial accounting standards and terminology rather than governmental accounting standards and terminology. This difference just makes governmental financial statements that much more fun to read!

Enterprise Funds   Enterprise funds account for activities that operate like business enterprises. These government-run businesses charge a fee for a service or product and can generate a profit. If they do generate a profit, their profits are often siphoned off to support other government activities. Examples of enterprise funds include public utilities and airports.

Be careful, however, not to assume that all enterprise funds generate a profit. Some show a loss every year and must be supported by appropriations from other governmental funds. An example of an enterprise fund that doesn't make money is a bus system. Tax revenues, federal grants, or private donations must supplement their operations.

Internal Service Funds   Internal service funds are businesses within the government. They do not transact with entities outside the government; instead, they support government operations. For example, the State of Texas has an agency whose function is to assist other state agencies in making purchases. It is called the Building and Procurement Commission. Instead of each state agency hiring staff to handle purchasing, the agencies can go to the commission, pay a little fee, and have it all taken care of. Other examples include print shops and motor pools.

Governmental Funds Supercategory

The governmental funds supercategory is the catchall category for any fund that isn't fiduciary or proprietary. This supercategory accounts for a variety of governmental operations.

General Fund   The general fund accounts for all resources not accounted for in any other fund. Governments have only one of these, and it usually accounts for a majority of the government's transactions. For most governments, this is the largest and most active fund.

Special Revenue Funds   Special revenue funds account for resources restricted for specific purposes. This restriction might be legal or administrative. For instance, a "sin tax" might be levied on cigarettes and the proceeds used to pay for ads to discourage teens from smoking. (Yes, this really is a true use of some of the cigarette tax in Texas.)

Or the federal government may grant funds to a state to be used for a special purpose, such as road construction. Many cities collect hotel and motel taxes and use the proceeds for economic development (a fancy way of saying that they use the money to bring more business into the area).

Capital Projects Funds   Capital projects funds account for resources being used to construct capital projects—one-time activities to acquire, construct, or improve (repair or renovate) facilities. For instance, the funds a town sets aside to build a town hall or remodel the library would be accounted for in this fund. In this way, the funds don't get lost or commingled in the general fund and possibly spent. This is where I wish my city had set aside funds to finish the road near my house.

Debt-Service Funds   Debt-service funds are like a savings account set aside to pay off bond debt. Instead of hoping that the general fund will have enough resources to cover the next bond payment, the government sets aside the money in a debt-service fund.

Think of the potential problems here if this money is not separate from the other funds. It might be time to make the bond payment, but the city is out of money because it just spent it paying payroll and utilities. Frequently, bondholders require the government to create a debt-service fund. If the government does not set the money aside, the bondholders have the right to call the entire debt immediately.

Permanent Funds   Here I think of the University of Texas, where I got my degree. A long, long time ago, the university took the proceeds from the oil wells it owned and created permanent funds. These permanent funds leave the principal always intact—hence the term *permanent*.

The earnings are used to support the operations of the school. For many years, the tuition was very low because of these permanent funds. Now the cost of running the school far exceeds the earnings of the permanent funds, and tuition has gone up exponentially.

Government Financial Statements

All these funds make government financial statements very, very thick.

In 2003, the State of Texas financial statements were 234 pages long—almost four times as long as Dell's 10-K. But why?

Well, it is the sheer number of financial statements. For one, each fund super-category gets its own set of financial statements. Add to this financial statements that combine various funds and financial statements that combine all funds. Before you know it, you have x financial statements instead of just three.

The GASB realized about a decade ago that these financial statements were getting out of hand: There were too many of them! So it set about looking for ways to make them more user friendly.

As a result of study and intense debate (yes, this got governmental accountants up in arms!), another, more user-friendly layer was added on top of the fund financial statements. This layer rolls up the entire government into one summary set of statements, in essence treating the operations of the government—no matter what fund they are in—as one large fund. This additional layer looks much like a proprietary entity's financial statements. It is called the *entitywide perspective*. So instead of shortening the financial statements, governments actually added pages, thereby lengthening the documents. Hmmm. Compromise has its price.

We Must Avoid the Word *Profit*

Governments are very careful to avoid the word *profit* when referring to themselves. If the government earned a profit, it would indicate to citizens that it was collecting too much in taxes. Citizens prefer that governments run lean and mean and tax as little as possible.

And because they also want to avoid the word *income*, governments renamed the income statement as the *statement of revenues, expenditures, and changes in fund balances*. And *net income* at the bottom of the statement was renamed as *excess (deficiency) of revenues over (under) expenditures* (Figure 12.1).

A New Financial Statement

The GASB also added a new type of financial statement to the mix called the *statement of activities*. So in addition to having a balance sheet, a statement of revenues and expenditures, and a cash-flow statement for most funds, we add a fourth perspective. The statement of activities is, in essence, another slice at the statement of revenues and expenditures (Figure 12.2 found on pages 188 and 189).

STATE OF TEXAS
Statement of Revenues, Expenditures and Changes in Fund Balances - Governmental Funds
For the Fiscal Year Ended August 31, 2009 (Amounts in Thousands)

	General	State Highway Fund	Permanent School Fund	Nonmajor Funds	Totals
REVENUES					
Taxes	$ 35,142,698	$ 39,631	$	$ 2,471,800	$ 37,654,129
Federal	32,848,427	2,820,154		30,540	35,699,121
Licenses, Fees and Permits	2,528,391	1,286,990		617,324	4,432,705
Interest and Other Investment Income (Loss)	321,190	102,635	(2,429,779)	48,931	(1,957,023)
Land Income	19,047	14,161	356,282	478	389,968
Settlement of Claims	554,004	1,531			555,535
Sales of Goods and Services	1,597,202	250,644	91,251	22,648	1,961,745
Other	3,132,589	4,506	2,596	52,033	3,191,724
Total Revenues	76,143,548	4,520,252	(1,979,650)	3,243,754	81,927,904
EXPENDITURES					
Current:					
General Government	2,777,816	11,622		235,178	3,024,616
Education	23,387,494	50,000	130,660	1,372,888	24,941,042
Employee Benefits	1,503			11,316	12,819
Teacher Retirement Benefits	1,728,959				1,728,959
Health and Human Services	37,897,642	60,163		30,089	37,987,894
Public Safety and Corrections	5,082,785	625,048		94,697	5,802,530
Transportation	4,630	3,376,214		18,267	3,399,111
Natural Resources and Recreation	1,524,645			81,607	1,606,252
Regulatory Services	334,495			99,832	434,327
Capital Outlay	133,481	3,443,634	33	161,181	3,738,329
Debt Service:					
Principal	1,566	205		594,035	595,806
Interest	584	66,941		445,304	512,829
Other Financing Fees		3,138		11,628	14,766
Total Expenditures	72,875,600	7,636,965	130,693	3,156,022	83,799,280
Excess (Deficiency) of Revenues Over (Under) Expenditures	3,267,948	(3,116,713)	(2,110,343)	87,732	(1,871,376)
OTHER FINANCING SOURCES (USES)					
Transfer In (Note 12)	4,147,551	2,875,959		2,713,445	9,736,955
Transfer Out (Note 12)	(9,311,339)	(433,462)	(716,534)	(3,571,625)	(14,032,960)
Bonds and Notes Issued		16,000		1,924,575	1,940,575
Bonds Issued for Refunding				270,920	270,920
Premiums on Bonds Issued				32,634	32,634
Payment to Escrow for Refunding				(308,736)	(308,736)
Sale of Capital Assets	11,060	5,149			16,209
Increase in Obligations Under Capital Leases	16				16
Insurance Recoveries	3,476	14,036		301	17,813
Total Other Financing Sources (Uses)	(5,149,236)	2,477,682	(716,534)	1,061,514	(2,326,574)
Net Change in Fund Balances	(1,881,288)	(639,031)	(2,826,877)	1,149,246	(4,197,950)
Fund Balances, September 1, 2008	10,655,166	778,471	25,227,185	7,344,259	44,005,081
Restatements (Note 14)	192,534		197,208	44,651	434,393
Fund Balances, September 1, 2008, as Restated	10,847,700	778,471	25,424,393	7,388,910	44,439,474
Fund Balances, August 31, 2009	$ 8,966,412	$ 139,440	$ 22,597,516	$ 8,538,156	$ 40,241,524

The accompanying notes to the financial statements are an integral part of this statement.

FIGURE 12.1 · Texas statement of revenues, expenditures, and changes in fund balance.

Still Struggling?

A Tour of the Statement of Activities

The statement of activities is the only GASB- or FASB-sanctioned financial statement that has to be read horizontally first and then vertically. It holds a lot of data, so it can be a bit intimidating to someone unfamiliar with its contents. Think of it as an upside down and sideways income statement!

Get a copy of a statement of activities in front of you as you read this, please.

Check out the rows on the left. The rows describe how much the different functions of government—general government, fire protection, health services, and so on—spent this year. So, unlike the income statement, we begin with expenses instead of income.

Now look at the column headers. The columns indicate where the different functions got the resources to pay for their operations. We are now piecing together the income. Did they get them from collecting fees or getting government grants? If you keep reading horizontally, you will see the total amount that the function still needs help paying for. In other words, its own activities and grants did not pay for everything it needed to operate.

After you see the deficits in each function in the columns on the right, you add up everyone's deficit and then begin asking who filled in the gap between expenses and revenues. First, we see whether our business activities were able to fill the gap. The answer is always, "Partially."

Now we start reading the statement vertically. Taxes, debt, and generic fees that the government collects cover the deficit. At the bottom of the statement, find the term *change in net assets*. Change in net assets is akin to the concept of net income. If it is negative, the government is spending more than it brings in.

A Turned-Around Balance Sheet

Governments also often play around with the balance sheet and put it into another format. The components are the same; the order is just switched around.

The formula of the balance sheet is *Assets = liabilities plus equity*. Governments prefer to express the ratio as *Assets − liabilities = net assets*. And one version of the balance sheet is called the *statement of net assets*. It is in essence a balance sheet with the elements flipped around (Figure 12.3 found on pages 190 and 191).

STATE OF TEXAS

Statement of Activities

For the Fiscal Year Ended August 31, 2009 (Amounts in Thousands)

Functions/Programs	Expenses	Charges for Services	Operating Grants and Contributions	Capital Grants and Contributions
			Program Revenues	
PRIMARY GOVERNMENT				
Governmental Activities:				
General Government	$ 3,052,177	$ 1,010,388	$ 821,206	$
Education	24,952,375	474,249	2,530,342	
Employee Benefits	220,272	109		
Teacher Retirement Benefits	1,667,325	33,624		
Health and Human Services	38,124,180	1,825,395	26,965,706	132
Public Safety and Corrections	6,026,868	354,117	1,354,652	
Transportation	4,025,226	1,920,123	167,551	2,619,499
Natural Resources and Recreation	1,673,915	574,032	568,414	
Regulatory Services	445,938	646,959	3,058	
Interest on General Long-Term Debt	525,648			
Total Governmental Activities	80,713,924	6,838,996	32,410,929	2,619,631
Business-Type Activities:				
General Government	180,543	42,147	214,121	
Education*	20,135,452	9,253,972	1,406,018	87,456
Health and Human Services	4,908,112	1,027,897	1,601,192	
Public Safety and Corrections	83,498	90,469		
Transportation	220,881	66,375	17	8,433
Natural Resources and Recreation	304,577	46,682	391,733	
Lottery	2,680,273	3,720,995	2	
Total Business-Type Activities	28,513,336	14,248,537	3,613,083	95,889
Total Primary Government	$ 109,227,260	$ 21,087,533	$ 36,024,012	$ 2,715,520
COMPONENT UNITS				
Component Units	$ 1,871,027	$ 1,515,317	$ 298,281	$
Total Component Units	$ 1,871,027	$ 1,515,317	$ 298,281	$ 0

General Revenues
  Taxes:
    Sales and Use
    Motor Vehicle and Manufactured Housing
    Motor Fuels
    Franchise
    Oil and Natural Gas Production
    Insurance Occupation
    Cigarette and Tobacco
    Other
  Unrestricted Investment Earnings
  Settlement of Claims
  Gain on Sale of Capital Assets
  Other General Revenues
Capital Contributions
Contributions to Permanent and Term Endowments
Transfers – Internal Activities (Note 12)
  Total General Revenues, Contributions and Transfers
  Change in Net Assets
Net Assets, September 1, 2008
Restatements (Note 14)
Net Assets, September 1, 2008, as Restated

Net Assets, August 31,2009

The accompanying notes to the financial statements are an integral part of this statement.
* Other postemployment benefits are not legally required to be provided by the state of Texas. The Texas Constitution does not allow the Legislature to impose financial obligations for a period longer than two years. See Note 11 for additional details.

FIGURE 12.2 · Texas statement of activities.

(Continued)

| | Net (Expense) Revenue and Changes in Net Assets | | | |
| | Primary Government | | | |
Governmental Activities	Business-Type Activities	Total	Component Units
$ (1,220,583)	$	$ (1,220,583)	$
(21,947,784)		(21,947,784)	
(220,163)		(220,163)	
(1,633,701)		(1,633,701)	
(9,332,947)		(9,332,947)	
(4,318,099)		(4,318,099)	
681,947		681,947	
(531,469)		(531,469)	
204,079		204,079	
(525,648)		(525,648)	
(38,844,368)	0	(38,844,368)	0
	75,725	75,725	
	(9,388,006)	(9,388,006)	
	(2,279,023)	(2,279,023)	
	6,971	6,971	
	(146,056)	(146,056)	
	133,838	133,838	
	1,040,724	1,040,724	
0	(10,555,827)	(10,555,827)	0
(38,844,368)	(10,555,827)	(49,400,195)	0
			(57,429)
0	0	0	(57,429)
21,026,034		21,026,034	
2,568,599		2,568,599	
3,155,941		3,155,941	
3,303,170		3,303,170	
1,335,296		1,335,296	
1,295,330		1,295,330	
1,564,061		1,564,061	
1,680,362		1,680,362	
178,470	129,445	307,915	34,918
555,626	14,691	570,317	
	609	609	1,707
1,769,051	156,903	1,925,954	19,937
1,554		1,554	
	120,404	120,404	
(4,268,014)	4,268,014		
34,165,480	4,690,066	38,855,546	56,562
(4,678,888)	(5,865,761)	(10,544,649)	(867)
100,671,188	42,152,308	142,823,496	959,017
(130,294)	(1,268,709)	(1,399,003)	13,279
100,540,894	40,883,599	141,424,493	972,296
$ 95,862,006	$ 35,017,838	$ 130,879,844	$ 971,429

STATE OF TEXAS

Statement of Net Assets
August 31, 2009 (Amount in Thousands)

| | Primary Government | | | Component Units |
	Governmental Activities	Business-Type Activities*	Total	
ASSETS				
Current Assets:				
Cash and Cash Equivalents	$ 20,460,254	$ 4,249,788	$ 24,710,042	$ 585,092
Short-Term Investments	581,985	1,318,156	1,900,141	807,796
Securities Lending Collateral	1,972,479	796,658	2,769,137	
Receivables:				
Taxes (Note 24)	2,321,689		2,321,689	
Federal	2,457,575	543,732	3,001,307	65,273
Other Intergovernmental	1,411,685	35,799	1,447,484	8,975
Accounts	819,326	589,266	1,408,592	105,997
Interest and Dividends	115,350	131,146	246,496	7,326
Gifts		134,692	134,692	
Investment Trades	5,336	169,840	175,176	
Other	46,288	1,015,763	1,062,051	166
From Fiduciary Funds	18,333	18,333		
Due from Primary Government (Note 12)				426
Due from Component Units (Note 12)		45	45	
Inventories	315,696	128,967	444,663	926
Prepaid Items	211	126,940	127,151	1,096
Loans and Contracts	87,567	334,864	422,431	9,633
Other Current Assets	47	334,446	334,493	1,569
Restricted:				
Cash and Cash Equivalents	150,019	1,431,711	1,581,730	21,777
Short-Term Investments		795,153	795,153	
Loans and Contracts	55,901	72,913	128,814	2,191
Total Current Assets	30,819,741	12,209,879	43,029,620	1,618,243
Noncurrent Assets:				
Internal Balances (Note 12)	4,845	(4,845)		
Loans and Contracts	832,513	3,901,063	4,733,576	68,300
Investments	22,998,121	4,092,652	27,090,773	9,426
Receivables:				
Taxes (Note 24)	346,919		346,919	
Federal	20,671		20,671	
Gifts		240,205	240,205	
Other	117,316	1,624	118,940	3,191
Restricted:				
Cash and Cash Equivalents		219,370	219,370	202
Short-Term Investments		17,321	17,321	
Investments		23,578,131	23,578,131	265,914
Receivables		198,754	198,754	
Loans and Contracts	810,068	3,362,723	4,172,791	12,580
Other	89,357	9,841	99,198	
Assets Held in Trust		3,125	3,125	
Net Pension Asset (Note 9)	5,131		5,131	
Deferred Charges	26,836	52,077	78,913	
Other Noncurrent Assets	15,921	46,209	62,130	5,379
Capital Assets: (Note 2)				
Nondepreciable	58,373,107	6,093,474	64,466,581	3,928
Depreciable	26,412,033	25,999,781	52,411,814	101,935
Accumulated Depreciation	(14,838,165)	(12,459,982)	(27,298,147)	(45,801)
Total Noncurrent Assets	95,214,673	55,351,523	150,566,196	425,054
Total Assets	126,034,414	67,561,402	193,595,816	2,043,297

The accompanying notes to the financial statements are an integral part of this statement.

* Other postemployment benefits are not legally required to be provided by the State of Texas. The Texas Constitution does not allow the Legislature to impose financial obligations for a period longer than two years. See Note 11 for additional details.

FIGURE 12.3 · Texas statement of net assets.

STATE OF TEXAS

Statement of Net Assets (concluded)
August 31, 2009 (Amount in Thousands)

| | Primary Government | | | |
	Governmental Activities	Business-Type Activities*	Total	Component Units
LIABILITIES				
Current Liabilities:				
Payables:				
Accounts	$ 4,795,531	$ 1,359,864	$ 6,155,395	$ 144,799
Payroll	650,350	663,685	1,314,035	143
Other Intergovernmental	287,085	15,409	302,494	14
Federal	1,339	34,448	35,787	50,026
Investment Trades	23,327	359,127	382,454	
Interest	353,090	61,072	414,162	2,083
Tax Refunds (Note 24)	1,173,821		1,173,821	
Annuities		12,173	12,173	
To Fiduciary Funds	191,596		191,596	
Internal Balances (Note 12)	815,672	(815,672)		
Due to Primary Government (Note 12)				45
Due to Component Units (Note 12)	426		426	
Unearned Revenue	4,030,800	2,435,022	6,465,822	58,446
Obligations/Reverse Repurchase Agreement	92,415		92,415	
Obligations/Securities Lending	2,081,057	801,356	2,882,413	
Short-Term Debt (Note 4)	300,000		300,000	
Claims and Judgments (Note 5)	55,023	103,843	158,866	
Capital Lease Obligations (Note 5,7)	1,667	2,408	4,075	164
Employees' Compensable Leave (Note 5)	482,070	309,721	791,791	3,369
Notes and Loans Payable (Note 5)	14,662	1,033,420	1,048,082	37,670
General Obligation Bonds Payable (Note 5, 6)	331,535	151,402	482,937	
Revenue Bonds Payable (Note 5,6)	175,148	1,905,342	2,080,490	9,540
Pollution Remediation Obligation (Note 5)	46,812	341	47,153	
Liabilities Payable from Restricted Assets (Note 5)		475,623	475,623	
Funds Held for Others		123,911	123,911	432
Other Current Liabilities	309,483	252,528	562,011	41,401
Total Current Liabilities	16,212,909	9,285,023	25,497,932	348,132
Noncurrent Liabilities:				
Claims and Judgments (Note 5)	107,935	51,766	159,701	
Capital Lease Obligations (Note 5,7)	6,406	10,137	16,543	111
Employees' Compensable Leave (Note 5)	329,914	351,902	681,816	1,993
Notes and Loans Payable (Note 5)	135,553	1,314,394	1,449,947	95,418
General Obligation Bonds Payable (Note 5, 6)	9,413,685	2,775,751	12,189,436	
Revenue Bonds Payable (Note 5,6)	3,111,973	13,582,628	16,694,601	322,766
Pollution Remediation Obligation (Note 5)	334,819		334,819	
Liabilities Payable from Restricted Assets (Note 5)		3,252,738	3,252,738	72,249
Assets Held for Others	691,328	691,328		
Net Pension Obligation (Note 9)	519,214		519,214	
Net OPEB Obligation (Note 11)		1,060,898	1,060,898	
Other Noncurrent Liabilities		166,999	166,999	231,199
Total Noncurrent Liabilities	13,959,499	23,258,541	37,218,040	723,736
Total Liabilities	30,172,408	32,543,564	62,715,972	1,071,868
NET ASSETS				
Invested in Capital Assets, Net of Related Debt	59,719,286	7,654,750	67,374,036	48,523
Restricted for:				
Education	807,687	2,315,160	3,122,847	84,851
Debt Service	220,794	207,892	428,686	
Capital Projects	284,951	386,555	671,506	
Veterans Land Board Housing Programs		659,010	659,010	
Economic Stabilization	6,734,165		6,734,165	
Funds Held as Permanent Investments:				
Nonexpendable	10,615,859	9,556,352	20,172,211	
Expendable	11,997,785	5,572,988	17,570,773	
Other	2,002,944	45,632	2,048,576	17,414
Unrestricted	3,478,535	8,619,499	12,098,034	820,641
Total Net Assets	$ 95,862,006	$ 35,017,838	$ 130,879,844	$ 971,429

Component Unit

Ever heard of a *quasi-governmental entity*? In Texas, we have a handful of quasi-government entities that are described in the state's financial statements as "component units." Texas Guaranteed Student Loan Corporation is one of these entities. It performs a government function by helping citizens finance their education. But it does not receive appropriations from the legislature. However, it is attached to the government because the governor appoints the board of directors. So it is quasi-controlled by the state.

It would be misleading to ignore quasi-government agencies completely, but it also would be misleading to integrate them into the primary government. In order to be listed as a component unit, the quasi-government entity must meet some GASB criteria that I will not bore you with here.

What Is *Fund Balance?*

Equity is not a meaningful concept in government because nothing is owned. Governments prefer to use the term *fund balance* or *net assets*. Fund balance and net assets are concepts similar to retained earnings. Which term you use depends on where you are in the financial statements. Some statements are presented on the full accrual basis of accounting and use the term *net assets*. Other statements use the modified accrual basis of accounting, a very conservative accounting method where revenues are not recognized until collected but expenses are recognized when incurred. *Fund balance* is used on statements requiring the modified accrual method of accounting, and the term *net assets* is used on statements using the full accrual method. Yes, the GASB requires the use of two accounting methods! It has its reasons. For more on this, you might want to check out guidance regarding GASB Pronouncement Number 34.

In general, fund balance and net assets represent the amount left in revenues after all the costs have been recorded plus the remaining excess from previous years. This year's little excess is added to last year's little excess to come up with the total little excess. (Remember, retained earnings work the same way—current earnings are added to previous earnings to come up with total retained earnings.)

What Is a Deficit?

The term *deficit* means "deficiency in amount or quality; a falling short; lack; as a deficit in taxes, revenue, etc." And it can be calculated in a variety of ways. This is why you will hear numbers for the federal deficit ranging widely.

David Walker, the former controller general of the United States, in his book *Comeback America*, estimates the federal deficit at $56 trillion. (Please notice I am saying *trillion*, not billion and not million. One trillion dollars has 12 zeros—$1,000,000,000,000!) Low estimates of the deficit only look at the current year's budget gap. The high-end estimates of deficit are created when economists don't look at just one year of operations but rather 5 or 10 years into the future.

What is incredible about the federal government is that its auditors—the Government Accountability Office—can't even express an opinion on the accuracy of the federal financial statements because financial systems and reports are so messy. So the deficit reported in the federal financial statements might not even be the right amount. And please recognize that the federal government isn't the only government entity that can put a debt burden on a citizen. A school district, a special district, a city, a county, or a state also can spend more than it brings in and issue debt to finance operations. Now that we are all frightened....

Not-for-Profit Accounting

Now, the not-for-profits did not fall into the fund trap, although they were using funds until relatively recently in their financial reports. Fortunately, the FASB put a stop to this. It said that not-for-profits can keep all these funds separate in their accounting system internally but could not create monstrously long, fund-based financial statements to share with the public. Thank goodness!

In terms of financial statements, not-for-profits operate out of one pool of resources, and you will have only one set of financial statements. So not-for-profit financial statements are quite a bit thinner and simpler than the government financial statements.

Accounting standards say that a not-for-profit possesses the following characteristics:

- Resource contributors do not expect commensurate or proportionate pecuniary return.

- The operating purpose is other than to provide goods or services at a profit.
- Ownership interest is absent.

Here are some examples of not-for-profits:

- Cemetery organizations
- Civic organizations
- Fraternal organizations
- Labor unions
- Libraries
- Museums
- Other cultural institutions
- Performing arts organizations
- Political parties

Not-for-Profits Have Unique Concerns

Because not-for-profits have unique concerns, they also have their own FASB pronouncements. Their financial statements are uniquely titled and formatted, although they, in essence, contain the same sorts of data that a proprietary business includes in its balance sheet, income statement, and cash-flow statement.

The not-for-profit's tax-exempt status is usually critical to its success. Each year, the not-for-profit must file Form 990 with the Internal Revenue Service (IRS). This is an extremely detailed form that asks for the not-for-profit's mission, balance sheet, income statement, and plenty of granular data on where the organization got its money and how it spent it. In order to complete the form, not-for-profits must break their expenditures into functional categories. See Figure 12.5 for a financial statement containing functional expenses that is designed to tie into the Form 990.

Donations

Not-for-profits are unique in that they might operate from donations—and donations cause all sorts of accounting trouble.

Some donations are made with stipulations that the donation be spent in a specific way. Some pledges are made and never collected. (A CPA with a public television station once told me that one-third of the pledges the station receives were never collected.) Some donations or pledges are not of cash but of time or other resources. These are just a few of the issues that cause revenue recognition to be a bit complicated.

You might hear terms thrown around such as *unrestricted funds, temporarily restricted funds*, and *permanently restricted funds*. This relates to whether the funds are spendable now or sometime in the future. Usually, the terms of the donation will dictate whether they are restricted or not.

Sales of Goods and Services

Other not-for-profits actually sell a product or a service to generate revenues but are not seeking earnings for an owner. All proceeds are to be used to further the mission of the not-for-profit. Such organizations run for the benefit of their clients.

Financial Statements

Not-for-profit financial statements need to demonstrate to their clients or beneficiaries that the organization is providing whatever services it can with the resources available—in other words, that beneficiaries are getting the most bang for the contributors' buck. However, this is often difficult to show with financial statements. It is possible, of course, to have accurate financial statements and spend all the contributions but still not be serving the clients in the most effective and efficient way.

This is why many not-for-profits include performance metrics in their annual reports. They might disclose how many clients were served and calculate a cost per client. They also might have metrics on how the quality of life of their clients has improved owing to their assistance.

Again, not-for-profits have financial statements that are similar to the three key financial statements of a business enterprise but with different names and in a slightly different format. Luckily for the reader, there are only a handful of statements, including our favorite three:

- Statement of financial position (the balance sheet)
- Statement of activities (the income statement)
- Statement of cash flows

The statement of financial position (Figure 12.4) is similar to a balance sheet. It must at least report the organization's total assets, liabilities, and net assets. Net assets are further broken out as to whether they are unrestricted, temporarily restricted, or permanently restricted.

The statement of activities (Figure 12.5) is a statement of revenues and expenses. It reports the change in the organization's net assets. The terms *fund balance* and *equity* are not used. The changes in net assets must be shown for each category: change in permanently restricted net assets, change in temporarily restricted net assets, and change in unrestricted net assets.

BIG BROTHERS/BIG SISTERS OF CENTRAL TEXAS INC.

Statement of Financial Position
December 31, 2009

ASSETS

CURRENT ASSETS

Cash	197,143
Investments	4,944
Contributions receivables, net	201,462
Government grants and contracts receivable	100,496
Prepaid expenses and other assets	22,515
Total Current Assets	526,528

FIXED ASSETS

Buildings	454,967
Furniture and fixtures	107,463
Computers and equipment	133,023
Land	43,355
Accumulated depreciation	(470,453)
Total Fixed Assets	268,065
TOTAL ASSETS	794,623

LIABILITIES AND NET ASSETS

CURRENT LIABILITIES

Accounts payable	86,801
Accrued expenses	49,860
Total Current Liabilities	136,661

NET ASSETS

Unrestricted	413,147
Temporarily restricted	244,815
Total Net Assets	657,962
TOTAL LIABILITIES AND NET ASSETS	794,623

FIGURE 12.4 · Central Texas Big Brothers/Big Sisters statement of financial position.

BIG BROTHERS/BIG SISTERS OF CENTRAL TEXAS, INC.

Statement of Activities
Year Ended December 31, 2009

REVENUE	Unrestricted	Temporarily Restricted	Total
Government grants	694,182	0	694,182
Other grants	631,088	0	631,088
Contributions, including goods and services of $34,007	191,466	98,733	290,179
Special events	257,090	4,980	262,070
Other	25,245	0	25,245
Net assets released from restriction	254,888	(254,888)	0
Total Revenue	2,053,939	(151,175)	1,902,764
EXPENSES			
Personnel	1,528,134	0	1,528,134
Contract labor	104,818	0	104,818
Insurance	70,759	0	70,759
Communication and printing	52,663	0	52,663
Transfers to other organizations (Note 2)	42,438	0	42,438
Occupancy	43,940	0	43,940
Membership dues	34,788	0	34,788
Contributed goods and services	34,006	0	34,006
Depreciation	33,000	0	33,000
Equipment rental and maintenance	32,204	0	32,204
Travel	31,157	0	31,157
Background checks	28,559	0	28,559
Supplies	25,878	0	25,878
Loss on disposal of fixed assets	16,341	0	16,341
Bad debt	2,538	0	2,538
Other	34,725	0	34,725
Total Expenses	2,115,948	0	2,115,948
CHANGE IN NET ASSETS	(62,009)	(151,175)	(213,184)
BEGINNING NET ASSETS	475,156	395,990	871,146
ENDING NET ASSETS	413,147	244,815	657,962

FIGURE 12.5 · Central Texas Big Brothers/Big Sisters statement of activities.

This statement most closely mimics the income statement we all know and love. Expenses are often grouped as management and general expenses, fundraising expenses, and membership development expenses.

Encumbrance

An *encumbrance* is an amount set aside for a commitment. For instance, a government might commit to hiring a trainer to come into an agency in four months to conduct a training session. The funds have not been paid to the trainer yet—and won't be until a month after delivery of the training session. So the cash won't actually go out for five months. However, this is not money that the government can spend on anything else. So the estimated obligation is *encumbered* or—the way I think about it—*burdened* by this commitment. It is recorded in the general ledger as encumbered so that government leaders and managers won't mistake the funds for something they can use.

A statement of cash flows (Figure 12.6) is no different from the statement used by proprietary entities.

BIG BROTHERS/BIG SISTERS OF CENTRAL TEXAS, INC. Statement of Cash Flows Year Ended December 31, 2009	
CASH FLOWS FROM OPERATING ACTIVITIES	
Change in net assets	(213,184)
Depreciation	33,000
Loss on disposal of fixed assets	16,341
Change in receivables	157,205
Change in other assets	12,159
Change in accrued expenses	13,129
Change in payables	27,200
Total Cash Flow from Operating Activities	45,850
CASH FLOWS FROM INVESTING ACTIVITIES	
Purchases of fixed assets	(23,119)
Purchases of investments	(4,944)
Total Cash Flows from Investing Activities	(28,063)
NET CHANGE IN CASH	17,787
BEGINNING CASH	179,356
ENDING CASH	197,143

FIGURE 12.6 · Central Texas Big Brothers/Big Sisters statement of cash flows.

All three of these statements also must disclose whether there are any donor restrictions on resources.

Internal Use of the Funds

If you work for a not-for-profit, you might hear the accountant throwing around names of the funds. Until the 1990s, many not-for-profits were using fund accounting—a similar method to the governmental accounting discussed earlier in this chapter. Now, a not-for-profit may use fund accounting internally to keep different resources pooled in different pots, but for external reporting purposes, all funds are combined into a single view of the entity. These funds are used for internal tracking and not reported in the financial statements given to stakeholders or external parties.

The funds that generally are needed by a not-for-profit include the following:

- Unrestricted fund
- Restricted funds
- Endowment fund
- Plant fund

The *unrestricted fund* is similar to the general fund in government. It is the money that the board of directors has to spend as it pleases. *Restricted funds* are funds that must be used only for specific purposes. An *endowment fund* is created when a donor gives cash, investments, and so on to a not-for-profit organization for the purpose of providing income. Sometimes the principal of the endowment is permanent; sometimes it reverts to the donor. The *plant fund* is where major capital assets and the debt incurred in obtaining them are reported.

Summary

If accounting can be viewed as language and rules that apply to tracking resources in a business, government and not-for-profit accounting can be viewed as special dialects of this language. The financial statements look a little different, contain a few different terms, but disclose similar core data that are common to all organizations. We all put on our pants one leg at a time. . . . or do we?

QUIZ

1. Governments collect taxes
   A. because they are in it for the money.
   B. to make their bottom line look better at the end of the year.
   C. to provide services to their owners, the citizens
   D. to make a profit from their collection.

2. Governmental entities such as municipalities, counties, and states use generally accepted accounting principles (GAAP) promulgated by which of the following agencies?
   A. AICPA
   B. FASB
   C. GASB
   D. SEC

3. Many not-for-profits follow GAAP, which is promulgated by which of the following agencies?
   A. AICPA
   B. FASB
   C. GASB
   D. SEC

4. IBM's financial statements look like all the revenues and expenditures are consolidated into one huge purse. However, a unique feature of government financial statements is that resources are tracked and reported using pools or funds. Why?
   A. So that they can prevent commingling.
   B. So that they can track expenditures for different projects and functions.
   C. So that they can track revenues for different projects and functions.
   D. All the above.

5. What are the three supercategories of funds for the government?
   A. Fiduciary, proprietary, capital
   B. Investment, proprietary, capital
   C. Fiduciary, permanent, governmental
   D. Fiduciary, proprietary, governmental

6. These are created when a government wants to invest on behalf of another government.
   A. Investment trust funds
   B. Special revenue funds
   C. Private-purpose trust funds
   D. Pension trust funds

7. **Building and procurement commissions, print shops, and motor pools are examples of what kind of funds?**
   A. Proprietary
   B. Enterprise
   C. General
   D. Internal service

8. **Money in this fund is used for construction or renovation projects?**
   A. General
   B. Special revenue
   C. Capital project
   D. Debt service

9. **Each year not-for-profits must share their mission, their balance sheet, and their income statements with whom?**
   A. Donors
   B. SEC
   C. IRS clients

10. **Funds that the not-for-profit board can use as it wishes are called**
    A. unrestricted funds.
    B. restricted funds.
    C. endowment funds.
    D. plant funds.

Part IV

Financial Indicators—Using Financial Information to Make Decisions

Cautions about Financial Analysis

Finance isn't the only thing that matters! You could even argue that financial health is the result of doing everything else right—pleasing customers, choosing a smart business model, and having your act together. In this chapter, we take the finance and accounting god off his throne and put him in a short chair at a table with a variety of other equally important factors that have an impact on an organization's success.

CHAPTER OBJECTIVES

- Summarize common theories of business success
- Examine other factors that contribute to organizational survival

In the remaining chapters we are going to look at how to conduct a financial analysis of an organization. After an introduction to the steps involved in an analysis, we are going to look at several tools for indicating the financial health of an entity. These tools include financial metrics. We will run financial metrics for two competing companies by using the financial data included in recent 10-K's. But first, let me share some cautionary comments about financial analysis.

There Isn't One Number That Indicates Health

Over the years, people have asked me, "What one number do I need to look at to determine whether my company is doing well or not?" Ah, if it were only that simple! There is not one magic number in the financial statements that will tell you how healthy an organization is.

You can be looking great on profit but have a weak cash flow. You might have a strong cash balance, but if it is all funded by debt, it will give you a weak balance sheet and affect your profitability because you have to pay interest.

All the financial information works together, so you must look at the three key financial statements together. Each has a unique perspective that is important to understanding the entity. If you rely on only one financial statement for all your decisions, you are likely to make a mistake.

So, in conducting a financial analysis, we are going to look at many metrics and many numbers, each derived from a different financial statement. After we have them all together, we can piece together a story and make some initial conclusions.

There Is No Such Thing As a Good or Bad Result

Anyone who tells you that there is a perfect range for ratios is full of it. I once taught a course in finance for nonfinancial managers for a savings and loan. I was there to teach the loan officers how to read the financial statements submitted by their clients who were asking for loans. (No, they didn't already know how to read financial statements!)

The loan officers would always run a standard set of 10 metrics to see if a client's results would fall within a certain acceptable range. When the metrics did not fall within an acceptable range, the client's loan was rejected.

The loan officers had no idea what they were looking at or what the metrics meant. They only knew that if a metric fell outside the range, it was bad.

This is a crazy way to do business. Obviously, they were not truly knowledgeable about how their clients' businesses worked. Each business has a unique business model and operating environment, and that must be taken into account when doing an analysis.

All the metrics do for you is paint you a picture of what is so. You cannot immediately judge a metric as good or bad based on some externally imposed scale. At the least, you must weigh it against other metrics, look at past results, and benchmark against competitors.

There Is No Standard That Dictates How Metrics Should be Calculated

There are no generally accepted accounting principles (GAAP) for metrics, no principles that guide how metrics should be calculated. One text will tell you that you should use an average; another will tell you to use a year-end figure. One text will add depreciation back when working with net income; another won't. It all depends on what you read and who you listen to.

It also depends on what makes sense for the organization you are analyzing. For instance, the metric *return on investment* (ROI) can be customized. The numerator of ROI is income, and the denominator is investment.

$$\frac{\text{Income (return)}}{\text{Investment}}$$

Which income figure are you going to use? Are you going to use net income after taxes or operating income? Or maybe earnings before interest and taxes (EBIT)?

How about the bottom figure? What do you consider the investment? Is it working capital plus equity? What are you including in working capital? Does it include rainy-day cash? This can make a big difference in the result.

One company I analyzed in the late 1990s revealed in its annual financial report that ROI was 316 percent. When I calculated it, using data from the annual report, I got 30 percent. I asked the accountants in the company to tell me why their number was so different, and they gave me a very detailed formula that had 20 components, not just the two I was working with. Is this kosher? Well, it is legal. Again, there is no standard against which to measure the measures.

This is why I recommend taking the metrics that companies disclose in their annual reports, on their Web sites, and in their investor relations marketing materials with a grain of salt. Recalculate them yourself.

Also, do not take the ratios we discuss in later chapters to be the gospel—the only way to approach the metric. Tweak them to your own needs because there is no standard that dictates how you have to do them. I do, however, strongly suggest that you document how you calculate the ratio and do the same thing consistently over time so that the numbers are comparable.

One of my students told me that she lost her job as a financial analyst because she couldn't answer a question posed by the chairman of the board. He thought that her calculations might be off and asked her how she came up with the results. She couldn't answer at the meeting, and when she went back to her desk, she still couldn't replicate the calculation because she didn't document her methodology. Save yourself a headache, and write the source of all your numbers down, describing how you calculated your numbers.

There Is More to Business than Finance

Finance is just one piece of the story of an organization's success. If you really think about it, good financial standing is a result of doing many other things in the organization well. You can't generate a profit over the long haul if you don't have a good product or if you frustrate and drive off customers and employees. Because this is a book about accounting, though, I am going to present only at metrics that can be measured with dollars.

All that financial analysis can do for you is to give you clues of something else happening. It may indicate that customers are being driven away, but it won't tell you what is driving them away. The financial statements won't say customers are being driven away by a bad jingle, for instance—all you will see is a decline in revenue over a period of years. When this happens, your next question is, "Why did revenues decline?" The financial results were a clue, and now you are going to have to do a little snooping around, asking tough questions of managers, customers, and possibly even suppliers.

The Balanced Scorecard Gives Us a Broader Perspective

To get a broader sense of how successful and stable a company is, you might want to use the structure of the balanced scorecard model.

Two professors at Harvard University, Robert Kaplan and David Norton, invented the *balanced scorecard model*. They argue that businesses should create goals and metrics in four categories, not just one.

We are very good, after decades and decades of compiling financial information, at generating financial metrics. Most organizations have pretty good systems in place to gather, compile, and summarize financial information. And many times, unfortunately, it is the only set of metrics that organizations use to determine whether they are successful.

In the balanced scorecard model, finance is just one of the four areas analyzed. Kaplan and Norton's balanced scorecard model includes four components:

- Financial
- Customer
- Internal business processes
- Learning and growth

The balanced scorecard encourages managers to take a more holistic view of the organization. Often, when companies are in a financial crunch, they put a stop to any training or travel for employees. While this results in better short-term financial results, it may have a negative long-term impact on the learning and growth area. It even may hurt customer relationships or allow internal business processes to deteriorate.

The balanced scorecard is just that, a scorecard—a report card, if you will—that looks at the balance of areas and metrics. Ideally, systems would be in place to compile information and report on metrics in each of these four areas as often as possible. One organization I consult with calculates certain metrics daily. Others may report on the metrics monthly or quarterly.

Financial Component

In Kaplan and Norton's model, the financial component of the balanced scorecard asks, "How do we look to our owners?" It asks, in essence, "Are the owners happy with the return they are getting on their investment in the organization?"

I teach a course on financial statement analysis to certified public accountants (CPAs), and in it, I cover more than 70 metrics—a really long day, to say the least! Accountants have been generating these types of metrics for centuries and are quite good at it now. It is the most fully developed area of the balanced scorecard. It includes the financial metrics discussed in the remaining chapters.

Customer Component

The customer component of the balanced scorecard asks, "How do customers see us?" Here we create goals and metrics to determine if we are doing a good job pleasing our customers. We might ask, for instance, if our customers are loyal, repeat customers.

Many organizations already do a good job at collecting this sort of information. We have been concerned about customer satisfaction in this country for several decades now. Examples of metrics in this area include

- Market share
- Customer acquisition
- Customer satisfaction
- Customer retention
- Shares of the customer wallet
- Response time
- Convenient access
- Brand recognition

Internal Business Processes Component

This component of the balanced scorecard asks, "What must we excel at?" In other words, how do our internal systems need to function for us to have happy customers and good financial results?

For instance, I was working for a high-tech company that had doubled in size in each of the preceding five years. At the quarterly meeting, the chief financial officer (CFO) congratulated everyone on the growth of the organization but redirected everyone's attention to the problems that would keep them from succeeding in the future.

He likened the company to a sleek rocket ship racing to the moon. From the outside, everything looks perfect. However, when you open the cockpit door, you see a little fire in the nose of the ship and thin, haggard mice running furiously in an attempt to keep the rocket moving.

Yes, the company had grown, but the internal processes had broken down. The wrong products were being shipped to customers, the quality of the products was slipping, and employees were not getting reimbursed for travel expenses for several months. He directed all managers to focus on cleaning up procedures and processes before chasing down additional market share and new products.

I once ordered all my family's Christmas presents from one fabulous-looking catalog. It was full of all sorts of fun outdoor items that I hadn't seen anyplace else. The catalog company gladly took my money and promised delivery a week before Christmas. We waited . . . and waited. Finally, the gifts arrived—around Valentine's Day. Great products, great marketing, horrible execution. I will never order from that company again, no matter how tempting its products are.

Examples of metrics for this component include

- Amount of research done on emerging and future customer preferences
- Percent of sales from new products
- New products introduced versus planned
- Percent defects
- Time customers must wait for delivery

Learning and Growth Component

This component of the balanced scorecard asks, "Can we continue to improve and create value?" Here we ask whether we have the infrastructure, the people skills, and the information systems to get us where we want to be in the future. This component asks whether we are set up for success. Are we investing in the skills of our people and in technology to get us where we want to be?

Under traditional, short-term financial measures, it is not in a manager's best interest to enhance the capabilities of subordinates, systems, or organizational processes. So sometimes this area is sacrificed to achieve short-term profit or cash flow.

For instance, a company might focus on profitability and cash flow to the detriment of long-term strategies. In one organization I worked with, the managers decided to stop offering employees training sessions because they were trying to cut expenses. In cutting expenses, they also were cutting customer service because the employees weren't being trained on how to handle customer complaints. Over time, the business lost several key customers, and hence the company's revenue went down even farther. What was the company's solution to this problem? Cut training even more to reduce expenses and make up for lost revenues—a nasty downward spiral, wouldn't you say?

Possible metrics include

- Employee retention
- Competency upgrades of employees
- Percent of employees who have access to customer information
- Number of suggestions per employee
- Percent of employees whose professional goals align with organizational goals
- Percent of team-based relationships with other business units

To learn more about the balanced scorecard, I suggest you go to the Harvard Business School Press Web site (www.hbsp.harvard.edu) and purchase some of Kaplan's other books or online courses.

Still Struggling?

Evolution of the Balanced Scorecard

Kaplan and Norton didn't let the balanced scorecard model rest—they kept working with it and working with it until they developed a relationship between the components. Their book, *Strategy Maps*, is an informative read.

A *strategy map* is a visual depiction of these relationships, and I've seen some crazy-looking, hard-to-decipher maps! The basic relationship, however, begins with our overall goal in the corporate world—more money!

Finance—Is the organization profitable and healthy?
Customers—You can't have a profitable and healthy organization without happy customers.

Internal business processes—You can't have happy customers unless you have smooth processes.

Learning and growth—You can't have smooth processes unless you have the technology and people to get you there (Figure 13.1).

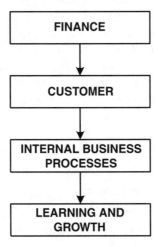

FIGURE 13.1 • Simple Strategy Map.

In the government version of a strategy map, customer is in the top box and finance is on the bottom!

There Is No Right or Wrong Way to Approach Business

Metrics will vary among competitors in the same industry for a variety of reasons. Consider this simple analogy: You don't live the same way your siblings live, but who is to say who is living the better life? You are all functioning members of society, I hope, and your choices are just as good as their choices.

As an investor, owner, or employee of a business, you are looking for an affinity with a company. Does the company seem wise to you? What is wise to you might look scary to me. Financial analysis will reveal some of the values and choices that a company has made.

Maturity of the Company Creates Different Results

The maturity of an organization makes a big difference in what you can expect financial ratios to look like and what the organization's goals are.

A Growing Firm

A growing firm often will consume more cash than it generates. It is like a baby needing to be fed all the time in hopes that one day it will become independent and be able to pay its own way. The company is fed by external investors, and all who are involved desire to grow the company's sales and market share. You often will see low profits, low cash, high debt, and high capital expenditures in a growing firm.

A Sustaining Firm

A sustaining firm has weathered childhood and is now just looking to clean up a few quirks here and there. You might liken this stage of maturity to a young adult who has a general sense of where he or she wants to go but hasn't learned some of the hard lessons of being a true adult. In these companies, the focus is on maintaining profitability and cash flow while cleaning up procedures, expanding capacity, and relieving bottlenecks. You often will see good profit, good cash flow, moderate debt, and high capital investments.

A Maturing Firm

A maturing firm is ready to reap the harvest, ready to take advantage of all the hard work of the earlier stages of its life and maximize cash flow and minimize investment. I liken a mature firm to a professional in her late fifties who is looking at retirement, is not looking for a career change, and wants to spend more time with her family and at her hobbies. You often will see good profit, good cash flow, low debt, and low capital investments.

What is a Business Model?

When you hear folks talking about the Google or eBay business models, they are talking about these companies' unique approaches to business. But the term *business model* doesn't mean anything specific—it isn't a specific formula or set of statements. Most descriptions of business models state what customers want, how they want it delivered, and how the company will organize to meet those needs. Most important, though, the business model describes how the company will get paid and earn a profit.

For instance, you might hear of a *brick-and-mortar business model*—which generally applies to a retailer that sells its products through stores. Or you might hear of a "freemium" model that offers online content for free but charges for premium content. Large companies often employ a variety of business models. For instance, Dell sells through a variety of channels. The company sells directly to consumers online and through big box stores. Dell also has a substantial sales force that creates customized computer solutions for corporations and governments.

As part of your financial analysis, find out what your subject's business model is, and think of the drawbacks and benefits to the model. And then do the same for its major competitors. Is everyone doing business the same way? If not, why not? Often you will find that the industry leader has thrown off the shackles of negative aspects of the industry's standard business model whereas its competitors have not.

Summary

Healthy financial results are just that—results, the results of a variety of other factors. As you will see in the remaining chapters, an organization's choices about which customers to serve and how to serve them affects financial metrics. But being in the right place at the right time matters, too.

QUIZ

1. Great profit means that a company is financially healthy. True or false?
   A. True
   B. False

2. The numerator of return on investment is income, and the denominator is
   A. total cost.
   B. investment.
   C. EBIT.
   D. equity.

3. Financial analysis can only give you clues about what is going on in an organization. True or false?
   A. True
   B. False

4. This component of the balanced scorecard model asks, "How do we look to our owners?"
   A. Customer
   B. Financial
   C. Learning and growth
   D. Internal business processes

5. Under traditional short-term measures of profitability, it is not in the managers' best interest to enhance the capabilities of employees or information systems. True or false?
   A. True
   B. False

6. The metrics market share, response time, brand recognition, and convenient access are included in what component of the balanced scorecard model?
   A. Financial
   B. Customer
   C. Internal business process
   D. Learning and growth

7. A growing organization often will consume more cash than it earns and rely on outside financing. True or false?
   A. True
   B. False

8. Your three-year-old birdbath company is now the biggest birdbath company in the United States. However, product is arriving broken to customers, wrong product is being shipped to customers, and employees are working lots of overtime per part. You meet with your managers and direct them to get control of themselves and their areas before you focus on growing any further. Which part of the balanced scorecard are you dealing with?

   A. Customer
   B. Financial
   C. Learning and growth
   D. Internal business process

9. All metrics should fall within a predetermined, standard range. True or false?

   A. True
   B. False

10. An example of an internal business process metric is

   A. new products introduced versus planned.
   B. the time a customer waits for delivery.
   C. employee retention.
   D. all the above.
   E. A and B.
   F. B and C.

11. The learning and growth component of the balanced scorecard asks whether we have the infrastructure, people skills, and information systems to get us where we want to go in the future. True or false?

   A. True
   B. False

Conducting a Financial Analysis—The Prep Work

In an ideal world, you have access to all sorts of wonderful information about a company before you start your financial analysis. In the real world, you may be lucky to get just a few things from the following list.

CHAPTER OBJECTIVE

- Review information you should gather before running a financial analysis on an organization

Just because you can't get some of this information doesn't mean that you should give up on running an analysis. Give it your best shot.

Also keep in mind the cost versus benefit of doing a superdetailed analysis of the organization. While it may be ideal to gather all the information I am recommending, it may be cost prohibitive in terms of time—and time is money!

You can subscribe to services that will do some of the data gathering and analysis for you. If you are going to make a habit of doing financial analyses, paying for the help may be wise. A company that does good work on gathering and analyzing financial information is Hoover's (www.hoovers.com).

Things to Gather in Order to Do an Analysis

Here is a list of things that would be ideal to have when doing an analysis. If you are a company insider, you should be able to get all this stuff. If you are doing an analysis from the outside, gathering this information will be a lot tougher and in some cases impossible.

Financing history. Find out how the organization has financed operations in the recent past, say, the last five years. Has it relied heavily on debt to keep running, has it sold shares in the business to investors, or has it been able to generate money on its own? Also, are there any restrictive debt covenants or shareholder obligations that could affect the organization?

Terms of loans. If the organization has any outstanding debt, what are the terms of the debt? When is it payable? Is the interest rate favorable? When does the organization project that it will retire the debt? To whom is the debt payable?

Distributions to owners. What is the organization's philosophy on sharing its wealth with owners? Many organizations like to plow their profits right back into the company in order to grow. Some prefer to give the owners the profits as they are made. Some are right in the middle: Some percentage is invested back in the company, and some is distributed. These decisions can make a huge difference in an organization's cash flow and equity position.

Ages and types of payables. To whom does the organization owe money? Who are their key vendors, and what are the terms with these vendors? Has the organization established credit with these vendors so that it can hold onto its cash longer?

Ages and types of receivables. Who owes the organization money? What is the mix of repeat versus new customers? Who are the organization's main customers, and how creditworthy are they? How long do receivables remain outstanding?

Ages and types of inventory. Does the organization hold a large amount of inventory? How old is this inventory? Do customers expect that products will be available to them immediately on demand? How does this affect inventory levels?

Details on cash—a cash-flow statement. Get an audited cash-flow statement. What does the organization do with its extra cash? Does the organization invest it or distribute it to owners? What does the organization invest in?

Details on income—an income statement. Get an audited income statement. What was the gross sales figure? How much of gross sales did the organization get to keep in net income? What are the types of expenses involved in running the organization?

Competitor information. Find out who the organization thinks its main competitors are, and get as much financial data on these competitors as possible. Gather all the items on this list for each competitor so that you will have plenty of information against which to benchmark.

Information on steady customers and steady vendors. Who are the significant vendors for this organization? How is the industry faring? How are other companies in the industry faring? Who are the organization's most significant customers? I know that if some of my steady customers go bust, I also will be in peril. Does the organization rely heavily on just one customer or one vendor? If so, how solid is that relationship?

Factors that dictate the success of the entity. Each organization has its own definition of success and the route to it. For instance, the reason that Krispy Kreme Doughnuts is successful is different than the reason that Dunkin' Donuts is successful. Find out, through reading corporate promotional literature, media interviews, Web sites, and just plain talking to managers, why the organization is successful. Your next question is, "How well is the organization doing at focusing on its success factors?"

Audited financial statements. I have to repeat it: *Audited* financial statements are infinitely more reliable than unaudited financial statements. Yes, auditors have been shown to be fallible in the past decade, over and over, but a little assurance is better than no assurance.

Business plan or strategic plan. If you can get hold of the long-term strategies that drive the organization and guide its leaders and employees, you will have a great deal of insight into why sacrifices are made and why the numbers look like they do. However, many organizations operate without business plans or strategic plans. (This is not recommended, by the way.) Organizations that operate using long-range planning of some sort often will sacrifice short-term returns for long-term goals. This will affect financial results.

Budget or standard to compare against. Budgets are simply translation of the future plans of an organization into financial terms. You can tell a lot about the priorities of an organization by looking at its budget.

Things that interest you. Do you have specific concerns about the organization that I haven't covered? See what kinds of data you can gather on these issues.

Financial Analysis, Step by Step

You can simply run a few metrics to start telling the story, but I want to teach you the "right" way to do it—the thorough way. This will yield the maximum amount of interesting data.

So here are the steps to conducting a thorough financial analysis:

1. *Consider the perspective of the users of your story.* What questions would they like your story to answer? Are the users of your analysis investors, managers, or bankers?

Your answer to this last question will dictate what sorts of metrics to run. For instance, investors are concerned mostly about profitability and return on their investment. Managers usually are concerned about such things as inventory levels, production, and sales. They also worry about how well working capital is being managed. Bankers care about whether the organization has the ability to repay a loan and as a result examine cash flow, other outstanding debt, and collateral.

2. *Gain an understanding of the business climate and market trends.* Here you are going to have to do some research outside the financial statements. The "Management's Discussion and Analysis" section of the 10-K and annual report may begin to give you clues about what is going on in the market, but you are going to have to do a little more work finding out the answers to the following questions. This is not a complete list; use your noggin and get creative.

- Who are the competitors?
- What is this organization's standing against these competitors? How much market share does it have?
- What are customer perceptions of the organization's product or service?
- Are the customers satisfied with the timeliness of service or product delivery?
- Is the demand for the organization's product or service declining or increasing? Is the organization making divining rods out of sticks or global positioning systems?
- Who are the customers for the product? What kind of buying power do they have?
- What markets remain unexplored? Is there potential for growth?
- What is the organization's plan for the future?
- Is the organization positioned for future success regarding its information systems and employee skills?
- What is the organization's reputation with suppliers?
- Have there been any major changes in management? Why?

Governments Give You More Information

Governments are great about sharing important nonfinancial information that helps you to understand how healthy they are. Governments share information in their financial statements about

- Overlapping tax rates
- Principal taxpayers
- Revenue base
- Ratios of total outstanding debt
- Overlapping debt
- Debt limits
- Total and per-capita personal income
- Unemployment rate
- Population
- Principal employers
- Government employees
- Demand for services
- Use and nature of capital assets

When evaluating a government, this information is key! Don't skip it.

3. *Determine what you think the financials should look like.* Here is where you apply all the knowledge you have learned so far in this book. You want to envision and physically sketch out what the balance sheet, income statement, and cash-flow statement should look like for this entity. An airline's balance sheet obviously will look much different than an accounting firm's balance sheet. Here are some questions to ask as you imagine and create the mock financial statements:

- How financially healthy is the organization?
- What would happen in case of liquidation?
- Where did the organization get its money, and what did it do with it?
- Who owns the organization?
- How profitable is the organization?
- Where does the profit come from? Operations? Investing? Other?
- How much investment must the organization make in its product or service?
- How much does the organization spend on overhead?
- Is this profitability sustainable or a one-time fluke?

- Where did the cash come from? Operations? Investing? Financing?
- Is the organization realizing its profits in cash?
- Is the organization in a better or worse cash position than in prior years?
- How liquid are the organization's resources?
- Are working capital items increasing or decreasing? Inventory? Accounts receivable? Accounts payable?
- Are sales increasing or decreasing?
- Is the organization realizing cost efficiencies?
- What stage of the life cycle is the organization in? Growth? Sustaining? Maturing? Declining?

Imagine and write out the balance sheet, income statement, and cash-flow statement on paper. Use both dollar figures and percentages. (The percentages will be very telling in your later analyses.) For example, you might say that you think that on the asset side of the balance sheet cash should represent 10 percent of the organization's assets, inventory 60 percent, and fixed assets 30 percent. You might predict that the cost of goods sold should be 70 percent of total sales. None of these documents has to be perfect; you are just doing an intuitive estimate.

Now, why are you doing this at all? Because you want to compare what you think the financials should look like with what they actually look like. If you are incredibly surprised, that tells you that either you really don't know a whole lot about how the organization runs (because you didn't do enough research) or something funny is going on in the organization.

Yes, it is a lot of work, but this is a high-yield activity!

4. *Run a flux analysis on the financial statements—both horizontal and common size. Fluctuation analysis*—or, in hip and cool accounting terms, *flux analysis*—is one of the best financial analysis tools around. In a fluctuation analysis, you stack up key numbers side by side to see how they have behaved over time.

Work with Both Dollars and Percentages

Relying on only dollars or only percentages can mislead you. For instance, you might see that sales have increased $1 million over the past year, but as a percentage, this is a minor 1 percent change because total sales are $100 million. Or the opposite might occur: You might see a huge percentage difference that is ultimately insignificant. For example, a 50 percent fluctuation in an account that has a very low dollar balance of $500 is only $250. So, if it goes up or down by $250, who cares?

There are two standard ways of doing a flux analysis—the common-size approach and the horizontal approach. You should run both. If you plug the data from the financial statements into an Excel spreadsheet and then ask it to do the same calculations for each year, it won't be that much manual work.

How to Express a Metric

Metrics can be expressed in five main ways:

As a fraction	¼
As a percentage	25 percent
As a decimal fraction	0.25
As a ratio	1:4 (read as "one to four")
As a multiplier	4 times per quarter

Each way of expressing the result is valid, but consider tradition and meaning when deciding on the method. For instance, return on investment (ROI) is best expressed as a percentage. You may hear, "ROI for the project is 25 percent." It would not be as meaningful to say, "ROI is 0.25" or "ROI is 1:4." You ultimately get to make the choice. Just try to be consistent in the way you express the metric so that you don't confuse yourself or the users of your analysis.

Common-Size Analysis

In common-size analysis, you turn everything into a percentage of a total. One item is 100 percent, and the rest are a portion of this 100 percent. On the income statement, you turn sales into 100 percent, and everything else becomes a percentage of total sales. Figure 14.1 shows an example.

Sales	$ 52,902	100%
Cost of goods sold	43,641	82.5%
Gross margin	9,261	17.5%
Operating expenses	7,089	13.4%
Operating margin	2,172	4.1%
Taxes and other	739	1.4%
Net income	1,433	2.7%

FIGURE 14.1 · Common-size analysis 2010.

I also think of this type of analysis as a *pie-chart analysis* (Figure 14.2). You are asking, "How much of the total sales pie was consumed by cost of goods and how much by operating expenses?"

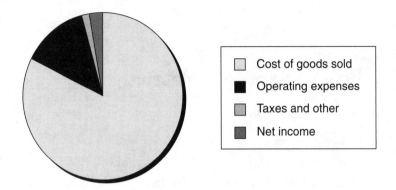

FIGURE 14.2 · Common-size analysis of the 2010 income statement.

Now, what do you do with this information? Well, you want the pie to look better and better, not worse.

Unfortunately, Dell's pie is not looking better. It is worse than last year (Figure 14.3). Last year, net income was 4 percent, and this year it is only 3 percent. This is due to cost of goods and operating expenses going up slightly in relation to income. However, keeping these figures so stable in a period of decreasing revenues is quite a feat. Total revenues have decreased from $61 billion in 2009 to $53 billion in 2010. This is a significant decrease in the size of the total pie. But Dell was able to match its volume of expenses to its volume of revenue, so it is still profitable. So, instead of losing money, Dell still earned $1.4 billion in profit. Of course, I am sure that the company would prefer last year's profit of $2.4 billion.

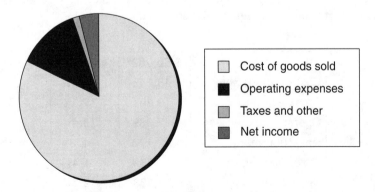

FIGURE 14.3 · Dell assets, common-size analysis, 2009.

When doing a common-size analysis of the balance sheet, total assets are 100 percent on the left side of the balance sheet, and total liabilities and equity are 100 percent on the right side of the balance sheet. You also can convert these figures to a pie chart. For our example, I ran a common-size analysis on just the asset side of the balance sheet (Figure 14.4).

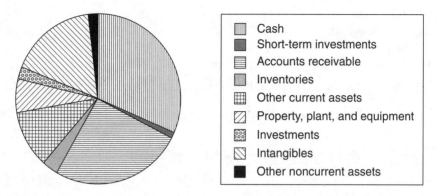

Cash
Short-term investments
Accounts receivable
Inventories
Other current assets
Property, plant, and equipment
Investments
Intangibles
Other noncurrent assets

FIGURE 14.4 · Dell's assets from the balance sheet, 2010 and 2009.

By running this common-size analysis, we become aware of some interesting choices that Dell has made during the year. Look at intangibles. Dell has been busy this year acquiring other companies. And when you pay more for a company than it is worth, you create an intangible called *goodwill* on your balance sheet.

And I'd like to look at Dell's liquid resources—its cash and short- and long-term investments. These are the monies the company can tap to respond to an emergency or purchase another company. In 2010, the sum of cash, short-term investments, and long-term investments was $11.9 billion. In 2009, the sum was $9.5 billion. So where is Dell getting the cash and extra income? If the company's total sales are going down and its profit is going down, you would expect that cash goes down, too. Obviously, something is happening on the liability side of the balance sheet. Debt is how the company is generating this extra cash. For one thing, accounts payable went up from $8.3 billion in 2009 to $11.3 billion in 2010.

We'd better run a common-size analysis on just the liability side of the balance sheet (Figure 14.5).

What do I see now? The other liabilities are relatively stable as a percentage of total liabilities, but I am still worried about that increase in accounts payable. Is the company stretching payments to vendors? That isn't very nice! This analysis raised a question that I think the ratios can answer better. We are building a pretty interesting story about Dell already. The company has been purchasing other companies, sales are down, profits are down, but cash is up because payables are significantly larger. To solve this mystery, let's keep going.

	2010		2009	
Short–term debt	$ 663	2%	$ 113	1%
Accounts payable	11,373	41%	8,309	37%
Accrued and other	3,884	14%	3,736	17%
Short–term deferred services revenue	3,040	11%	2,701	12%
Long–term debt	3,417	12%	1,898	9%
Long–term deferred services revenue	3,029	11%	3,000	13%
Other noncurrent liabilities	2,605	9%	2,472	11%
Total liabilities	28,011	100%	22,229	100%

FIGURE 14.5 · Common-size analysis of Dell's liabilities.

Take a Gander at the Cash-Flow Statement

Running a common-size analysis on a cash-flow statement is difficult because some of the numbers are negative (uses of cash) and some are positive (inflows of cash). I don't recommend doing a common-size analysis for a cash-flow statement. However, simply reading it yields quite a few interesting tidbits. See Figure 14.6. Looking under "Cash flows from operating activities," you'll see significant fluctuations year over year in accounts payable. And then looking under "Cash flow from investing activities," you'll see the acquisition of another business. And under "Cash flows from financing activities," you'll find a trend over the three-year period from $66 million in debt to taking on $2 billion in debt. Also notice that Dell has stopped using its cash to buy back and retire its own stock—which has been its habit for the past decade.

Horizontal Analysis

With this second flux analysis technique, you choose one year as a base year, and every other year is fluctuated off that year. In this case, a picture will substitute for a thousand words (Figure 14.7).

Be careful which years you compare! Be careful that you compare valid numbers. Compare the fluctuating years only with the base year, not with each other.

So I chose 2008 as my base year. Every account in 2008 is 100 percent. Then 2009 and 2010 are fluctuated off this base year—not off each other.

Because of this, you cannot compare the 2009 numbers with the 2010 numbers. You can't say that sales in 2009 were 99 percent and sales in 2010 were 86.5 percent, so sales went down between 2009 and 2010 by 12.5 percent. This is not valid mathematically or logically because sales between 2009 and 2010 actually decreased by 13.4 percent [(61,101 − 52,902)/61,101]. You can say that sales in 2009 were very close to 2008 sales—down only 0.1 percent—but that sales in 2010 were 13.5 percent lower than the 2008 numbers.

DELL INC.

CONSOLIDATED STATEMENTS OF CASH FLOWS

(in millions)

	Fiscal Year Ended		
	January 29, 2010	January 30, 2009	February 1, 2008
Cash flows from operating activities:			
Net income	$ 1,433	$ 2,478	$ 2,947
Adjustments to reconcile net income to net cash provided by operating activities:			
Depreciation and amortization	852	769	607
Stock-based compensation	312	418	329
In-process research and development charges	-	2	83
Effects of exchange rate changes on monetary assets and liabilities denominated in foreign currencies	59	(115)	30
Deferred income taxes	(52)	86	(308)
Provision for doubtful accounts — including financing receivables	429	310	187
Other	102	32	30
Changes in operating assets and liabilities, net of effects from acquisitions:			
Accounts receivable	(660)	480	(1,086)
Financing receivables	(1,085)	(302)	(394)
Inventories	(183)	309	(498)
Other assets	(225)	(106)	(121)
Accounts payable	2,833	(3,117)	837
Deferred services revenue	135	663	1,032
Accrued and other liabilities	(44)	(13)	274
Change in cash from operating activities	3,906	1,894	3,949
Cash flows from investing activities:			
Investments:			
Purchases	(1,383)	(1,584)	(2,394)
Maturities and sales	1,538	2,333	3,679
Capital expenditures	(367)	(440)	(831)
Proceeds from sale of facility and land	16	44	-
Acquisition of business, net of cash received	(3,613)	(176)	(2,217)
Change in cash from investing activities	(3,809)	177	(1,763)
Cash flows from financing activities:			
Repurchase of common stock	-	(2,867)	(4,004)
Issuance of common stock under employee plans	2	79	136
Issuance of commercial paper (maturity 90 days or less), net	76	100	(100)
Proceeds from debt	2,058	1,519	66
Repayments of debt	(122)	(237)	(165)
Other	(2)	-	(53)
Change in cash from financing activities	2,012	(1,406)	(4,120)
Effect of exchange rate changes on cash and cash equivalents	174	(77)	152
Change in cash and cash equivalents	2,283	588	(1,782)
Cash and cash equivalents at beginning of the year	8,352	7,764	9,546
Cash and cash equivalents at end of the year	$ 10,635	$ 8,352	$ 7,764
Income tax paid	$ 434	$ 800	$ 767
Interest paid	$ 151	$ 74	$ 54

The accompanying notes are an integral part of these consolidated financial statements.

FIGURE 14.6 · Dell's cash-flow statement.

	2010		2009		2008	
Sales	$52,902	86.5%	$61,101	99.9%	$61,133	100%
Cost of goods sold	43,641	88.2%	50,144	101.4%	49,462	100%
Gross margin	9,261	79.4%	10,957	93.9%	11,671	100%
Operating expenses	7,089	86.1%	7,767	94.4%	8,231	100%
Operating margin	2,172	63.1%	3,190	92.7%	3,440	100%
Taxes and other	739	149.9%	712	144.4%	493	100%
Net income	1,433	48.6%	2,478	84.1%	2,947	100%

FIGURE 14.7 · Horizontal analysis, Dell's income statement, 2010, 2009 and 2008.

So this analysis helps us to see that the decline in profitability we saw in our two-year common-size analysis is a recent event. The 2009 numbers are similar to the 2008 numbers, although I do see an unpleasant bump in the cost of goods sold between the years, which Dell compensated for by decreasing operating expenses. In 2010, however, Dell's operating margin is down to 63 percent of its 2008 levels. Dell has always been a master at scaling. *Scaling* means that you are able to spend proportionally fewer dollars to make proportionally more income. Dell scaled quite nicely on the way up from a sales of $18 billion in 1999 but now has to practice scaling back as top-line revenues decrease.

After performing a common-size analysis and a horizontal analysis, make notes about what you are seeing so far.

5. *Decide which ratios are meaningful to the organization.* Choose at least five ratios from each category—liquidity, profitability, and financing—and calculate them for the past three years.

You can ratio any number against any other number in the financial statements. You can generate numbers and metrics until you are blue in the face. Some of the metrics will tell an interesting story, and some will be entirely meaningless.

Be choosy about the metrics you run on your organization. Not all ratios will tell an interesting story about an organization. Some ratios may not even apply to the organization at all. So what you want to do is to look over the lists of ratios in Chapters 15 through 18 and decide which ones make sense to you.

For our case study, I am going to run every metric listed in the chapter, whether or not it is a good, meaningful metric for our companies. I am doing this to drive home the point that not all metrics will work and not all metrics are worth working with.

The three categories of ratios are liquidity, profitability, and financing.

- *Liquidity* ratios tell us how flexible and powerful the organization is. Does the organization have enough liquid resources to cover its obligations?

- *Profitability* ratios tell us what kind of return the organization brings for its owners. Does the organization generate enough of its own funding to make it worth it for the owners to be in business?
- *Financing* ratios tell us how the organization is getting resources to operate. Is the organization generating its own resources, borrowing the resources, or selling equity to generate resources? Does the organization fund its growth and/or operations through profit *or* debt *or* contributions from owners?

6. *Investigate.* Now that you have raised so many questions with your flux analysis and ratio analysis, you need to start investigating why the numbers look as they do. If you are an outsider to the organization, you may not have any other source to turn to. You are then left to make educated guesses about what may have happened. You also can come up with a hypothesis and then watch to see if your hypothesis holds in future periods.

If you are on the inside, you should be able to ask questions of the accountant and managers and get answers. But this is not always the case because some organizations do their best to keep financial information secret.

If the organization is a publicly traded company, read the "Management's Discussion and Analysis" section of the financial reports to see if the questions are answered. As we discussed in Chapter 7, the "Management's Discussion and Analysis" section of the financial statements is one of most important parts of the 10-K. It is the top managers' explanation of what happened over the past period and even may contain a little projection about where the organization is going in the near term.

Often, closely held organizations are also closed lipped. The owners are not accustomed to answering your questions, nor are they required to do so. For many managers, this is one of the biggest drawbacks of becoming a public company. When you go public, you have to answer the shareholders' questions. When you are private, you only have to answer to a few folks.

Even when you are analyzing a public company that issues 10-Ks and other annual reports, the numbers are so summarized or rolled up that it is hard to get at the root cause of an issue.

 ## Open-Book Management

A company might benefit from sharing financial results with its employees. A philosophy called *open-book management* recommends that managers educate employees about how the business makes money and the tools used to track business success. It also recommends that employees be told how the company is doing as often as possible and that employees share in the ownership of the company.

(Continued)

A man named Jack Stack popularized this philosophy. Stack was the manager of a division of a huge conglomerate. His division retooled engines. The huge conglomerate had decided that his division was not profitable and was planning to shut it down. It was the largest employer in a small town, and this would have had a disastrous impact on the whole community.

Stack was up nights worrying about what to do when he realized that he was doing everyone a disservice by keeping this problem to himself. He realized that only three other managers in the company understood what was going on and that the employees would be completely shocked when they lost their jobs. The employees would blame Stack for all their troubles because they were being kept in the dark.

Stack decided to open up the books to his employees and train them how to understand what was going on. He told them that to save their jobs, they would have to become owners of the company, and as owners, they needed to concern themselves with the financial success of the company.

Jack came up with procedures, meetings, and even games that kept his employees involved. Once they understood the situation, the employees came up with a multitude of ideas to keep the business profitable. After two decades of open-book management, the company is still going strong.

If you want to read more on this topic, pick up Stack's book, *The Great Game of Business*. It is fun to read—and educational to boot.

7. *Make general conclusions about liquidity, profitability, and financing.* Remember to highlight both the positive and negative trends. Run more ratios if necessary.

I recommend actually documenting your conclusions. Write down what you see in terms of liquidity, profitability, and financing. If you are anything like me, your memory is short. (I can't remember what I had for lunch last Wednesday.) And writing things down and stepping away for a little while will help you to see themes or patterns in the data.

So do yourself a favor in each of these steps: Write your conclusions down so that you will have something to refer to.

8. *Compare with benchmarks.* The numbers, sitting alone, mean little. You must compare them with something—competitors, industry averages, or past history—in order to tell if the numbers are happy or sad.

My favorite comparison is against the company itself over time. As your mother always said, "Do your best!" Is the company doing its best? Are results improving over time?

No other company in the world operates exactly like the company you are examining, so comparisons with other companies are sometimes futile.

I was once tasked with summarizing the financial health of the State of Texas government in a magazine-style report, complete with graphics and color, for the legislature. My boss asked me to benchmark Texas against other states.

This turned out to be an impossible task. No other state runs like Texas. The other big states, such as California, Florida, Pennsylvania, and New York, have completely different bureaucratic structures. The way they present their financial results is quite different. Some states allow local government more of a hand in operations; some are highly centralized. I had to give up on other-state comparisons.

It is like this in industry too. In my class on financial statement analysis, I compare Dell, Apple, and Hewlett-Packard (HP). All are computer manufacturers, but comparison is still challenging. For instance, HP has a top-line revenue of $114 billion, and until 2010, Apple was significantly smaller. Apple's 2007 revenues were $24.5 billion. This comparison yields some interesting results, but it isn't completely meaningful because the companies don't employ the same business model or even sell the same products. HP sells lots of software and printers as well as computers. And while Dell also sells phones and tablet PCs, it has nowhere near the market share of the iPhone and iPad.

Other problems with benchmarking may arise when you are trying to benchmark in the following situations:

- *The company is part of a conglomerate*. In this case, the financial results may be impossible to separate from the mother company.
- *The company uses different accounting policies*. It might use last in, first out (LIFO) instead of first in, first out (FIFO) or recognize stock options.
- *The company is a different size*. Sheer size of the organization may affect the way operating expenses, depreciation, and fixed assets look on the financial statements.
- *The company calculates its metrics differently*. There is no standard for calculating financial metrics. In other words, there is no GAAP for financial ratios. I recommend that you calculate them for yourself rather than relying on the organization's disclosure. The metrics the organization calculates always will present the prettiest picture possible.
- *The company delays publication of results or does not publish at all*. You may want to benchmark against your toughest competitor but cannot get any financial data on that competitor because it does not share its results with the public.
- *The company likes to dress up its financial results*. Everyone likes to dress up! Many companies take action at the end of a quarter or a year to make their financial results as pretty as they can be. This may not hold in the middle of the period. So what anyone presents has to be taken with a grain of salt.

If you want to compare with industry averages, take a look at these resources:

- Dun and Bradstreet (www.dnb.com/us/)
- Risk Management Association (www.rmahq.org)
- *Forbes* magazine (www.forbes.com)
- *Fortune* magazine (www.fortune.com)

- CFO magazine (www.cfo.com)
- PricewaterhouseCooper's industry reports (www.pwcglobal.com)
- *Almanac of Business and Industrial Financial Ratios* (annual, Prentice-Hall)

9. *Represent these conclusions graphically and narratively.* Depending on whom you are creating this analysis for, you may want to represent your conclusions graphically and narratively. You may want to create a user-friendly report summarizing your conclusions. The pictures, colors, and short stories I used in my magazine-style financial report went a long way toward helping the legislature understand Texas finances.

Before embarking on this task, I recommend that you do some reading about what makes reports and graphics user friendly. If you present too much data, you can overwhelm and turn off your audience. One of my favorite books on the subject is *Say It with Charts: The Executive's Guide to Visual Communication*, by Gene Zelazny (McGraw-Hill).

10. *Consider making recommendations for improvements.* Depending on your relationship with the organization, you even may go as far as to point out weaknesses and make recommendations for improvement.

Case Study—Dell and Apple, 2010

Why Did I Choose Dell and Apple for Our Analysis?

I've been teaching financial analysis courses to CPAs for about 15 years now. Originally, in 1998, I started using Dell, Gateway, and Compaq financial statements for my classes. I asked the CPAs to run some metrics and piece together a story about the companies. The first edition of this book compared Dell with Gateway. But did you notice anything about that list? Two of the original companies are missing: Gateway came close to going bankrupt before it was purchased by a Chinese manufacturer, and HP purchased Compaq.

Over time, I switched to analyzing Dell, HP, and IBM during my classses. But IBM was impossible to analyze because it is such a diverse, complex conglomerate that the results are meaningless. I decided in 2006 to replace IBM with Apple, which up to that point had been too small to include in the mix. As of this writing, Apple is poised to overtake Dell in total revenue.

Notice that I have never considered taking Dell out of the mix because I am selfish. Dell is a major employer in my hometown of Austin, Texas, and many of my neighbors' livelihoods depend on the company. At one point, mine did. I want to keep an eye on Dell.

What Do We See?

Year after year, Dell has come out smelling like a rose. Its revenues climbed steadily and then plateaued at a healthy level. The company has always been great at stockpiling cash and keeping expenses down. That is, until 2010. As we have already seen, Dell had a bad year, and it is hard to say whether the downward trend will continue.

HP has much more volatile profitability than Dell. Sometimes HP makes money; sometimes it doesn't. And because of its enormous size and various product lines, it is hard to tell which product is actually doing well and which is taking HP down. The company also is in the habit of buying other companies and occasionally restating its financial statements, making year-over-year comparisons more challenging.

But Apple has been very fun to watch and analyze. Its revenues have grown exponentially, it is skilled at accumulating cash, and it has financial statements that are easy to work with.

Why and how is this? I mentioned in Chapter 13 that financial results are just that—results. Finances don't drive success. Remember the balanced scorecard? Business starts by making the customer happy. And Apple's customers are very happy. I wasn't so happy being a Dell customer because the company refused to fix a broken computer and made me negotiate with its managers in India for several days before the issue was resolved. Add customer happiness to innovation and good financial management, and presto! Profit! Okay, nothing in business is this simple, but I think you get my opinionated point.

But my, how quickly things change. Gateway had a store with an inflatable cow on the roof near my house 12 years ago. And now the company and the cow are gone. Poof!

Poof! Presto! … We have a regular magic show going on here!

We Are Going to Do Every Ratio

I am going to run every ratio whether or not it makes sense. Why? So that you can see why some metrics are not all that meaningful. I will take the more meaningful metrics and summarize them at the end of each chapter and make conclusions.

I am going to look at profitability metrics in Chapter 15, liquidity metrics and working capital in Chapter 16, liquidity metrics and cash in Chapter 17, and financing metrics in Chapter 18. I will conclude each chapter with one piece of the story for Dell and one piece of the story for Apple. At the end of the last chapter, I will present my overall findings.

Summary

Taking time to understand your subject will give context to your analysis and help you to piece together the story of your subject's financial success or failure. Common-size analysis is used frequently because it is powerful and meaningful. But common-size and horizontal analyses can be misleading and need to be tempered or rounded out with ratios.

QUIZ

1. These kinds of financial statements offer more assurance than other ones.
   A. Most recent
   B. Audited
   C. Balance sheet
   D. Annual report

2. Banks are concerned about this kind of metric the most.
   A. Return on investment (ROI)
   B. Profitability
   C. Inventory
   D. Cash flow

3. This is simply a translation of future plans of an organization into financial terms.
   A. A budget
   B. A strategic plan
   C. A market trend
   D. Financial health

4. You do this to compare what you think the financials should look like with what they actually are.
   A. Financial history
   B. Scratch financial statements
   C. Financial analysis
   D. Flux analysis

5. The common-size approach and the horizontal approach are two standard ways of doing what?
   A. Scratch financial statements
   B. Flux analysis
   C. The budget
   D. The balance sheet

6. In a common-size analysis, you turn everything into a _____ of the total.
   A. fraction
   B. percentage
   C. whole number
   D. ratio

7. **When you pay more for a company than what it is worth, you create an intangible called**
   A. investments.
   B. a stack.
   C. prepaid expense.
   D. goodwill.

8. **Which of the following is the most relevant for comparing a company's results against?**
   A. Its largest competitor
   B. Itself over time
   C. Industry averages
   D. The newest competitor

9. **All metrics are not meaningful to all organizations. True or false?**
   A. True
   B. False

10. **How a company decides to distribute its profits can have an impact on its cash flow and equity position. True or false?**
    A. True
    B. False

Chapter **15**

Profit Ratios

Profit. Yeah! That's what capitalism is all about—taking something raw and/or unformed and turning it into something that others will pay a premium for. Profitable businesses put a little in and get a lot out; very profitable businesses put a dime in and get a dollar out.

The main financial statement that indicates profit is the income statement, sometimes called the *profit and loss statement* (P&L). So many of our ratios work from numbers derived from this statement.

CHAPTER OBJECTIVES

- Calculate profitability ratios for two organizations
- Interpret the results of the ratios

The three categories of profit ratios are

- Margin ratios
- Return ratios
- Shareholder earnings ratios

Margin Ratios

Margins are subtotals. We already talked about gross profit and operating profit in Chapter 3 when we were discussing the income statement. The margins tell us how much of our bar of soap (total sales revenue) we have left after whittling down the bar by taking out all expenses. Maybe you have a hotel-size bar of soap; maybe you have a sliver. These metrics turn the dollars into percentages.

Net Profit Margin Percentage

$$\frac{\text{Net income}}{\text{Net sales}}$$

The questions this margin answers include, "What percentage of sales was retained by the time we got to the bottom line of the income statement?" and "How much profit did we walk away with at the end of the day?"

Margins vary widely by industry. Some organizations have a very high net profit percentage, such as custom home builders. They might generate 20 percent profits, *but* they might experience low dollar volume. So, although they retain a high percentage, they don't realize much in cold, hard cash. Some bigger operations, such as Walmart, do not have huge profit margin percentages. They might generate only a 3.5 percent profit, but 3.5 percent profit when you sell $408 billion is $14 billion. $14 billion is not easy to generate in any business.

Results for Dell

What is Dell's net profit margin percentage for some recent periods?

2010: Net income of $1,433,000,000/net sales of $52,902,000,000 = 2.7 percent

2009: Net income of $2,478,000,000/net sales of $61,101,000,000 = 4.1 percent

Results for Apple
Here are Apple's figures:

> 2009: Net income of $8,235,000,000/net sales of $42,905,000,000 = 19.2 percent

> 2008: Net income of $6,119,000,000/net sales of $37,491,000,000 = 16.3 percent

Conclusions
Apple's profit margins are incredibly high: almost 20 percent in the computer industry—amazing. Even at its peak, Dell achieved an 8 percent profitability. And while Apple's net profit margin is improving, Dell's is declining.

Dell's 2.7 percent of a bar of soap is better than no soap at all! Net profit margin percentage is such a summarized figure. We need to break it down to diagnose whether it is component costs or operating expenses that are eating away at Dell's profits. This is what gross profit margin and operating profit margin do for you.

Gross Profit Margin

$$\frac{\text{Gross profit}}{\text{Net sales}}$$

Gross profit margin in dollars is one of the subtotals on the way to the bottom of the income statement. Sales less cost of goods sold equals gross margin. So gross margin tells us how much the organization has to work with after it pays direct expenses for creating its product or service. The gross margin percentage converts the gross margin dollars into a percentage. So if the gross margin percentage is 45 percent, this means that the organization consumed 55 percent of total sales revenue in order to pay for the direct expenses of making its product. A gross margin percentage of 45 percent indicates that the organization still has 45 percent of total sales left to pay operating expenses, taxes, and other expenses. Hopefully, after all the expenses are subtracted, the organization still has a little left. The little bit left is net income. So, to get it, we take the gross margin dollars and divide by total sales dollars.

Results for Dell
What is Dell's gross profit margin percentage for some recent periods?

> 2010: Gross profit of $9,261,000,000/net sales of $52,902,000,000 = 17.5 percent

2009: Gross profit of $10,957,000,000/net sales of $61,101,000,000 = 20.9 percent

Results for Apple
Here are Apple's figures:

2009: Gross profit of $17,222,000,000/net sales of $42,905,000,000 = 40.1 percent

2008: Gross profit of $13,197,000,000/net sales of $37,491,000,000 = 35.2 percent

Conclusions
Gross profit is the result of subtracting cost of goods sold from total sales. When Dell does this, it is left with a 17.5 percent gross profit margin percentage. In other words, Dell has 17.5 percent left of its bar of soap after cutting off cost of goods, and Apple has 40 percent left. Two main factors are at play in Apple's very happy result; either the company has been able to charge more for its products because of its premium or luxury brand or it is using inexpensive components and labor or both. Again, Dell's margins are slipping in the wrong direction. But we also need to remember that its total revenue declined by $8 billion between periods. The company may not have had time to scale back expenses to match the decline in sales.

Operating Profit Margin

$$\frac{\text{Operating profit}}{\text{Net sales}}$$

Operating profit margin percentage tells us what percentage of our sales revenue we still have on hand after paying for cost of goods sold and operating expenses. Operating income equals gross margin less operating expenses. More formally, operating income equals sales revenue less cost of goods sold less operating expenses. Operating profit margin converts the dollars left after paying those two major expense categories (cost of goods sold and operating expenses) into a percentage. If this is still a bit fuzzy, refer back to the income statement discussion in Chapter 3, and focus on the explanation of gross margin and operating profit margin.

Still Struggling?

Three Common Margins

Gross sales

Less cost of goods

Equals gross profit margin (number 1)

Less operating expenses

Equals operating profit margin (number 2)

Less taxes and other

Equals net income or net profit margin (number 3)

These figures can be extracted from the income statement in dollars. Then you can easily take the dollars and convert them to percentages by dividing all items by gross sale dollars. Remember the formula that I will ask you to recite when I see you on the street? Revenues − expenses = profit. This is the same formula—just in more detail with more subtotals!

Results for Dell

2010: Operating income of $2,172,000,000/net sales of $52,902,000,000
= 4.1 percent
2009: Operating income of $3,190,000,000/net sales of $61,101,000,000
= 5.2 percent

Results for Apple

2009: Operating income of $11,740,000,000/net sales of $42,905,000,000
= 27.4 percent
2008: Operating income of $8,372,000,000/net sales of $37,491,000,000
= 22.2 percent

Conclusions

Again, Apple is ahead. Operating income is a key measure for all organizations because it indicates how well the business part of the business is doing—how well operations are going. It does not tell you how much the organization is paying in taxes or interest or any other semiuncontrollable aspect of being in business. Many organizations bonus their employees based on operating income instead of net income because operating income is under the control of the employees, and items below operating income on the income statement are not.

Relative Research and Development (R&D)

$$\frac{\text{R\&D expense}}{\text{Sales}}$$

This ratio asks, "How much is the organization investing in creating future products and services?" Again, we will get a percentage here. If you see that the organization invests practically nothing in new-product development, you might be concerned. This might mean trouble in the future. But then again, it might not mean anything. If the organization is a retailer, it might not spend any money on R&D because it does not develop products; it sells other people's products. Again, choose to run the ratio only if it makes sense to you.

Results for Dell

2010: R&D investment of $624,000,000/sales of $52,902,000,000 = 1.2 percent
2009: R&D investment of $663,000,000/sales of $61,101,000,000 = 1.1 percent

Results for Apple

2009: R&D investment of $1,333,000,000/sales of $42,905,000,000 = 3.1 percent
2008: R&D investment of $1,109,000,000/sales of $37,491,000 = 3 percent

Conclusions

Wow, Dell spends very little on R&D—around 1 percent. It makes sense for Dell because it is not an innovator; it is an assembler. The company takes whatever is selling on the market and packages it and sells it. Dell doesn't invent much.

Contrast this with Apple. Apple is an innovator. Its investment in R&D was over $1.3 billion, or 3 percent of total sales. If Dell invested another 2 percent of its sales in R&D, it would barely break even. I am actually surprised that Apple's R&D expense isn't higher. In years past, I've seen it as high as 8 percent, but that was when its total sales were under $1 billion. Thus $1.3 billion is a lot to spend on thinking up new stuff.

Return Metrics

In these metrics, we contrast profit with the investments that went into creating that profit. We want to invest as little as possible and generate the highest possible profit.

Return on Assets

$$\frac{\text{Net income}}{\text{Total assets}}$$

Return on assets asks, "What sort of return did we generate for our investment in assets?" It is a very similar metric to return on investment (ROI). Some industries are very asset-heavy. For instance, the airline industry will have a huge investment in fixed assets in the form of jets and planes. This metric asks how much return or net income was generated as a result of putting those assets to work.

Results for Dell

2010: Net income of $1,433,000,000/total assets of $33,652,000,000 = 4.3 percent

2009: Net income of $2,478,000,000/total assets of $26,500,000,000 = 9.4 percent

Results for Apple

2009: Net income of $8,235,000,000/total assets of $47,501,000,000 = 17.3 percent

2008: Net income of $6,119,000,000/total assets of $36,171,000,000 = 16.9 percent

Conclusions

Because Apple is so unreasonably profitable, this metric looks much better for it. Dell's numbers are worsening because its profit is worsening while its asset balances are increasing. A bigger bottom number makes this metric worse, and Dell increased its assets by going into debt to buy another company and keep its cash balances high.

Sales to Fixed Assets

$$\frac{\text{Sales}}{\text{Fixed assets}}$$

This may be a more meaningful ratio for an airline than return on total assets. Here we are asking about the relationship between fixed assets and sales. Hopefully, the top of this ratio is large in relationship to a lean fixed asset balance. This would tell us that the organization is using its resources efficiently to generate sales.

Results for Dell

2010: Sales of $52,902,000,000/fixed assets of $2,181,000,000 = 2,425.6 percent

2009: Sales of $61,101,000,000/fixed assets of $2,277,000,000 = 2,683.4 percent

Results for Apple

2009: Sales of $42,905,000,000/fixed assets of $2,954,000,000 = 1,452.4 percent

2008: Sales of $37,491,000,000/fixed assets of $2,455,000,000 = 1,527.1 percent

Conclusions

These are silly numbers! Neither company invests much in fixed assets. I have been inside Dell's headquarters just outside of Austin, and the company isn't what I would call posh. As a matter of fact, Dell is as basic and inexpensive as it can manage. Multiple-story boxes with unfinished ceilings and concrete floors. Apple also has offices here in Austin, but I'm pretty sure that it rents. In the notes to Apple's financial statements, the company discloses that it has $1.6 billion in leasehold improvements but less than $1 billion in land and buildings. When I talk about liquidity in Chapter 16, I'll explore this rent versus buy issue again.

DuPont Analysis

DuPont analysis gets very granular. It allows you to diagnose the underlying causes of a change in return metrics. Return on equity (net income/equity) is the most common metric analyzed, but you also can use DuPont analysis for return on invested capital and return on assets. If I explain it to you clearly, it would take me a whole chapter—so I'm just going to bring it to your attention in case someone mentions it to you.

Both components of the equation—net income and equity—are products of other accounts such as revenues and expenses. So if the top part of the return-on-equity equation changed, was it because total sales changed or expenses changed? DuPont analysis will tell you which factors changed—although it won't tell you why. Figure 15.1 is a graphic that will either scare you or intrigue you. If it intrigues you, check out http://home.ximb.ac.in/~slramana/AFDMCourseWeb/Dupont%20Analysis.htm.

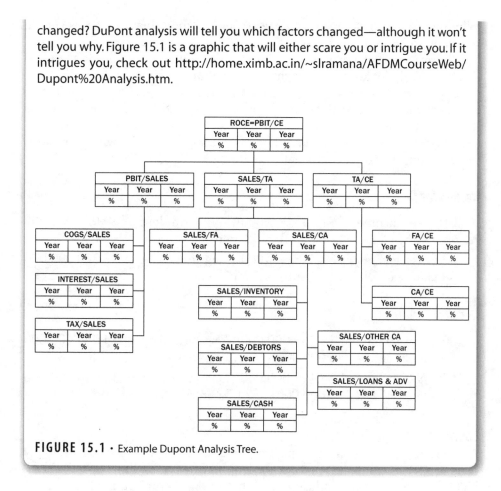

FIGURE 15.1 · Example Dupont Analysis Tree.

Return on Investment

$$\frac{\text{Net income}}{\text{Long-term debt + equity}}$$

I have seen this ratio calculated in a variety of ways. In this particular example, we have net income (our return) on the top and our investment (long-term debt and equity) on the bottom.

The result will be a percentage that indicates how well the investment in the company is doing at generating a profit. Ideally, you would like to see the percentage return higher than the percentage return you would get if you put your money in the bank, say, in a certificate of deposit (CD) or some other conservative instrument. If a CD rate is beating your company's return on investment, it may indicate that investors could do better investing their money elsewhere.

Why should they risk giving you the resources when they can get as good a return on something much less risky and with a guaranteed payoff?

Why are long-term debt and equity considered our investment in the organization? Well, looking at the right-hand side of the balance sheet, the only major thing we left out of the bottom of this equation is accounts payable. The argument might be that this should not be considered an investment because it has short turnaround: It will be paid off in the current quarter. I also have seen this ratio calculated with accounts payable included, so do whatever makes sense to you—but do it consistently!

Results for Dell

2010: Net income of $1,433,000,000/(long-term debt of $9,051,000,000 + equity of $5,641,000,000) = 9.8 percent

2009: Net income of $2,478,000,000/(long-term debt of $7,370,000,000 + equity of $4,271,000,000) = 7.3 percent

Results for Apple

2009: Net income of $8,235,000,000/(long-term debt of $4,355,000,000 + equity of $31,640,000,000) = 22.9 percent

2008: Net income of $6,199,000,000/(long-term debt of $2,513,000,000 + equity of $22,297,000,000) = 24.7 percent

Conclusions

A 7 percent return on investment is nothing to sneeze at, especially when my bank is paying less than 2 percent for long-term CDs. Again, Apple is ahead. I like this metric for this industry much better than return on fixed assets.

Return on Equity

$$\frac{\text{Net profit}}{\text{Equity}}$$

This ratio asks, "Was the investment in the organization, in terms of equity, worth it?" Equity tells us how much of the company the owners own through stock and retained earnings. It contrasts return with total equity. Total equity will include stock and retained earnings.

Results for Dell

2010: Net profit of $1,433,000,000/equity of $5,641,000,000 = 25.4 percent

2009: Net profit of $2,478,000,000/equity of $4,271,000,000 = 58 percent

Results for Apple

2009: Net profit of $8,235,000,000/equity of $31,640,000,000 = 26 percent

2008: Net profit of $6,199,000,000/equity of $22,297,000,000 = 27.04 percent

Conclusions

This is an interesting decline for Dell—but we know one of the causes of this already. The decline highlights another aspect of the balance sheet we haven't talked about much—equity. Dell earned $309 million in other comprehensive income in 2009 but lost $37 million in 2010. This is not a huge amount, but it does affect this metric.

Shareholder Earnings Ratios

The following two ratios are very popular with shareholders. Undoubtedly, you've encountered both if you've read any books on investing.

Earnings per Share

$$\frac{\text{Earnings available to common stockholders}}{\text{Number of common shares outstanding}}$$

This is a favorite metric of Wall Street. It simply expresses profitability in per-share terms. You may hear that earnings per share (EPS) were 20 cents this past quarter. This metric simply takes the total dollar amount of profit and divides it by the number of shares outstanding during the period.

Companies love to project their earnings per share and announce their projections to the public and to Wall Street. If a company does not meet its projection, the selling price of its stock might suffer. This metric can be manipulated by changing the number of shares outstanding. The company can buy back and retire shares. And it is not comparable between corporations because some corporations will have earnings in pennies and others in dollars because of the denominator. The best use for it is as a basis for the price/earnings ratio, which we will calculate next.

I got the shares outstanding from the bottom of the first page of the 10-K for both companies.

Results for Dell

2010: Earnings available to common shareholders of $1,433,000,000/shares outstanding 1,957,000,000 = 73 cents

2009: Earnings available to common shareholders of $2,478,000,000/shares outstanding 1,944,000,000 = $1.27

Results for Apple

2009: Earnings available to common shareholders of $8,235,000,000/shares outstanding 890,000,000 = $9.25

2008: Earnings available to common shareholders of $6,119,000,000/shares outstanding 888,000,000 = $6.89

Conclusions

So, is it bad that Dell's earnings are around a dollar and Apple's are over $9. Not necessarily. Apple has fewer shares outstanding than Dell, making the denominator smaller. I am not a big fan of this metric because it is useful only if compared with the company's projections.

Still Struggling

What Is the Big Deal about EPS?

EPS is one of the key ratios for Wall Street analysts and investors, and it is mostly about expectations.

Public companies project what their earnings will be for the upcoming four quarters. Those projections are communicated to the big investors—such as the California Public Employees' Retirement System (CalPERs) and Fidelity Investments. These big investors can swing the price of the stock with one big purchase or sale.

If the company believes that it might fall short of its earning projections, it starts communicating its shortfall to these institutional investors early. In this way, the big investors are not surprised and make any fast moves in or out of the stock. If the justification for not meeting projections sounds reasonable to them, a shortfall may not affect the stock price very much. This is what the company hopes, anyway. If earnings are way under projections and the large institutional investors do not appreciate the reasons, share price can drop precipitously.

And the reason the company cares about the stock price? Well, it affects the company's ability to get future financing, but its mostly because the people who run the company also personally own serious amounts of stock. If the company does well, their personal portfolios do well, and vice versa.

Most public companies have a division called *investor relations*. Communicating with the large investors is one of the investor relations department's main jobs.

Price/Earnings(P/E) Ratio

$$\frac{\text{Market price per share of common stock}}{\text{Earning per share}}$$

This metric asks, "How much are the stockholders paying for the earnings?" Another way to look at this is, "How expensive are the earnings? What multiple did the stockholders have to pay to own the shares?" It takes the market price of the share of stock and compares it with the earnings per share. You may get a result such as 35. This means that investors are willing to pay 35 times current earnings to purchase the stock. Is this good or bad? Again, it is subject to market conditions, the economy, and Wall Street's perceptions of the value of the stock.

Results for Dell

2010: Market price of $11.60 per share (aggregate market value of $22.7 billion from the cover of the 10-K/1.957 billion shares)/earnings per share of 73 cents = 15.84

2009: Market price of $16.87 per share (aggregate market value of $41.8 billion from the cover of the 10-K/1.954 billion shares)/earnings per share of $1.27 = 16.87

Results for Apple

2009: Market price of $133.38 per share (aggregate market value of $94.5 billion from the cover of the 10-K/890 million shares)/earnings per share of $9.25 = 14.41

2008: Market price of $106.28 per share (aggregate market value of $118.4 billion from the cover of the 10-K/888 million shares)/earnings per share of $6.89 = 15.43

Conclusions

I have seen Dell's P/E ratio over 40. And I was expecting Apple's to be high also—but the recession kept investors calm and paying reasonable amounts for their stock.

The P/E ratio supposedly tells you that an investor is willing to pay around 16 times the earnings for the stock. But this number is affected by many factors.

Dell's earnings per share were up in 2010 but the number of shares outstanding is down by over 37 million. Market price is affected by many things other than the profitability of a company. It is affected by investor's vision of the companies future, its leadership, and its position in relationship to its competitors. More and more global events beyond the control of the company in question can impact Wall Street's mood. My conclusion: Take any metric that integrates the mood of Wall Street within it with a grain of salt. The elements of the equation are possibly more interesting and more informative than the results of the equation.

Uncomfortable with Market Price per Share Information

We have all had a good dose of craziness in the 1990s. We saw how perceptions and hype can affect the price of stock. One good magazine article can send the price of stock soaring. One small mistake can send stock prices down, down, down. We have seen companies sell their stock at exorbitant prices without any real profitability to back it up. We have seen liars and swindlers take their employees' benefit plans and cruelly zero them out.

After the stock market downturn in the early 2000s, many companies that had gone public in the previous five years went private again so that they would not have to tolerate and bow to the expectations of uninformed investors and Wall Street. It is unrealistic to expect double-digit growth in sales and revenue every single quarter and every single year; however, this is what Wall Street often expects.

I am much more comfortable calculating metrics that have to do with an organization's internal operations and management decisions than I am with data that are easily manipulated by the company and by investor expectations. For instance, I am wary of EPS and the P/E ratio because, in effect, they are out of the control of the organization's managers. These numbers can be manipulated by a stock split in the case of EPS or by a negative press release.

What Can We Conclude about Profitability for These Two Companies?

Apple is making hay while the sun shines! This is a hot time for the company, and profits are unusually high. And in a period of just a few years, it has grown exponentially. In 2005, Apple revenues were $14 billion. In five years, revenues grew to $42.9 billion.

Dell was hot in the late 1990s, experiencing similar growth but never the levels of profitability we saw at Apple. Dell seeks to be a low-cost provider of computers. This caps the price it can charge customers and squeezes its margins. Apple positions itself as a premium brand and is not as hemmed in by customer expectations of low prices. To be profitable, an organization needs to manage its working capital wisely, sell a large volume of products, or sell products for plenty more than it takes to make them. At this time, Apple is able to do all three. Dell is still relying on volume as a driver of its profitability, but its volume is decreasing.

Ratios for Projects

Internal rate of return (IRR), return on investment (ROI), and dollar value added (DVA) are used commonly to evaluate the wisdom of projects. For instance, if you were going to purchase a new machine to increase production, you would evaluate whether it actually was going to make a positive difference to your organization in terms of profit and cash flow.

One organization I work with uses all three metrics to evaluate projects. If the metrics do not meet certain minimum thresholds, the project is rejected.

Internal Rate of Return (IRR)

The formal definition of *internal rate of return* is "the rate of return that would cause the present value of all future cash flows to be $0." Ha! That's not very helpful!

The reason the definition sounds so bad is that IRR takes into account the time value of money, which is one of those concepts that has caused many an accounting student to abandon the business school and go study English. The time value of money concept argues that $1 today is worth more than $1 five years down the line because you could have put that dollar to work and it would be worth more than $1.00 five years down the line.

IRR asks us, "What kind of return are we making on the project in the long run?" For our example, we have a software manufacturer that takes two years to create the software and then sells it for four years before it has to be revised or updated. So the life cycle of the software is six years. The first two years, the software developer experienced negative cash flow because it was paying to develop the software. Then the developer got an ROI investment in the product.

The result of calculating this metric is a percentage return. In our case (below), we end up with a 20 percent IRR on a software project.

IRR is a very complex formula and not something you should try to calculate by hand. I suggest using an Excel spreadsheet command that will calculate the return for you given a series of future cash flows because you get the number by taking each of the cash flows and discounting it back to the present. The interest rate that you have to assume to get all those future cash flows to equal zero in the present is the IRR. Was that Greek? You are not alone.

Here is what you really need to know about IRR:

- It gives us a sense of the return we will make on a project over a long period of time.
- It gets higher or better the faster the project recovers the cash. If the project recoups a huge amount of cash in the first few years of the project, IRR will be high. Conversely, if the project recoups a little cash in the first few years and the majority of cash in later years, IRR will be low.

- It gets higher or better the more cash the project earns. If the project recoups just a little cash throughout its life, IRR will be low.
- The less you invest in the project, the better IRR will be because it is a rate of return. The less investment you have to cover with profits, the better.

Return on Investment (ROI)

$$\frac{\text{Net operating profit after tax}}{\text{Invested capital}}$$

This is another way to look at return on a project, but it does not take into account the time value of money. It doesn't matter when the funds come in or in what amounts. All that matters is the final total return in dollars.

Hence, this metric is best used on short-term projects. If you are like our software developer and your projects have a long life cycle, ROI possibly could mislead you. If all your cash flows come in year six and until then you are paying out cash, ROI will give you the same results as you would get if all your money came in years one and two and none came in year six. Obviously, you would rather have your money today than have to wait six years for it.

In our first case study below, we have an IRR of 20 percent but a ROI of 40 percent. Quite a difference—and it is all due to the time value of money.

Dollar Value Added (DVA)

$$\text{Net operating profit after tax} - (\text{cost of capital} \times \text{capital employed})$$

Would you rather earn 12 percent or 55 percent? If you have your thinking cap on, the answer is, "It depends!" It depends on the size of the project. I'd rather have a 12 percent return on a $10,000 project ($1,200) than a 55 percent return on a $1,000 project ($550).

DVA is another way of looking at return. Instead of asking what percentage return is garnered on a project, DVA gives us a dollar figure. In its simplest terms, it is just the total dollars generated by a project. It does not take into account the time value of money either. It asks, "How much profit did you generate versus how much the project cost you to implement?"

The tricky thing about DVA can be in calculation of the cost of capital. But determining how much it actually costs a company to get more capital (i.e., the cost of capital) can be a complicated study.

If the company has limited resources, which we can assume is the case for almost all organizations, there is an opportunity cost involved in using resources on any particular project.

In other words, if the money is used for project A, then it can't be used for project B. The opportunity cost is the return that could have been generated on project B.

Along with opportunity cost, you have to factor in the cost of debt and equity, making the calculations even more complicated.

Using the Three Metrics to Make a Decision

In our first case study below, DVA is $1,184, assuming a simple 12 percent cost of capital.

So these three metrics together give us a pretty good picture of the profitability of any project or undertaking. IRR is a great metric to use if you have a long life cycle. Because ROI does not take into account the time value of money, it is best used on short-term projects and decisions. And DVA gives you an actual dollar return.

Just like the fluctuation analysis we discussed earlier in this chapter, you want to run both dollars and percentages. For instance, a project might give you an IRR of 50 percent but a DVA of only $50. Thus it is probably not worth your time.

Here are some data from a mock company. Let's say that it creates software that takes two years to develop and then the software sells for four years after that. So the product's life cycle is six years. Figure 15.2 is a simple projection of the cash flows. What happens to IRR, ROI, and DVA in each of the scenarios in the figure?

Base case study—6-year software project							
Cash Flows	**Year 1**	**Year 2**	**Year 3**	**Year 4**	**Year 5**	**Year 6**	**Totals**
Cash collected	—	—	$1,000	$2,000	$2,000	$1,000	$6,000
Cash paid out	$1,000	$1,500	$300	$600	$600	$300	$4,300
Net cash	($1,000)	($1,500)	$700	$1,400	$1,400	$700	$1,700
						IRR	20%
						ROI	40%
					DVA = 6,000 − (4,300 x 1.12) =	$1,184
Instead of $1,000 cash out in year 1—spend only $500							
Cash collected	—	—	$1,000	$2,000	$2,000	$1,000	$6,000
Cash paid out	$500	$1,500	$300	$600	$600	$300	$3,800
Net case	($500)	($1,500)	$700	$1,400	$1,400	$700	$2,200
						IRR	32%
						ROI	58%
					DVA = 6,000 − (4,300 x 1.12) =	$1,744

FIGURE 15.2 · Case study: IRR, ROI, and DVA.   *(Continued)*

Instead of $1,000 cash out in year 1—earn $2,000 in year 3. In year 5, earn only $1,000 so that total cash flow remains the same							
Cash Flows	**Year 1**	**Year 2**	**Year 3**	**Year 4**	**Year 5**	**Year 6**	**Totals**
Cash collected	—	—	$2,000	$2,000	$1,000	$1,000	$6,000
Cash paid out	$1,000	$1,500	$300	$600	$600	$300	$4,300
Net cash	($1,000)	($1,500)	$1,700	$1,400	$400	$700	$1,700

IRR	25%
ROI	40%
DVA = 6,000 − (4,300 x 1.12) =	$1,184

Instead of only costing $1,000 in year 1, cash out is $1,500 in year 1							
Cash collected	—	—	$1,000	$2,000	$2,000	$1,000	$6,000
Cash paid out	$1,500	$1,500	$300	$600	$600	$300	$4,800
Net cash	($1,500)	($1,500)	$,700	$1,400	$1,400	$700	$1,200

IRR	12%
ROI	25%
DVA = 6,000 − (4,300 x 1.12) =	$624

Cost of goods sold—cash paid out in years 3-6 increases by 20% each year							
Cash collected	—	—	$1,000	$2,000	$2,000	$1,000	$6,000
Cash paid out	$1,000	$1,500	$360	$720	$720	$360	$4,660
Net cash	($1,000)	($1,500)	$,640	$1,280	$1,280	$640	$1,340

IRR	15%
ROI	29%
DVA = 6,000 − (4,300 x 1.12) =	$780.80

FIGURE 15.2 · *(Continued)*

Summary

Profit funds operations and fuels growth. Profit also allows the owners of an organization to personally enjoy the success of the organization either through distributions or a rising value of their investment in the organization. Profitability ratios allow analysts to compare key numbers from the income statement with key numbers on the balance sheet and the cash-flow statement.

QUIZ

1. **Many of the profit ratios are derived from which financial statement?**
   A. The balance sheet
   B. The cash-flow statement
   C. The income statement
   D. The statement of net assets

2. **Who will have the highest net profit percentage?**
   A. Target
   B. Custom home builder
   C. Dell

3. **Net profit is the same as**
   A. net sales.
   B. net income.
   C. gross profit.
   D. operating profit.

4. **Margins are**
   A. subtotals.
   B. the result of taking revenues less expenses.
   C. what is left over after expenses are taken out.
   D. all of the above.

5. **The difference between gross profit margin and operating profit margin is**
   A. total sales.
   B. cost of goods sold.
   C. operating expenses.
   D. net profit.

6. **What do we divide by total assets to get our return on asset metric?**
   A. Gross profit
   B. Total sales
   C. Net income
   D. Fixed assets

7. **IRR is a great metric to use if you have a long life cycle for your product or service. True or false?**
   A. True
   B. False

8. **EPS is**
    A. profit divided by number of shares outstanding.
    B. gross margin divided by number of shares outstanding.
    C. gross margin divided by profit.

9. **To increase IRR,**
    A. invest less on the front end.
    B. get cash out earlier.
    C. get more cash out in total.
    D. all of the above.

10. **ROI takes into account the time value of money. True or false?**
    A. True
    B. False

Chapter **16**

Liquidity and Financial Flexibility

There are three ways in which a company can use its money—spend it on fixed assets, spend it on working capital, or let it sit around as cash or investments. In order to respond to unexpected opportunities or needs, the business needs to be as liquid as possible. Liquid means as flexible and as near cash as possible.

CHAPTER OBJECTIVES

- Calculate liquidity ratios for two organizations
- Interpret results of the ratios

This might be a good time for you to revisit the scale of liquidity discussed in detail in Chapter 2. Fixed assets are definitely not liquid (see Figure 16.1).

Cash — **Most Liquid**
Investments
Accounts Receivable
Raw Materials Inventory
Finished Goods Inventory
Office Equipment
Manufacturing Equipment
Headquarters Building
Manufacturing Building
Birdbath Designs
Brand Names — **Least Liquid**

FIGURE 16.1 · Scale of liquidity.

A building or vehicles will take awhile to sell, and you might not get your cash for days, maybe months. *Working capital* is the money you have tied up in things that you hope to sell. It is more liquid than fixed assets but still not as liquid as our favorite asset—cash.

In this chapter we are going to look at ratios that have to do with working capital. In Chapter 17 we will look at ratios that address cash balances only.

Working Capital

Current assets – current liabilities

Current assets are cash, accounts receivable, and inventory. *Current liabilities* are accounts payable. So another way to express the calculation is

Cash + accounts receivable + inventory – accounts payable = working capital

Working capital is the money we have tied up in things that we hope to sell. If we take out rainy-day cash from the equation, this number should be as small as possible because we want to minimize current assets (i.e., day-to-day cash needs, accounts receivable, and inventory) and maximize current liabilities (i.e., accounts payable).

If we have money tied up in working capital, we don't have that money tied up in cash—and when given the choice, we always prefer that money be in cash.

Now here is the dilemma if you are calculating this metric as an outsider to an organization. It will be virtually impossible for you to figure out how much of the cash is necessary for current needs and how much is rainy-day or reserve cash. So you are going to have to use the entire cash balance. This causes some of our metrics to be skewed for both Apple and Dell because they both have a high proportion of pure cash on their balance sheets. If you are monitoring working capital from the inside, you should be able to get at the true daily cash needs.

Still Struggling?

How to Make Happy Working Capital

Wise working capital management can make or break a company. So just keep these simple rules in mind:

- Minimize inventory.
- Minimize daily/weekly/monthly cash needs (in other words, be cheap, and don't hire too many folks).
- Minimize accounts receivable.
- Stretch payments to vendors without injuring those vendors.

So again, if we have the information to do so, we should run the majority of metrics in this chapter using daily-needs cash, not rainy-day cash. This makes the metrics much more meaningful. But we are stuck with calculating them as an outsider.

Rainy-Day Cash versus Daily-Needs Cash

There is a difference between the cash you need to have on hand to help you through a rainy day and the cash you need to operate on a day-to-day basis. When we are looking at liquidity metrics, it would be great to know how much of a company's cash is in each category. In this way, we could get a better sense of how much it actually costs to run the organization, and we could contrast that with its ability to generate cash or meet its debt obligations.

I know how much I need to keep my household going as well as how much it takes to keep my small business going. Anything in excess of those needs can be set aside for savings and is not capital I need "working" in my life and business on a regular basis.

Results for Dell

2010: Current assets of $24,425,000,000 – current liabilities of $18,960,000,000 = $5,285,000,000

2009: Current assets of $20,151,000,000 – current liabilities of $14,859,000,000 = $5,292,000,000

Results for Apple

2009: Current assets of $31,555,000,000 – current liabilities of $11,361,000,000 = $20,049,000,000

2008: Current assets of $30,006,000,000 – current liabilities of $11,361,000,000 = $18,645,000,000

Conclusions

Cash is skewing these results. In 2010, Dell had $11 billion in cash short-term investments, and Apple had well over $23 billion in cash and short-term investments. If you take cash out of the working capital amount, both Dell and Apple will have had negative working capital. And regardless of what the banks want to see when they run their list of standard ratios, negative working capital is good. It means that working capital is contributing to the company—not consuming and taking from it. This idea will become clearer as we proceed with the other ratios in this chapter.

Also know that this total can be altered easily by either company's investment policy. If Dell chooses not to keep its excess cash in current assets but instead invest it in long-term assets, working capital will be smaller.

How Hard Is Working Capital Working?

The next four ratios tell us how hard working capital is working at generating revenues. They indicate how lean and mean the organization is running.

Working Capital to Sales

$$\frac{\text{Working capital}}{\text{Total sales}}$$

This metric indicates how well working capital worked in generating sales. Ideally, you'd like to invest very little in working capital in order to make a load of sales.

Results for Dell

2010: Working capital of $5,285,000,000/total sales of $52,902,000,000 = 10 percent

2009: Working capital of $5,292,000,000/total sales of $61,101,000,000 = 9 percent

Results for Apple

2009: Working capital of $20,049,000,000/total sales of $42,905,000,000 = 47 percent

2008: Working capital of $18,645,000,000/total sales of $37,491,000,000 = 50 percent

Conclusions

This indicates that Dell had to make a very small investment in working capital—but remember that Apple has an enormous amount of cash that is skewing this number. And Dell has significantly increased its accounts payable. Unless we can get at a truer figure of how much each organization has to put to work in the organization, this metric is meaningless. I told you I was going to run them anyway!

Working Capital Turnover

$$\frac{\text{Sales}}{\text{Working capital}}$$

This is the same ratio as working capital to sales expressed in a different way. It is simply flipped. This tells you how efficiently working capital was used to generate sales. A lean, mean fighting machine of a company would have a high turnover rate. This would mean that the organization put a little in and got out a lot.

Results for Dell

2010: Sales of $52,902,000,000/working capital of $5,285,000,000 = 10 times

2009: Sales of $61,101,000,000/working capital of $5,292,000,000 = 11.5 times

Results for Apple

2009: Sales of $42,905,000,000/working capital of $20,049,000,000 = 2.1 times

2008: Sales of $37,921,000,000/working capital of $18,645,000,000 = 2 times

Conclusions

Again, this is not a good comparison because Apple's huge cash balance is skewing the numbers. But I would like to express admiration for Dell's numbers. Even with a significant cash balance, Dell has a nice turnover rate. Another way we could express the 2010 Dell rate is to say that for every dollar of working capital invested in the company, Dell generates $10 of sales.

Working Capital Contrast Ratios

Current Ratio

$$\frac{\text{Current assets}}{\text{Current liabilities}}$$

The way this equation looks depends on whether you include or exclude rainy-day cash. If you leave rainy-day cash in, you want current assets—cash, inventory, and accounts receivable—to be larger than current liabilities. This would indicate that you have enough current resources to meet current obligations.

However, if you take out rainy-day cash from the top, you want current assets to be small and you want current liabilities to be big so that the equation will not look as lopsided. Yes, the top may be slightly larger but not terribly larger. To me, a very close ratio—say, 1:1—would indicate a healthy consciousness of the need to minimize inventory and receivables and maximize payables

Results for Dell

2010: Current assets of $24,245,000,000/current liabilities of $18,960,000,000 = 1.27:1

2009: Current assets of $20,151,000,000/current liabilities of $14,589,000,000 = 1.35:1

Results for Apple

2009: Current assets of $31,555,000,000/liabilities of $11,506,000,000 = 2.74:1

2008: Current assets of $30,006,000,000/liabilities of $11,361,000,000 = 2.64:1

Conclusions

Dell is closer to the 1:1 ratio that I think is good to see. Apple's huge amount of cash is skewing its number again, making comparison silly.

Quick Ratio

$$\frac{\text{Current assets} - \text{inventory}}{\text{Current liabilities}}$$

This ratio is also called the *acid test*. This is the same ratio as the current ratio except that it takes inventory out of the top of the equation, leaving only accounts payable and cash. It is called *quick* because it takes the slow-moving asset—inventory—out of current assets. Inventory may or may not be liquid. Some of the inventory may be obsolete or unsellable.

I like to run both the current ratio and the quick ratio together. If there is a vast difference between the two, say, the current ratio is 2:1 and the quick ratio is 0.5:1, this would tell me that the organization has a large proportion of its resources tied up in inventory—maybe dangerously so.

Results for Dell

2010: Current assets of $24,245,000,000 – inventory of $1,051,000,000/ current liabilities of $18,960,000,000 = 1.22:1

2009: Current assets of $20,151,000,000 – inventory of $867,000,000/ current liabilities of $14,589,000,000 = 1.29:1

Results for Apple

2009: Current assets of $31,555,000,000 – inventory of $455,000,000/ liabilities of $11,506,000,000 = 2.70:1

2008: Current assets of $30,006,000,000 – inventory of $509,000,000/ liabilities of $11,361,000,000 = 2.59:1

Conclusions

In 2010, Dell's current ratio was 1.27:1 and the quick ratio was 1.22:1. Apple's current ratio in the most current period was 2.74:1 and its quick ratio was 2.70:1. This shows that neither company has much tied up in inventory, another hint at very efficient working capital management.

Inventory Component of Working Capital

Inventory to Current Assets

$$\frac{\text{Inventory}}{\text{Current assets}}$$

Total current assets is made up of all sorts of happy things—cash, short-term investments, receivables, and inventory. Inventory is the least liquid component, and it is best to minimize it.

Results for Dell

2010: Inventory of $1,051,000,000/current assets of $24,245,000,000 = 4 percent

2009: Inventory of $867,000,000/current assets of $20,151,000,000 = 4 percent

Results for Apple

2009: Inventory of $455,000,000/current assets of $31,555,000,000 = 1 percent

2008: Inventory of $509,000,000/current assets of $30,006,000,000 = 2 percent

Conclusions

Both companies are keeping a slim balance of inventory. Nice. But the next metric, days' supply of inventory, is more compelling and finally removes cash from our consideration.

Days' Supply of Inventory

$$\frac{\text{Inventory}}{\text{Cost of goods sold}/365}$$

This is a very relevant metric for our companies. It measures how many days' worth of inventory are sitting around. Obviously, you want this number to be as small as possible. With my clients, I have seen it as high as 400 (for a school textbook publisher who has since gone bankrupt) and as low as 2. When your money is in inventory, it isn't in cash—our favorite asset. The client with 400 days of inventory is constantly in a cash dilemma, whereas the client with 2 days of inventory is a cash-generating machine. If you are in the service business, you obviously don't have inventory. So instead use *days between billings* or *days to bill*. Your accumulated time is your inventory, and unless you bill frequently, you are letting your time build up and adding to the length of time it takes you to convert your efforts into incoming cash.

Results for Dell

2010: Inventory of $1,051,000,000/cost of revenue of $43,641,000,000/365 days = 8.79 days

2009: Inventory of $867,000,000/cost of revenue of $50,144,000,000/365 days = 6.31 days

Results for Apple

2009: Inventory of $455,000,000/cost of revenue of $25,683,000,000/365 = 6.47 days

2008: Inventory of $509,000,000/cost of revenue of $24,294,000,000/365 = 7.65 days

Conclusions

Dell's inventory balance is creeping up, whereas Apple's is declining. Dell's higher days' supply of inventory could be triggered by a variety of events: lower demand for its products, slower manufacturing times, and use of slower channels to distribute its goods (such as retail operations) It is hard to say without being an insider—but given that Dell used to disclose a days' supply of inventory of 4, this is not a positive trend.

Inventory Turnover

$$\frac{\text{Cost of goods sold}}{\text{Inventory}}$$

This is another way to look at days' supply of inventory. Instead of saying that days in inventory is 30 (a month's worth of inventory), you can say that inventory turned 12 times or once each month.

Results for Dell

2010: Cost of goods (cost of revenues) of $43,641,000,000/inventory of $1,051,000,000 = 41 times

2009: Cost of revenues of $50,144,000,000/inventory of $867,000,000 = 57 times

Results for Apple

2009: Cost of goods (cost of revenues) of $25,683,000,000/inventory of $455,000,000 = 56 times

2008: Cost of revenues of $24,294,000,000/inventory of $509,000,000 = 48 times

Conclusions

This is just another way of expressing days' supply of inventory, our previous ratio, so the same conclusions as for days' supply of inventory apply here.

Accounts Receivable Component of Working Capital

Accounts Receivable to Current Assets

$$\frac{\text{Accounts receivable}}{\text{Current assets}}$$

This ratio tells you about the makeup of current assets. I often see analysts calculate accounts receivable to working capital. I don't like using working capital in the denominator because it has both positive and negative components. And when you calculate it for a company that has very lean working capital, it can even look bad when compared with an organization that has inflated working capital. So I prefer to keep it simple.

Results for Dell

2010: Accounts receivable of $5,873,000,000/current assets of $24,245,000,000 = 24.2 percent

2009: Accounts receivable of $4,731,000,000/current assets of $20,151,000,000 = 23.5 percent

Results for Apple

2009: Accounts receivable of $3,361,000,000/current assets of $31,555,000,000 = 10.6 percent

2008: Accounts receivable of $2,422,000,000/current assets of $30,920,000,000 = 8.1 percent

Conclusions

This is another ratio that can be skewed by cash. Cash is a component of current assets, and Apple has so much cash that it makes any number involving cash questionable. We need a more absolute number indicating the wisdom of the organization's accounts receivable balance. And the next metric, days' sales outstanding, does a good job indicating the health of accounts receivable while not involving Apple's troublesome amount of cash. I should make sure that you know that by *troublesome*, I mean for analysis only. Having so much cash is brilliant, admirable, and powerful for every other reason!

Days' Sales Outstanding (Days of Accounts Receivable)

$$\frac{\text{Accounts receivable}}{\text{Net sales/365}}$$

This is another of my favorite metrics. Here we are asking how long it takes us to collect from our customers. In the United States, we tend to work on 30-day terms—meaning that we expect payment in 30 days. We definitely want this number to be as low as possible.

Results for Dell

2010: Accounts receivable of $5,873,000,000/net sales of $52,902,000,000/365 = 40.5 days

2009: Accounts receivable of $4,371,000,000/net sales of $61,101,000,000/365 = 28 days

Dell revealed in the "Management's Discussion and Analysis" section of its 10-K that days' sales outstanding were 31 and 28 for the same periods. Again, our calculation is close.

Results for Apple

2009: Accounts receivable of $3,361,000,000/net sales of $42,905,000,000/365 = 28.6 days

2008: Accounts receivable of $2,422,000,000/net sales of $37,491,000,000/365 = 23.6 days

Conclusions

This is an interesting trend. Apple collects from its customers faster—significantly faster than Dell. Dell collects in 40.5 days and Apple in 28.6 days. If customers use credit cards, the numbers will look better. If customers pay on terms and wait out the 30 days, the number will look worse. And, as you can imagine, you don't want to hold your breath while waiting to get paid by institutional clients such as the government or large corporations. And if you sell products overseas, the accounts payable cycle is abysmal. It is customary for Europeans to pay in 120 days, and South Americans can be even worse. Possibly, as both companies expand into international markets, the average number of days it takes to collect will worsen.

It also may be procedural. Maybe the companies aren't dedicating enough resources to collection. Sometimes you have to hire a team of irritating accounts receivable collection staff to follow up with slow-paying customers.

Also, Dell has gone from selling most of its products to customers directly to selling through retailers. Savvy retailers—such as Walmart and Best Buy—pay a few months after the item has sold. So if it doesn't sell, the accounts receivable numbers get worse and worse.

If I were a manager inside Dell, I would investigate and see if I have any control over the negative trend in this metric.

Accounts Receivable Turnover

$$\frac{\text{Net credit sales}}{\text{Accounts receivable}}$$

This metric is similar to days' sales outstanding, except that it is not expressed in days but in turns. So if it takes on average 60 days to collect from customers, accounts receivable turns is 6, one turn every two months.

Results for Dell
For this metric to work for Dell, I had to assume that all sales were credit sales, that no one paid cash. I do not have access to the information on proportions of cash versus credit sales.

> 2010: Sales of $52,902,000,000/accounts receivable of $5,873,000,000 = 9 times
>
> 2009: Sales of $61,101,000,000/accounts receivable of $4,371,000,000 = 12 times

Results for Apple

> 2009: Sales of $42,905,000,000/accounts receivable of $3,361,000,000 = 12.7 times
>
> 2008: Sales of $37,491,000,000/accounts receivable of $2,422,000,000 = 15 times

Conclusions
This metric shows, using another expression of the same figures, that Apple is better at collecting its receivables than Dell. However, its ability to collect is slowing from 15 to 12.7 times. I would watch this figure in future years. This difference between the two might be due to its customer base. Customers who pay with credit cards will pay within three days. Corporate clients pay in 30 or more days. If you do business in foreign countries, you can expect the collections to be much slower.

Bad Debt Percentage

Allowance for doubtful accounts
—————————————————————
Gross accounts receivable

This metric might give us an indication of how unreliable the companies' customers are. Every time the financial statements are created, the company must estimate how much of its accounts receivable will go uncollected. I have—knock on wood—never experienced a bad debt; none of my customers has ever stiffed me. However, many organizations experience bad debt or sell to unqualified customers who didn't have the ability to pay in the first place. This metric tells us a little about the quality of the receivables.

You can imagine that a rent-to-own business that rents appliances might have plenty of customers who end up not paying. This is part of the reason it costs $300 a month to rent a couch!

Allowance for doubtful accounts has its own schedule in the notes to the 10-K. It showed up in different spots for Dell and Apple but can be uncovered easily by scanning the notes through the final pages of the 10-K.

Results for Dell

2010: Allowance for doubtful accounts of $194,000,000/accounts receivable of $5,873,000,000 = 3.3 percent
2009: Allowance for doubtful accounts of $181,000,000/accounts receivable of $4,371,000,000 = 3.8 percent

Results for Apple

2009: Allowance for doubtful accounts of $52,000,000/accounts receivable of $3,361,000,000 = 1.5 percent
2008: Allowance for doubtful accounts of $47,000,000/accounts receivable of $2,422,000,000 = 1.9 percent

Conclusions

Both companies allow for less than 4 percent of their accounts receivable to go bad or be uncollectible. But Dell's numbers are significantly higher. This could mean that Apple makes more credit card sales than sales on terms. This would jive with our days' sales outstanding metric. Or it could mean that Apple does a better job qualifying its customers. In other words, maybe Apple isn't as loose with granting credit. Or it could mean that the chief financial officer (CFO) at Apple is more optimistic than the CFO at Dell—because this is a guess at what will happen in the future. Or it could be a combination of all these factors.

Accounts Payable Component of Working Capital

Accounts Payable to Working Capital

$$\frac{\text{Accounts payable}}{\text{Working capital}}$$

This metric tells us the portion of working capital that is made up of accounts payable. As I explained for the ratios of accounts receivable to working capital and inventory to working capital, working capital is a mix of positive and negative numbers (rainy-day cash plus inventory plus accounts receivable less accounts payable). I think this makes this number squirrelly. But again, it is used quite a bit, so it is good to know of it. Let's see what it looks like.

Results for Dell

2010: Accounts payable of $11,373,000,000/working capital of $5,285,000,000 = 2.15:1

2009: Accounts payable of $8,309,000,000/working capital of $5,292,000,000 = 1.57:1

Results for Apple

2009: Accounts payable of $5,601,000,000/working capital of $20,049,000,000 = 0.27:1

2008: Accounts payable of $5,520,000,000/working capital of $18,645,000,000 = 0.30:1

Conclusions

Here is a perfect example of a silly metric. It is incomparable between the two organizations. It would lead you to believe by its wording that we are looking for the portion of working capital that is composed of accounts payable. But because accounts payable is a negative number—or is subtracted from working capital—it just doesn't work. So, although you can pair any combination of numbers from the financial statements to run ratios, sometimes the results are just plain dumb and so not worth the effort. Let's simply rack this up as an example of what not to do. Have you ever seen those motivational posters in someone's office titled "Teamwork" and "Excellence"? A company here in Austin took this concept and turned it around. My favorite poster is titled "Failure" and pictures a ship sinking. The motto is, "Sometimes your role in this world is to show other people what not to do." It is good to know that all my screw ups are benefiting someone. This silly, meaningless metric is my gift to you.

Days' Payables Outstanding (DPO)

$$\frac{\text{Accounts payable}}{\text{Sales}/365}$$

This measures the number of days that it takes you to pay your vendors. In general, you want to keep your own resources for as long as possible. So it is best to stretch accounts payable as far as you can without ruining your relationship with your vendors.

Results for Dell

2010: Accounts payable of $11,373,000,000/sales of $52,902,000,000/365 = 78.5 days

2009: Accounts payable of $8,309,000,000/sales of $61,101,000,000/365 = 49.6 days

Results forApple

2009: Accounts payable of $5,601,000,000/sales of $42,905,000,000/365 = 47.6 days

2008: Accounts payable of $5,520,000,000/sales of $37,491,000,000/365 = 53.7 days

Conclusions

Whoa! Dell is asking a lot of its vendors in 2010. Why would a vendor put up with this? If a vendor of liquid-crystal display (LCD) screens wants to sell a lot of screens, it likely will put up with Dell paying it later than the industry norm.

Apple is also paying beyond normal 30-day terms. Remember that this is an average, which means that some vendors get paid faster and some slower. Often, large organizations will lord their status over smaller organizations. Vendors with weak cash flows will have to get a loan to stay in business. Loans are expensive. The one-two punch of an expensive loan and a weak cash flow can put a vendor out of business very quickly. You do not want to do business with either of these companies if you aren't big enough to handle these late payments.

Accounts Receivable to Accounts Payable

$$\frac{\text{Accounts receivable}}{\text{Accounts payable} + \text{accrued expenses}}$$

This is another way to look at liquidity or working capital items. In a traditional interpretation, you would want to see accounts receivable balanced by accounts payable. In this way, accounts receivable could fund accounts payable. However, if you are managing your working capital items wisely, you would have a stretched-out or relatively large accounts payable and a relatively small accounts receivable.

Results for Dell

2010: Accounts receivable of $5,873,000,000/accounts payable of $11,373,000,000 + accrued expenses of $3,384,000,000 = 0.32:1
2009: Accounts receivable of $4,371,000,000/accounts payable of $8,309,000,000 + accrued expenses of $3,736,000,000 = 0.32:1

Results for Apple

2009: Accounts receivable of $3,361,000,000/accounts payable of $5,601,000,000 + accrued expense of $3,852,000,000 = 0.35:1
2008: Accounts receivable of $2,422,000,000/accounts payable of $5,520,000,000 + accrued expenses of $4,224,000,000 = 0.24:1

Conclusions

I don't see either of these results as remarkable for these companies. Yes, accounts receivable is smaller than accounts payable—and this is how it should be. I would not run this metric for these companies on a regular basis.

How All the Elements of Working Capital Add Up

Cash Conversion Cycle

Days' supply of inventory (DSI) + days' sales outstanding (DSO)
– days' payables outstanding (DPO)

This adds three key metrics for determining how well the organization is managing its working capital items—inventory, receivables, and payables. We want to minimize inventory balances, minimize receivables, and maximize payables.

When you add DSI and DSO and subtract DPO, you end up with the number of days it takes the organization to turn an investment in its products and services into cash.

The components of this metric, as well as the metric itself, are my favorite metrics in this chapter. They are universally applicable to all organizations and tell volumes about how well the organization is managing its working capital.

Remember, if inventory is not relevant to your business, you need to replace DSI with another number. In my business, how frequently and quickly I bill affects my cash conversion cycle. If I wait a month to bill, I am adding a month onto my cash conversion cycle. After having suffered from a few dry periods caused by my own laziness, I learned to bill after every gig and after every sale. This keeps the cash flowing and keeps the bills paid.

Results for Dell

2010: DSI of 9 + DSO of 40 − DPO of 78 = −29 days
2009: DSI of 6 + DSO of 28 − DPO of 50 = −16 days

Results for Apple

2009: DSI of 6 + DSO of 28 − DPO of 48 = −14
2008: DSI of 8 + DSO of 24 − DPO of 54 = −22

Conclusions

What does Dell's −29 mean, anyway? It means that Dell has the use of other people's money for 29 days. In essence, Dell never has to reach into its own pockets to finance operations. It uses other people's money to finance operations and growth. Apple is also efficiently managing working capital so that it has use of other people's money, but its number is not as deeply negative. It is now −14, Having a negative cash conversion cycle is ideal, and both have it.

Back in 1996, Dell was a nearly $8 billion company. In 2010, it was a $53 billion company. A day's worth of other people's money when you are operating at a $53 billion sales volume is enormous. This is where Dell gets its $11 billion in cash and short-term investments.

And although Apple's cash conversion cycle isn't as negative, its explosive sales growth has contributed to its $23 billion in cash and short-term investments.

Overall Conclusions for Working Capital for Dell and Apple

Both Dell and Apple are masters at managing their working capital. Neither company gives customers leeway or is easy on vendors. Both are great at keeping inventory levels low.

When I performed the financial analysis on Dell's 2004 numbers in the first edition of this book, the company was stronger in working capital management across the board. But its current position is still enviable.

If Apple continues to grow market share, it will outpace Dell and have a healthier balance sheet than Dell in future years. It will be very interesting to watch!

Summary

Working capital management is firmly in the control of the organization. Wise working capital management indicates that the managers of the organization are aware of the power of working capital and are financially savvy. Profitability is less controllable. The organization can set prices only as high as the market will bear, and costs can be slashed only so far. I recommend running DSO, DSI, and DPO every time you want to determine the financial health of an organization.

QUIZ

1. **Which of the following personal items is most liquid?**
   A. Car
   B. Home
   C. Checking account
   D. Cash
   E. Furniture

2. **Which of the following business items is the most liquid?**
   A. Accounts receivable
   B. Cash
   C. Finished goods inventory
   D. Building
   E. Work-in-progress materials

3. **Working capital is**
   A. current assets less current receivables.
   B. current assets less current liabilities.
   C. rainy-day cash plus daily-needs cash.

4. **Accounts receivable over (net sales/365) is the formula for**
   A. days' sales outstanding.
   B. accounts receivable to current assets.
   C. accounts receivable turnover.

5. **Allowance for doubtful accounts is a projection (sophisticate guess) that may or may not come to fruition. True or false?**
   A. True
   B. False

6. **A negative cash conversion cycle means that other people are using the organization's money. True or false?**
   A. True
   B. False

7. **What is the equation for the cash conversion cycle?**
   A. DSI + DPO − DSO
   B. DSO − DPO − DSI
   C. DSI + DSO − DPO
   D. DSI + DSO + DPO

8. **Working capital is monies you have tied up in things that you hope to sell. True or false?**
    A. True
    B. False

9. **Current liabilities include**
    A. accounts payable.
    B. inventory.
    C. accounts receivable.

10. **The quick ratio is also called**
    A. the acid test.
    B. the accounts payable turnover ratio.
    C. the inventory turnover ratio.

Chapter 17

Cash Ratios

Cash is our favorite asset because we can do so much with it. It is so flexible, so accommodating, so green. This chapter is all about examining our cash position. Many of the ratios use information from the cash-flow statement.

But before we do the ratios, though, we should spend a little time eyeballing the cash-flow statement. This will give us some insight into what Dell and Apple are doing with the cash they have.

CHAPTER OBJECTIVES

- Calculate cash ratios for two organizations
- Interpret results of the ratios

Categories of the Cash-Flow Statement

Every cash-flow statement is divided into three categories of flows (both inflows and outflows): operating cash flows, investing cash flows, and financing cash flows.

Operating cash flows tell us how the company generated and used cash in creating products or providing services. Investing cash flows tells how the company used its rainy-day cash to invest in other entities. This category also tells us whether the company has used its cash to buy fixed assets or gained any cash from the sale of fixed assets. Fixed assets are considered a long-term investment. (I think this is a confusing and strange categorization of fixed asset purchases and sales, but I didn't write the accounting rules.) Financing cash flows tell us how the company got financing to operate other than through operations. So this includes any debt or equity financing the company uses or pays back.

For more on this topic, you might want to revisit Chapter 4.

Eyeballing Dell's Cash-Flow Statement

Let's first look at Dell's cash-flow statement for fiscal year (FY) 2010 (Figure 17.1).

First Category—Operating Cash Flows

Dell generated $1.4 billion in net income in 2010 but had a positive effect on cash flows of $3.9 billion for the same period. Cool. Cash flows exceeded net income.

Remember that the accrual method of accounting will always result in a difference between net income and cash. This is what all that detail is in between the top line of the cash-flow statement and the net cash provided by operating activities line. It is a reconciliation of net income generated under the accrual method to true cash.

I don't want you to concentrate on the reconciling items. That can get pretty technical, and it even confuses accountants! [I know this because I teach the statement of cash flows to certified public accountants.] Luckily for the whole world of financial statement users, the new international accounting standards will take these silly items off the statement of cash flows and instead disclose normal categories of cash flows such as cash from customers, cash paid to vendors, and so on.

What we need to do is notice that cash from operations exceeds net income. This is a good trend and is due in large part to Dell's fabulous management of working capital, as described in Chapter 16.

DELL INC.

CONSOLIDATED STATEMENTS OF CASH FLOWS

(in millions)

	Fiscal Year Ended		
	January 29, 2010	January 30, 2009	February 1, 2008
Cash flows from operating activities:			
Net income	$ 1,433	$ 2,478	$ 2,947
Adjustments to reconcile net income to net cash provided by operating activities:			
Depreciation and amortization	852	769	607
Stock-based compensation	312	418	329
In-process research and development charges	–	2	83
Effects of exchange rate changes on monetary assets and liabilities denominated in foreign currencies	59	(115)	30
Deferred income taxes	(52)	86	(308)
Provision for doubtful accounts –including financing receivables	429	310	187
Other	102	32	30
Changes in operating assets and liabilities, net of effects from acquisitions:			
Accounts receivable	(660)	480	(1,086)
Financing receivables	(1,085)	(302)	(394)
Inventories	(183)	309	(498)
Other assets	(225)	(106)	(121)
Accounts payable	2,833	(3,117)	837
Deferred services revenue	135	663	1,032
Accrued and other liabilities	(44)	(13)	274
Change in cash from operating activities	3,906	1,894	3,949
Cash flows from investing activities:			
Investments:			
Purchases	(1,383)	(1,584)	(2,394)
Maturities and sales	1,538	2,333	3,679
Capital expenditures	(367)	(440)	(831)
Proceeds from sale of facility and land	16	44	–
Acquisition of business, net of cash received	(3,613)	(176)	(2,217)
Change in cash from investing activities	(3,809)	177	(1,763)
Cash flows from financing activities:			
Repurchase of common stock	–	(2,867)	(4,004)
Issuance of common stock under employee plans	2	79	136
Issuance of commercial paper (maturity 90 days or less), net	76	100	(100)
Proceeds from debt	2,058	1,519	66
Repayments of debt	(122)	(237)	(165)
Other	(2)	–	(53)
Change in cash from financing activities	2,012	(1,406)	(4,120)
Effect of exchange rate changes on cash and cash equivalents	174	(77)	152
Change in cash and cash equivalents	2,283	588	(1,782)
Cash and cash equivalents at beginning of the year	8,352	7,764	9,546
Cash and cash equivalents at end of the year	$ 10,635	$ 8,352	$ 7,764
Income tax paid	$ 434	$ 800	$ 767
Interest paid	$ 151	$ 74	$ 54

The accompanying notes are an integral part of these consolidated financial statements.

FIGURE 17.1 • Dell's cash-flow statement FY 2010

Second Category—Investing

Dell bought and sold investments in other organizations. Over the year, it bought $1.3 billion worth of investments and sold $1.5 billion worth. Not a dramatic change.

But the acquisition of $3.6 billion in other businesses is interesting. Investors should consider whether this purchase will have a positive long-term impact on Dell's financial results. Since I am not tech savvy, I am not sure whether Dell's purchase is wise. So I'm just going to stick to the numbers and point out the purchase. Dell discusses its reasons for the purchase in the "Management's Discussion and Analysis" section of the 10-K.

So Dell also used some cash to buy equipment and sold off some facilities and land. All these activities give us a net effect of using $3.8 billion of cash in investing activities.

Third Category—Financing

Here we see that Dell used its cash in the past two years to buy back and retire its stock. Not so in 2010. Also, we see debt increasing significantly over the three-year period. This is allowing Dell to buy other companies without dipping into its liquid resources. Currently, interest rates are very favorable, so maybe Dell reasoned that it is better to go into debt at a low interest rate than to consume its excess cash. I am sure that managers thought through all their options thoroughly, aren't you?

Eyeballing Apple's Cash-Flow Statement

Let's check out Apple's cash-flow statement (Figure 17.2).

First Category—Operating

Whereas Apple generated $8.2 billion in 2009, it generated $10 billion in operating cash. Some of this is due to differences between accrual accounting—which takes into account noncash transactions such as depreciation and deferred taxes. Most of the difference is due to Apple's excellent management of working capital, as we discussed in Chapter 16.

Second Category—Investing

Apple has been busy investing its extra cash. The first three lines of this section of the cash-flow statement conglomerate its investing activities—Apple's purchase, sales, and maturities of investments. The net effect of these transactions was to allow Apple to sock away $16 billion ($46,724,000 in

CONSOLIDATED STATEMENTS OF CASH FLOWS

(In millions)

Three years ended September 26, 2009	2009	2008	2007
Cash and cash equivalents, beginning of the year	$ 11,875	$ 9,352	$ 6,392
Operating activities:			
Net income	5,704	4,834	3,496
Adjustments to reconcile net income to cash generated by operating activities:			
Depreciation, amortization and accretion	703	473	317
Stock-based compensation expense	710	516	242
Deferred income tax (benefit)/expense	(519)	(368)	78
Loss on disposition of property, plant and equipment	26	22	12
Changes in operating assets and liabilities:			
Accounts receivable, net	(939)	(785)	(385)
Inventories	54	(163)	(76)
Other current assets	(1,050)	(1,958)	(1,540)
Other assets	(1,346)	(492)	81
Accounts payable	92	596	1,494
Deferred revenue	6,908	5,642	1,139
Other liabilities	(184)	1,279	612
Cash generated by operating activities	10,159	9,596	5,470
Investing activities:			
Purchases of marketable securities	(46,724)	(22,965)	(11,719)
Proceeds from maturities of marketable securities	19,790	11,804	6,483
Proceeds from sales of marketable securities	10,888	4,439	2,941
Purchases of other long-term investments	(101)	(38)	(17)
Payments made in connection with business acquisitions, net of cash acquired	–	(220)	–
Payment for acquisition of property, plant and equipment	(1,144)	(1,091)	(735)
Payment for acquisition of intangible assets	(69)	(108)	(251)
Other	(74)	(10)	49
Cash used in investing activities	(17,434)	(8,189)	(3,249)
Financing activities:			
Proceeds from issuance of common stock	475	483	365
Excess tax benefits from stock-based compensation	270	757	377
Cash used to net share settle equity awards	(82)	(124)	(3)
Cash generated by financing activities	663	1,116	739
(Decrease)/increase in cash and cash equivalents	(6,612)	2,523	2,960
Cash and cash equivalents, end of the year	$ 5,263	$11,875	$ 9,352
Supplemental cash flow disclosures:			
Cash paid for income taxes, net	$ 2,997	$ 1,267	$ 863

See accompanying Notes to Consolidated Financial Statements.

FIGURE 17.2 · Apple's cash-flow statement.

purchases, less $19,790,000 in maturities and $10,888,000 in sales of investments) in long-term investments. Apple did not use this cash this year to buy another company and spent $1 billion on stuff—or in fancier terms, property, plant, and equipment.

Third Category—Financing

Apple issued 475 million in common stock. Since Apple is not exactly strapped for resources, this stock was issued as part of employee stock plans. This information is disclosed on the statement of shareholders' equity.

Cash Ratios

Operating Cash Index

$$\frac{\text{Cash from operations}}{\text{Net income}}$$

Now this is a good metric. If the numerator is substantially different from the denominator, this may indicate that the organization has a hard time converting its profits into cash. Maybe it has difficult, slow-paying customers or it doesn't make much of an effort at collecting.

Results for Dell

2010: Cash from operations of $3,906,000,000/net income of $1,433,000,000
= 2.73:1

2009: Cash from operations of $1,894,000,000/net income of $2,478,000,000
= 0.76:1

Results for Apple

2009: Cash from operations of $10,159,000,000/net income of $8,235,000,000
= 1.23:1

2008: Cash from operations of $9,596,000,000/net income of $6,119,000,000
= 1.57:1

Conclusions

Dell's results are inconsistent on this metric. Looking closer at the cash-flow statement, I see wild fluctuations in receivables and payables. As we saw in Chapter 16, Dell is stretching its payables to vendors as its total revenue is declining. This is something worth watching in future years. Apple is consistent in it ability to realize its sales in cash. Consistency is comforting if it is for the right reasons.

Cash Ratio

$$\frac{\text{Cash equivalents} + \text{marketable securities}}{\text{Current liabilities}}$$

This ratio is the quick ratio less accounts receivable. It is truly just your current liquid resources contrasted against current liabilities. Again, the question this metric is supposed to answer is, "Do we have enough liquid resources to cover our current obligations?"

Results for Dell

2010: Cash of $10,635,000,000 + marketable securities of $373,000,000 + $781,000,000/current liabilities of $18,960,000,000 = 0.53:1

2009: Cash of $8,352,000,000 + marketable securities of $740,000,000 + $454,000,000/current liabilities of $14,859,000,000 = 0.61:1

Results for Apple

2009: Cash of $5,263,000,000 + marketable securities of $18,201,000,000 + 10,528,000,000/current liabilities of $11,506,000,000 = 2.04:1

2008: Cash of $11,875,000,000 + marketable securities of $10,236,000,000 + $2,379,000,000/current liabilities of $940,349,000 = 1.95:1

Conclusions

This is a fascinating metric to me. Notice how Apple could pay off its obligations to vendors twice with its current cash resources. But Dell can't. This may be the most telling ratio in the whole book about Dell's current situation. In your personal life, I am sure that you have had moments when your monthly bills exceeded your ability to pay and you had to dip into your savings to cover expenses. This ratio, in a limited way, says that Dell has to keep selling in order to pay its obligations. If the sales cycle stops or slows, Dell will struggle to meet its current obligations. You've heard of living paycheck to paycheck? Since Dell is experiencing a decreasing market share, it is stretching payments to vendors to stay ahead. I've done that in my personal life. Maybe I'll just let that credit card bill ride another month. See the problem?

Cash to Total Assets

$$\frac{\text{Cash}}{\text{Total assets}}$$

This metric tells how much of the happy side of the balance sheet (the asset side) is made up of cash. I am going to change this ratio just a tad to include short-term investments.

$$\frac{\text{Cash} + \text{short-term investments}}{\text{Total assets}}$$

Why did I add short-term investments? Because they are very close to cash and will give us a more accurate picture of the liquid resources of both organizations. Apple has more in short-term investments than it does in cash—so I think that it would be misleading to leave them out of this calculation.

Results for Dell

2010: Cash of $10,635,000,000 + short-term investments of $373,000,000/ total assets of $33,652,000,000 = 32.7 percent

2009: Cash of $8,352,000,000 + short-term investments of $740,000,000/ total assets of $1,015,023,000 = 34.3 percet

Results for Apple

2009: Cash of $5,263,000,000 + short-term investments of $18,201,000,000/ total assets of $ 47,501,000,000 = 49.4 percent

2008: Cash of $11,875,000,000 + short-term investments of $10,236,000,000/ total assets of $36,171,000,000 = 61.1 percent

Conclusions

Yes, it is unusual for 60 percent or more of a company's balance sheet to be held in cash. Apple is on a roll for sure. Dell appears to be consistent regarding the amount of cash it holds in relation to the rest of the balance sheet, that is, until you consider how it keeps that cash consistent. In 2010, to hold it steady, Dell stretched payables and took out debt.

Cash Turnover Ratio

$$\frac{\text{Sales}}{\text{Cash} + \text{marketable securities}}$$

This asks, "How many times was the investment in cash realized in sales?" and "How hard did your cash work for you in generating sales?" What you will get here is a multiple, such as cash turned over 5 times or 10 times or 100 times. In other words, the higher the turnover rate or the bigger the multiple, the better. It means that your cash is working hard, not just lollygagging around. This ratio is kin to the working capital turnover ratio we discussed in Chapter 16.

Results for Dell

2010: Sales of $52,902,000,000/cash of $10,635,000,000 + short-term investments of $373,000,000 = 4.8 times

2009: Sales of $61,101,000,000/cash of $8,352,000,000 + short-term investments of $740,000,000 = 6.7 times

Results for Apple

2009: Sales of $42,902,000,000/cash of $5,263,000,000 + short-term investments of $18,201,000,000 = 1.8 times

2008: Sales of $37,491,000,000/cash of $11,875,000,000 + short-term investments of $10,236,000,000 = 1.7 times

Conclusions

This number is skewed by Apple's enormous cash balances and really isn't that meaningful for either company.

Cash-Flow Ratio

$$\frac{\text{Cash flow from operations}}{\text{Current liabilities}}$$

This contrasts operating cash with current liabilities. The numerator is refined—not all cash but only operating cash. So it is asking if the organization is generating enough cash from selling its products and services to meet current obligations.

Results for Dell

2010: Cash from operations of $3,906,000,000/current liabilities $18,960,000,000 = 0.21:1

2009: Cash from operations of $1,894,000,000/current liabilities $14,859,000,000 = 0.13:1

Results for Apple

2009: Cash from operations of $10,159,000,000/current liabilities of
$11,506,000,000 = 0.88:1

2008: Cash from operations of $9,596,000,000/current liabilities of
$11,361,000,000 = 0.84:1

Conclusions

Again, we see Dell living paycheck to paycheck! Apple is generating enough
from operations to pay for its current liabilities. Dell is not. But Dell is choosing
to make its liabilities larger by stretching its payments to vendors. But so is
Apple.

Cash-Flow Adequacy Ratio

$$\frac{\text{Cash from operations}}{\text{Capital investments + inventory additions + dividends + debt uses}}$$

The denominator in this equation is a laundry list of all the desirable ways that
a company could spend its cash. This equation asks, "Is cash flow from selling
our product or service enough to get us the extra goodies we need to grow and
keep our owners happy?" and "Do we have enough cash from operations to buy
additional capital equipment, to expand our inventory, to pay dividends to our
owners, and to meet additional debt obligations if we decide to take on an
expansion loan or a loan for a special project?" This metric is one that I recommend that you customize for your own situation.

Still Struggling

Is That Behavior Sustainable?

Which events from this list are least likely to occur again next year?

- Sale of common stock to investors
- Sale of the headquarters building
- Sale of memberships

The cash-flow statement divides the cash flows up into sustainable and unsus-
tainable activities. Selling memberships, if that is your primary business, is sustainable and gets classified into operating cash inflows. Sales of stock happen rarely,

and this gets classified in the financing category. And the cash inflows from selling your headquarters may occur only once in your lifetime. Sales of fixed assets are investing inflows of cash.

Sustainable, stable behavior can best be measured by the operating cash flows—not investing cash flows or financing cash flows. This is why operating cash is such an important number!

Results for Dell

2010: Cash from operations of $3,906,000,000/capital investments of $367,000,000 (from the cash-flow statement) + inventory increase of $183,000,000 (from the cash-flow statement) + $0 dividends + $122,000,000 in debt uses (from the cash-flow statement) = 5.8 times

2009: Cash from operations of $1,894,000,000/capital investments of $440,000,000 + inventory decrease of $309,000,000 + $0 dividends + $237,000,000 debt uses = 5.14 times

Results for Apple

2009: Cash from operations of $10,159,000,000/capital investments of $1,144,000,000 (from the cash-flow statement) + inventory decrease of $54,000,000 (from the cash-flow statement) + $0 dividends + $0 in debt uses = 10.4 times

2008: Cash from operations of $9,596,000,000/capital investments of $1,091,000,000 + inventory increase of $163,000,000 + $0 dividends + $0 in debt uses = 7.6 times

Conclusions

While Dell is living paycheck to paycheck, it has kept its discretionary expenses such as generous nights on the town with friends (dividends), new shoes (inventory), and tricked-out houses (capital investments) to a bare minimum. Apple has invested a bit this year in tricked-out houses but also keeps its discretionary spending to a minimum. And it has no old credit card balances from previous overspending to pay off.

Depreciation Impact Ratio

$$\frac{\text{Depreciation}}{\text{Cash from operations}}$$

This ratio helps to refine your diagnosis of what might be going amiss in the operating cash index. Depreciation is a noncash expense, so it reduces net income but not cash. This equation might tell you whether the difference between cash from operations and net income is largely made up by depreciation expense.

Results for Dell

2010: Depreciation of $852,000,000/cash flow from operations of $3,906,000,000 = 21.8 percent

2009: Depreciation of $769,000,000/cash flow from operations of $1,894,000,000 = 40.6 percent

Results for Apple

2009: Depreciation of $734,000,000/cash flow from operations of $10,159,000,000 = 7 percent

2008: Depreciation of $496,000,000/cash flow from operations of 9,596,000,000 = 5 percent

Conclusions

The impact of depreciation on cash flows is significant for Dell and minimal for Apple. This is due, in part, to Dell's relatively low cash flow from operations. This is another revealing metric for Dell. Dell has very little in the way of fixed assets to depreciate. But Dell also has very lean profit margins. If Dell owned fancier or more expensive facilities and equipment, depreciation's impact on net income would be devastating and could wipe it out completely. Dell has never been an extravagant spender, and now I see how this behavior is keeping it afloat during a low period for the company.

Apple's generous cash flow from operations gives it much more flexibility at this moment in time. But the company is buying billions in fixed assets, which could, as we see from this metric, hurt it in a future and inevitable declining market.

Depreciation to Total Fixed Assets

$$\frac{\text{Accumulated depreciation}}{\text{Total fixed assets}}$$

This metric indicates the age of fixed assets.

Results for Dell

2010: Accumulated depreciation of $2,471,000,000 (from the notes to the financial statements)/total property, plant, and equipment of $4,642,000,000 (from the notes to the financial statements—not netted as on the balance sheet) = 53 percent

2009: Accumulated depreciation of $2,233,000,000/total property, plant, and equipment of $4,510,000,000 = 50 percent

Results for Apple

2009: Accumulated depreciation of 1,713,000,000/fixed assets of $4,667,000,000 = 37 percent

2008: Accumulated depreciation of $1,292,000,000/fixed assets of $3,747,000,000 = 34 percent

Conclusions

For Dell, half the useful life of the fixed assets has expired. This means that these assets are pretty old and could indicate that they need to be replaced soon. Apple has fully depreciated a third of its assets.

For Dell, in looking at the components of fixed assets or of property, plant, and equipment in the notes to the financial statements, I see that in 2010 computer equipment makes up $2.1 billion of the company's fixesd assets, land and buildings $1.6 billion, and machinery and equipment $0.8 billion. I would imagine that the computer equipment is totally depreciated because it depreciates so quickly. Does this mean that Dell will have to replace it all soon? I won't be able to tell from the outside.

In 2009, Apple held $0.9 billion in land and buildings, $1.9 billion in machinery and equipment, $0.1 billion in office equipment but $1.6 billion in leasehold improvements. So, while Apple holds less in buildings and land, it more than makes up for that in leasehold improvements. Leasehold improvements generally depreciate much faster than land and buildings because they correspond to the lease terms. Buildings take almost 40 years to depreciate. As an interesting tidbit, Guinness Beer has a $9,000-year lease that would turn this analysis on its ear!

Cash Ratios That Won't Work for Our Two Companies

The following ratios tell interesting stories. The only problem is that they aren't relevant to our companies or we don't have the data to calculate them. I thought I'd mention them here anyway, in case they are relevant to you as you analyze your target organization.

Cash-to-Cash Dividends

$$\frac{\text{Operating cash flow} - \text{preferred dividends}}{\text{Common stock cash dividends}}$$

This is asking us to determine if the entity has enough cash to meet dividend obligations. Since neither of our organizations pays dividends, this is not relevant to us.

Dividend Payout of Cash from Operations

$$\frac{\text{Dividends}}{\text{Cash from operations}}$$

This metric gives us another perspective on dividend obligations and cash. How able is the organization to generate enough cash from operations to pay dividends? Neither of our companies pays dividends.

Mandatory Cash Flows Index

$$\frac{\text{Cash used in operations} + (\text{cash used for financing activities} - \text{dividends})}{\text{Total sources of cash}}$$

This metric contrasts the cash that the organization is obligated to use on a regular basis with the total cash generated. Cash used in operations to make and sell products or services is a mandatory expenditure, as is cash used to repay loans.

Notice that dividends have been taken out of the cash flow used for financing activities because dividends are not mandatory in many cases. If push came to shove and the organization were in cash-flow trouble, it could delay or cancel the dividends.

This is a metric that is hard to get at from outside the company. The two components—cash from operations and cash from financing—are hard to access.

Cash from operations is total cash less rainy-day cash. From the cash-flow statement, we cannot derive the cash used in operations. It discloses only the net effect on cash of operations, and it is a positive number—termed *cash provided*, not *cash used*. Because we don't know what rainy-day cash is, we can't get at this number. If you are inside the organization, this could be a great metric to calculate.

Defensive Interval

$$\frac{\text{Current assets} - \text{inventory}}{\text{Daily cash operating expenses}}$$

This is a great ratio to calculate if you have the information. It would, in essence, show you how many days you could make it—pay your cash operating expenses—before you would run out of cash. Notice that inventory is taken out of current assets because we might not be able to sell our inventory fast enough to make that daily cash payment. Unfortunately, we have no way to accurately figure daily cash operating expenses for either company.

Overall Conclusions about the Cash Positions of Dell and Apple

In the first edition of this book, Dell looked like such a star in comparison with Gateway Computers that it was almost a pitiful comparison. And while the comparison between Dell and Apple is not pitiful, it is clear that Apple is in a much stronger cash position than Dell. Dell is still plugging along, but in 2010 Dell experienced a decline in sales and profitability. This had a corresponding negative effect on its cash flows. While Dell still has a healthy cash balance, the source of the cash flows may not be sustainable. Dell has some buffer against hard times, but this buffer is created only with the permission of its vendors and lenders. Dell will be interesting to watch in the coming years.

Apple is in a sweet spot. Growing market share, high profitability, and low operating costs all contribute to a healthy cash flow. The company has kept its discretionary spending in check and is poised to take full advantage of its moment in the sun.

Summary

Cash flow and cash holdings are such a significant determinant of financial health and flexibility that they deserve to be scrutinized closely. Pick a handful of cash ratios that are meaningful to your organization, and run them often to stay on top of your most important asset.

QUIZ

1. The accrual method of accounting will always cause a difference between
    A. cash from operations and net income.
    B. cash and net income.
    C. net cash and cash.
    D. assets and liabilities.

2. The operating category of the cash-flow statement discloses how much cash the organization generated in creating and selling its products and services. True or false?
    A. True
    B. False

3. This ratio asks, "Do we have enough liquid resources to cover current obligations?" And this might be the most telling ratio in the whole book for Dell.
    A. Operating cash index
    B. Cash ratio
    C. Cash to total assets
    D. Cash-flow adequacy ratio

4. Common shareholders always receive dividends. True or false?
    A. True
    B. False

5. The investing category of the cash-flow statement discloses how much the organization has invested in inventory. True or false?
    A. True
    B. False

6. This metric asks, "Is cash flow from selling our product or service enough to get us the extra goodies we need to grow and keep our owners happy? Do we have enough cash from operations to buy additional capital equipment, to expand our inventory, to pay dividends to our owners, and to meet additional debt obligations if we decide to take on an expansion loan or a loan for a special project?"
    A. Operating cash index
    B. Cash ratio
    C. Cash to total assets
    D. Cash-flow adequacy ratio

7. **The cash-flow statement divides cash flows into which of the following three categories?**
   A. Investing, financing, and asset purchases/disposals
   B. Investing, financing, and operating
   C. Financing, operating, and equity

8. **When dividends are paid, they are classified in which category of the cash-flow statement?**
   A. Investing
   B. Financing
   C. Operating

9. **When fixed assets are purchased, they are classified in which category of the cash-flow statement?**
   A. Investing
   B. Financing
   C. Operating

10. **The operating cash index contrasts net income with operating cash. True or false?**
    A. True
    B. False

Chapter 18

Financing Ratios

There are three ways to finance your organization. You can get a loan, you can sell equity or ownership in your company, or you can generate your own resources by selling your product or service at a profit. Each type of financing has advantages and disadvantages. In this chapter we will examine ratios that help us to understand whether an organization is reliant on debt and equity financing to stay in business.

CHAPTER OBJECTIVES

- Calculate cash ratios for two organizations
- Interpret results of the ratios

Debt

Debt is incurred when you arrange for someone, such as a bank, to give you resources now with the understanding that you will pay them back later, often with a little fee—interest. The lender can require you to conform to a myriad of requirements. If you take the money, you also take on whatever requirements the lender imposes. Examples include being required to keep a certain amount of cash in the bank at all times, keeping inventory levels within an acceptable range, and undergoing quarterly audits. Usually debt financing requires you to make periodic payments and to pay interest.

Debt is not inherently bad. Debt can be a very useful tool. Debt might allow you to take advantage of opportunities that you otherwise would have to pass up. So debt itself is not bad. What is bad is being burdened by such a large amount of debt that all you can do is keep up with the obligation each month.

An advantage of debt financing is that it is often cheaper than equity financing because equity investors often expect a higher return. They expect a higher return because equity holders get paid last in case of liquidation, and they demand a higher return for this risk. Also, the interest on loans is tax deductible.

Equity

The disadvantage of equity is that you have to answer to the people to whom you sell it. They become owners of the organization and therefore have a say in how the organization is run.

They also expect a return for their investment in the organization either in terms of an increase in the value of the stock or in terms of distributions or dividends. Either one of these needs can be hard to satisfy.

If you are expected to make the value of the stock go up, then you are also expected to earn profits and maintain happy financial metrics. You may have to sacrifice long-term goals for short-term profitability. If you are expected to pay dividends, you must have the cash available every quarter to do so.

The advantage of equity is that you might not be expected to pay dividends, and it might be easier to attract investors than to generate a profit. If you are in the early years of building your company, you might not be profitable at all, and debt or equity financing are your only sources of money.

Earnings

Ideally, you run on your own steam. You generate enough resources through the sale of your product or service to pay for the things you need to operate and expand. If you generate your own resources through sales, you do not have to answer to either lenders or equity holders. However, making a profit is not that easy. As you have seen from reading earlier chapters, many factors can affect an organization's ability to generate a profit.

I once met a man who was a financial analyst for a venture capitalist. He spent all his time investigating and analyzing companies to determine if they were worthy of investment. Each quarter, out of the hundreds of companies he evaluated, he recommended that his investors put their money into only 10 companies.

He said that of this 10, 5 would fail in the first year, 2 would fail in the first five years, 2 would generate a decent return for the rest of their existence, and only 1 would be a star—worth the investment in the other 9. The big companies that we all know and love now—IBM, Microsoft, and General Motors—are all stars. Many a company has failed in its quest to make it to that size.

My point? Generating a profit and staying in business are not as easy as they sound.

The following ratios help to give us a picture of what sort of external financing the company is relying on. We looked at earnings in Chapter 15 under profitability ratios. Good management of working capital is also a source of resources, and we discussed those ratios in Chapter 16. Another source is cash balances brought forward from previous years.

This chapter looks at how else we finance companies with external resources—debt or equity financing. I've grouped the ratios into three sets: debt ratios, equity ratios, and fixed asset/capital investment ratios.

Debt Ratios

These ratios tell us if a company is comfortably handling its debt obligations.

Debt to Equity

$$\frac{\text{Total debt}}{\text{Total equity}}$$

This is a very straightforward ratio. It asks us to contrast the components of the right side of the balance sheet. The right side of the balance sheet tells us where the organization gets money to operate—through debt, stock, or retained earnings.

So this ratio contrasts debt with the combination of stock and retained earnings. Ideally, because we like retained earnings so much, we would like the bottom to be larger than the top. If the top is larger, we may have hit on a hint that the organization is overburdened with debt.

Results for Dell

2010: Total liabilities of $28,011,000,000/total equity of $5,641,000,000
= 4.9:1

2009: Total liabilities of $28,011,000,000/total equity of $5,641,000,000
= 5.2:1

Results for Apple

2009: Total liabilities of $15,861,000,000/total equity of $31,640,000,000
= 0.5:1

2008: Total liabilities of $13,874,000,000/total equity of $22,297,000,000
= 0.6:1

Conclusions

The number for Dell surprised me. I expected equity to be on a par with debt, and I expected Dell to be in a better position than this. But there are several factors at play here. For one, Dell stretches its accounts payable out quite a bit. For another, Dell has been buying back its stock and thus decreasing its equity.

Equity is also affected by profit. Apple's superhealthy profit margins contribute to an exemplary equity balance.

Maybe the remaining ratios will give us better, more meaningful results. We need to keep on this track to see what is really going on.

Still Struggling?

Equity—Personal versus Corporate

If you own your home, you know how debt and equity works. For me to purchase my home, I put 10 percent down and took on a mortgage for the rest. The equity in my home is the difference between the value of my house and the debt I still owe on it. Equity in my house rises as I pay down the debt or the value of my house appreciates.

In accounting for corporate equity, however, the value of the corporate assets is whatever the organization paid for them minus depreciation and amortization. It has nothing to do with the assets' true value in the marketplace. Equity on the balance sheet of a corporation is the difference between assets and liabilities: equity = assets – liabilities. So in order to enhance equity, corporations have to earn more and puff up their asset balances (i.e., cash, investments, inventory, accounts receivable, fixed assets, and intangibles) and decrease the debt corresponding to said assets.

Debt Ratio

$$\frac{\text{Total liabilities}}{\text{Total assets}}$$

Here is another way of looking at the debt burden. Instead of contrasting the debt against equity, we contrast it against the total resources we have available to pay off that debt. Obviously, we want the bottom to be larger than the top; this would indicate that the organization has the resources necessary to meet its debt obligation. If we see the top bigger than the bottom, we are likely in serious trouble because that would mean that equity was negative (assets = liabilities + equity).

Results for Dell

2010: Total debt of $28,011,000,000/total assets of $33,652,000,000 = 0.83:1

2009: Total debt of $22,229,000,000/total assets of $26,500,000,000 = 0.84:1

Results for Apple

2009: Total debt of $15,861,000,000/total assets of $47,501,000,000 = 0.33:1

2008: Total debt of $13,874,000,000/total assets of $36,171,000,000 = 0.38:1

Conclusions

Dell's numbers are significantly higher than Apple's. This metric is, again, being affected by Apple's huge cash balance as a component of assets. I am a bit concerned that Dell's debt is so close to its assets—but I am not surprised by it because Dell has taken on long-term debt and stretches its payables.

Cash to Long-Term Debt

$$\frac{\text{Cash and cash equivalents}}{\text{Long-term debt}}$$

I like this ratio because it is getting a little more specific than the first two we looked at. It is looking only at long-term debt. Total debt would include accounts payable, and we have seen in previous chapters how both Dell and Apple are stretching accounts payable.

This contrasts the amount of cash the organization holds with its debt obligation. This gives us an indication of the power of the organization to pay off its debt with the cash it holds.

You may not see the top being bigger than the bottom because long-term debt may be a huge 30-year obligation and the organization holds only enough cash to meet the currently due portion of that debt plus some to pay current bills. So this might not be as meaningful a ratio as cash to current maturities of long-term debt. Again, you need to choose the ratios that make sense for your particular situation. In our case, Apple does not have any long-term debt, so the metric is not relevant to Apple at all.

Results for Dell

2010: Cash and cash equivalents of $10,635,000,000/long-term debt of $3,417,000,000 = 3.1:1

2009: Cash and cash equivalents of $8,352,000,000/long-term debt of $1,898,000,000 = 4.4:1

Results for Apple

This metric is not relevant to Apple because Apple does not have any long-term debt. Instead, Apple is funding its growth through profits.

Conclusion

Dell is taking on an increasing amount of debt. 2010 was an opportune time to take on debt because the interest rates were very low. However, Dell historically has financed its growth without debt or equity financing. The company was able in recent years to buy back and retire significant amounts of stock. This debt burden is something to keep an eye on. Apple is financing its growth and operations with profits.

Long-Term Debt Payment Ratio

$$\frac{\text{Cash applied to long-term debt}}{\text{Cash supplied by long-term debt}}$$

This is an interesting ratio. It asks us, for the current year, how much cash we got by issuing long-term debt versus how much cash we had to pay out in our obligations on long-term debt. This information comes from the cash-flow statement and may not be relevant if the organization did not receive any cash from long-term debt this year.

Results for Dell

2010: Cash applied to long-term debt of $122,000,000/cash supplied by long-term debt of $2,058,000,000 = 0.06:1

2009: Cash applied to long-term debt of $237,000,000/cash supplied by long-term debt of $1,519,000,000 = to 0.15:1

Results for Apple

This ratio isn't applicable to Apple because Apple doesn't have long-term debt.

Conclusions

Dell either took on a loan late in the year or is in no hurry to pay it off. With such low interest rates, the company may not have a goal to pay it off. Apple funds its growth through profit and has no debt.

Short-Term Debt to All-Debt Ratio

$$\frac{\text{Short-term debt}}{\text{Short-term debt} + \text{long-term debt}}$$

This ratio separates short-term debt from long-term debt. Why does this matter? Well, it gives the analyst another piece of information about how the company is financed. Does the company prefer to operate on short-term debt—on lines of credit, for example—or on longer obligations?

Which type of debt is more costly to the organization right now? What does this tell us about the operating philosophy of its managers? (Do you get the feeling, as I do, that more often than not these ratios raise more questions than they answer? This is the nature of financial analysis.)

Results for Dell

2010: Short-term debt of $663,000,000/short-term debt of $663,000,000 plus long-term debt of $3,417,000,000 = 16 percent

2009: Short-term debt of $113,000,000/short-term debt of $113,000,000 plus long-term debt of $1,898,000,000 = 6 percent

Results for Apple

Apple does not have short- or long-term debt.

Conclusions

As of the balance sheet date, Dell had a minor amount of short-term debt in relation to its long-term debt. But we need to realize that short-term debt is often renewed and then paid off throughout the year. Dell could be relying heavily on short-term financing to operate its business day to day, but we will not necessarily see that in our analysis. Apple is free and clear of debt as of the balance sheet date.

Receivables to Long-Term Debt

$$\frac{\text{Accounts receivable}}{\text{Long-term debt}}$$

This ratio is a little abstract. It is just another indicator of how easily the organization can meet its long-term debt obligations with current resources. Instead of using cash as a current asset, we use accounts receivable. This may make more sense for organizations that prefer to distribute cash earnings to owners and hence have a small cash balance. Accounts receivable eventually will be collected and can be used to pay the long-term debt obligations.

Results for Dell

2010: Accounts receivable of $5,873,000,000/long-term debt of $3,417,000,000 = 1.7:1
2009: Accounts receivable of $4,791,000,000/long-term debt of $1,898,000,000 = 2.5:1

Results for Apple
Apple does not have long-term debt.

Conclusions
For Dell, this metric tells us that it could pay off long-term debt 1.7 times with its current accounts receivable. Contrast this with its ability to pay off long-term debt with cash balances. Dell could pay the long-term debt off 3.1 times in 2010 with cash. Both metrics are meaningful to track.

External Financing Index

$$\frac{\text{Cash from operations}}{\text{Total external financing sources}}$$

We want to generate as much cash on our own as possible, and this is what the cash from operations figure tells us. We contrast this with the cash that we generated from sources other than operations, which would include cash from financing activities and cash from investing activities.

This gives us a sense of whether the company is running on its own steam or running on the steam of external parties. Both Dell and Apple have sought external financing recently—but they sought it from different sources. Dell earned financing through debt, and Apple used equity financing. So the bottom of our ratio will be long-term debt plus equity.

Results for Dell

2010: Cash from operations of $3,906,000,000/long-term debt of $3,417,000,000 + issuance of stock of $0 = 1.9:1
2009: Cash from operations of $1,894,000,000/long-term debt of $1,898,000,000 + issuance of common stock of $0 = 1.2:1

Results for Apple

2009: Cash from operations of $10,159,000,000/long-term debt of $0 + issuance of common stock of $475,000,000 = 21.4:1
2008: Cash from operations of $9,596,000,000/long-term debt of $0 + issuance of common stock of $483,000,000 = 19.9:1

Conclusions

Again, Apple leads and clearly does not rely on outside financing to operate.

Ratios That We'd Like to Calculate but Can't Because We Don't Have the Data or the Ratio Is Not Applicable to Either Company

Cash to Current Maturities of Long-Term Debt

$$\frac{\text{Cash + cash equivalents}}{\text{Current maturities of long-term debt}}$$

Now here is a specific ratio. It asks how much a company is obligated to pay on its long-term debt right now versus how much cash it has available. To find out how much is due, we have to look at the notes to the financial statements. And note 3 to Dell's 2010 10-K informs us that Dell is not obligated to pay on its loans at all in 2011. So we can't run this ratio.

In 2012, Dell must pay $24 million, and then in 2013, it is obligated to pay $400 million! The peak for the current debt outstanding is $600 million in 2014. This is a sizable obligation. Given that Dell's net income in 2010 was $1.4 billion and the debt payment in 2014 is $0.6 billion, I am a little worried about Dell's profitability in 2014. The company is gambling that things will improve for it. Maybe this debt is giving the company the impetus it needs to gain market share. I don't know Dell's strategy from reading the financials. I hope the gamble pays off.

Again, Apple has no long-term debt.

Fixed Charge Coverage

$$\frac{\text{Earnings before interest, taxes, and lease payments}}{\text{Interest expense and lease payments}}$$

Interest and lease payments are obligations that an organization can't get out of. Organizations must pay off the interest on a loan or the bank will call the loan. They must pay their lease or they will get kicked out of their facility.

Again, this should be a multiple. Earnings should be able to cover the basic obligations—the fixed charges—of the organization many times over.

This ratio screams for customization. You can add anything you like as a fixed charge and contrast that with the earnings that will be paying the fixed charges.

We can't derive these numbers from outside the company with much accuracy. This one is a good one to calculate if you are internal to the company.

Dividend Payout

$$\frac{\text{Dividends per common share}}{\text{Earnings per share}}$$

Once a company starts paying dividends, equity investors come to expect it. This contrasts how much the company earned—on the bottom of the ratio—and how much it distributed to owners. This will tell you that 40 percent of the wealth was distributed and 60 percent was retained, for example. Since neither Dell nor Apple pays dividends, we can't apply this ratio to them.

Percentage of Earnings Retained

$$\frac{\text{Net income} - \text{all dividends}}{\text{Net income}}$$

This is another way of looking at what was paid out versus what was retained by the organization. Since neither company distributes earnings to its shareholders, we can't calculate this ratio.

Reinvestment Ratio

$$\frac{\text{Capital investments}}{\text{Depreciation} + \text{sale of assets}}$$

The point of this ratio is to give us an indication of whether the organization is keeping its capital investments fresh. The top of the ratio is what the organization spent this period on new equipment, and the bottom of the ratio shows the depreciation of the equipment. Depreciation or the sale of equipment reduces the value of capital investments. This ratio would make a lot of sense to use in a capital-intensive industry such as an airline or a steel manufacturer.

I can't tell how much in fixed assets the company disposed of during the year. This could be an interesting ratio to run if you are in a capital-intensive industry and you are an insider and can get at the information!

Conclusions on Financing

Dell has been relying more on debt in the past few years than it has in its entire history. Because it took on debt during a downturn in its sales, the ratios are not stellar. Apple, again, is in a sweet spot and is able to finance its operations using its own resources. It does not have to reach outside its organization to get financing and will not experience negative consequences of its choices to take on debt in the future in case the market turns downward. Dell may have a plan to avoid the negative impact of its ballooning debt on its cash flow and profit in 2014.

Overall Conclusions for Dell and Apple

Apple is living large. It is gaining market share, earning high profits, managing its working capital wisely, and running on its own steam.

2009 and 2010 were not good at Dell. Sales declined along with profitability. And although Dell still does quite well managing its working capital, none of the components of working capital are as shining as they have been in the past. Days' sales of inventory is longer, days' sales of receivables is climbing, but Dell is trying to compensate by stretching payments to vendors. Much of this change is due to Dell's exploration of new distribution channels to regain market share.

Dell made significant purchases of other companies in the past few years and went into debt to do it. This debt obligation will balloon in 2014 and will have a negative impact on Dell's cash flow and profitability. The depth of the negative impact depends on whether Dell is able to get its profits back into the 4 or 5 percent range.

Dell's frugal choices are serving it well in this down period and allow the company to still earn a profit as market share declines. Because Dell is so integral to the financial health of my community, I am going to keep a close eye on it in the next few years and hope that it can turn things around.

Summary

Everyone needs a little help sometimes! Debt and equity financing can help organizations do things they can't fund using their own profits. But the key to managing these external sources is to not let them overwhelm an organization and cause the organization to make choices that center around paying back debt or making short-term shareholders happy.

QUIZ

1. Debt and equity are the same thing; you just get the money from different people. True or false?
   A. True
   B. False

2. The ratio of cash to long-term debt contrasts current cash balances with all debt. True or false?
   A. True
   B. False

3. The best part about financing your company this way is that you do not answer to anybody.
   A. Debt
   B. Equity
   C. Earnings

4. Equity owners are owners of the organization and have a say in how the organization is run. True or false?
   A. True
   B. False

5. This ratio ask us to contrast the components of the right side of the balance sheet.
   A. Debt to equity ratio
   B. Equity to cash ratio
   C. Cash to long-term debt ratio
   D. Long-term debt payment ratio

6. If Dell's debt to equity ratio is about 5:1, what does that tell us about Dell?
   A. It has five times as much equity as debt.
   B. Twenty percent of its balance sheet is debt.
   C. It has five times as much debt as equity.

7. Debt should be avoided at all times. True or false?
   A. True
   B. False

8. Reinvestment ratio is a relevant ratio to run in a capital-intensive industry such as airlines or steel manufacturing. True or false?
   A. True
   B. False

9. **Which of the following ratios would indicate whether the organization had enough resources to pay its debt?**

    A. Gross profit margin
    B. Cash to current maturities of long-term debt
    C. Earnings per share
    D. Return on investment
    E. Days' sales outstanding

10. **Equity tells us how much of the company the owners own through stock and retained earnings. True or false?**

    A. True
    B. False

Final Exam

1. **The balance sheet**
   A. is the supersummary of the general ledger.
   B. is the mother of all financial statements.
   C. must balance.
   D. All of the above

2. **Aliases for the income statement include**
   A. the P&L.
   B. the profit and loss statement.
   C. the statement of earnings.
   D. All of the above

3. **Master these three financial statements and you will have mastery of 80 percent of the business lingo used to analyze a business. They are**
   A. the balance sheet, income statement, and earnings statement.
   B. the balance sheet, income statement, and cash-flow statement.
   C. the general ledger, balance sheet, and earnings statement.
   D. the balance sheet, cash-flow statement, and general ledger.

4. **This is the mother of all financial statements.**
   A. The general ledger
   B. The profit and loss statement
   C. The balance sheet
   D. The earnings statement

5. **The double-entry accounting system is called such because**
   A. it was invented by an Italian.
   B. it was invented during the Renaissance.
   C. you have to enter every transaction two or more times.
   D. each entry has two sides to it—a debit and a credit.

6. **GAAP stands for**
    A. generally accepted auditing practices.
    B. generally accepted accounting practices.
    C. generally accepted accounting principles.
    D. government-accepted accounting procedures.
    E. generally accepted accounting procedures.

7. **Which of the following is the most liquid asset?**
    A. Building
    B. Equipment
    C. Inventory
    D. Cash
    E. Accounts receivable

8. **Assets are**
    A. happy things that you own.
    B. sad amounts that you owe other people.
    C. disclosed on the cash-flow statement.
    D. highly liquid.

9. **A business can raise money by**
    A. selling stock.
    B. taking out a loan.
    C. selling goods and services.
    D. All of the above

10. **Working capital**
    A. is current assets minus current liabilities.
    B. should be as small as possible.
    C. is the resources, or capital, you have working for you.
    D. All of the above

11. **Long-term debt appears on which statement?**
    A. The balance sheet
    B. The income statement
    C. The cash-flow statement

12. **The classic accounting equation is**
    A. assets = short-term liabilities + long-term liabilities.
    B. assets = working capital − equity.
    C. assets = liabilities + equity.

13. **What is a disadvantage to financing your operations with debt?**
    A. You must pay interest.
    B. You must make periodic payments.

C. You must comply with bank convenants.

D. All of the above

14. **When an entity does not have enough resources to pay off its lenders or the bank, it is called**

A. liquidation.

B. bankruptcy.

C. claim management.

15. **In general, inventory balances should be**

A. high.

B. low.

C. stable.

16. **In general, accounts receivable balances should be**

A. high.

B. low.

C. stable.

17. **Your house, car, computer, and some jewelry minus your mortgage, car note, and credit card debt equals what?**

A. Assets

B. Liabilities

C. Equity

D. Fixed assets

18. **Which of the following is least liquid?**

A. Cash

B. Finished goods inventory

C. Accounts receivable

D. Raw materials inventory

19. **You have liquidated your entire business, and now it is time to pay off the owners. Who gets paid first?**

A. Common stockholders

B. Preferred stockholders

C. Bank

20. **When might you factor your accounts receivable?**

A. When you are balancing your books

B. When you want a cheap loan

C. When you need cash

D. When you want good customer relations

21. **The formula for the income statement is**
    A. cash − expenses = profit.
    B. revenues − cost of goods = profit.
    C. revenues − expenses = profit.
    D. cash − cost of goods = profit.

22. **EBIT stands for**
    A. everything before income taxes.
    B. earnings before income taxes.
    C. earnings before interest and taxes.

23. **The subtotal on the income statement that is the result of subtracting cost of goods sold from sales is**
    A. operating margin.
    B. gross margin.
    C. net income.

24. **In general, direct costs go into which category of expenses?**
    A. Cost of goods sold
    B. Operating expenses
    C. Capital expenditures
    D. Unusual items

25. **Total sales revenue appears on which statement?**
    A. The balance sheet
    B. The income statement
    C. The cash-flow statement

26. **Which of the following likely would be a direct cost?**
    A. Materials
    B. Manufacturing labor
    C. Utilities
    D. Rent
    E. Legal fees
    F. Marketing expenses
    G. A and B
    H. A, B, and C
    I. A, E, and F

27. **To which margin should managers be held accountable?**
    A. Net margin
    B. Gross margin
    C. Operating margin
    D. Profitability margin

28. **Cash receipts from borrowing are classified on the cash-flow statement as**
    A. cash inflow from operating activities.
    B. cash inflow from financing activities.
    C. cash inflow from investing activities.

29. **Profit and cash are different because of**
    A. timing.
    B. the double-entry system of accounting.
    C. banking regulations.
    D. Internal Revenue Service (IRS) rules.

30. **The cash method of accounting is the most commonly used method among large corporations. True or false?**
    A. True
    B. False

31. **If operating cash from the cash-flow statement and operating income from the income statement are vastly different, this may indicate that**
    A. the entity is not realizing its sales in cash.
    B. the entity is using the cash method of accounting.
    C. the entity has a large balance of fixed assets.
    D. the entity is being investigated by the Securities and Exchange Commission (SEC).

32. **The three categories of cash flow described on the cash-flow statement are**
    A. operating, financing, and investing.
    B. operating, purchasing, and net income.
    C. financing, investing, and day-to-day purchases.

33. **How does the cash-flow statement link to the balance sheet?**
    A. Through the retained earnings account
    B. Through the cash account
    C. Through the fixed asset account

34. **When we collect on an account receivable,**
    A. the income statement records a sale.
    B. the cash-flow statement records an increase in cash.
    C. the income statement is not affected.
    D. the cash-flow statement is not affected.
    E. B and C are correct.
    F. C and D are correct.

35. **Retained earnings appear on which statement?**
    A. Balance sheet
    B. Income statement
    C. Cash-flow statement

36. **When we make a cash sale,**
    A. the income statement records a sale.
    B. the cash-flow statement records an increase in cash.
    C. the income statement is not affected.
    D. the cash-flow statement is not affected.
    E. A and B are correct.
    F. B and C are correct.

37. **When we make a sale on credit,**
    A. the income statement records a sale.
    B. the cash-flow statement records an increase in cash.
    C. the income statement is not affected.
    D. the cash-flow statement is not affected.
    E. A and B are correct.
    F. B and C are correct.
    G. A and D are correct.

38. **The frequency and accuracy of information cost time and money. True or false?**
    A. True
    B. False

39. **Which type of budget links the strategic plan to the budget?**
    A. The line-item budget
    B. The zero-based budget
    C. The performance-based budget

40. **A budget is**
    A. the translation of the future plans of the company into financial terms.
    B. operating expenses from last year decreased by 10 percent.
    C. a listing of all the expenses of the organization.

41. **ABC stands for**
    A. action-based communication.
    B. activity-based costing.
    C. activity-biased costing.

42. **The general ledger tracks how many hours were spent manufacturing a product. True or false?**
    A. True
    B. False

43. **Taxable income is often different than income calculated in the general ledger because of differences between GAAP and the tax code. True or false?**
    A. True
    B. False

44. **To get the 10-K, you can**
    A. print it from the company's Web site.
    B. print it from the SEC Web site.
    C. call investor relations at the company to request a copy.
    D. e-mail investor relations at the company to request a copy.
    E. All of the above

45. **MD&A stands for**
    A. Minor Disclosures and Analysis.
    B. Management's Disclosures and Analysis.
    C. Management's Discussion and Analysis.

46. **The best opinion an auditor can issue on the financial statements is**
    A. an unqualified opinion.
    B. a qualified opinion.
    C. an adverse opinion.

47. **The auditor issues an adverse opinion when the entity does not follow GAAP and it results in a material misstatement in the financial statements. True or false?**
    A. True
    B. False

48. **SG&A and R&D are subcategories of what?**
    A. Gross margin
    B. Operating expense
    C. Operating income
    D. Net income

49. **This section of the financial statements has five years' worth of financial data and a narrative version of the financial information.**
    A. Management Disclosure and Analysis
    B. Financial Conditions Analysis
    C. Management Discussion and Analysis
    D. Financial Results of Operations

50. **The annual report is the same thing as the 10-K. True or false?**
    A. True
    B. False

51. **The SEC was created after the Enron debacle. True or false?**
    A. True
    B. False

52. **Accumulated depreciation is a contra account to fixed assets. True or false?**
    A. True
    B. False

53. **When you buy a copier, you debit fixed assets. True or false?**
    A. True
    B. False

54. **When you purchase an item instead of leasing it, you record the purchase on the balance sheet under fixed assets. True or false?**
    A. True
    B. False

55. **The three phases of inventory are**
    A. raw, work in progress, and finished.
    B. raw, work in process, and done.
    C. raw, work in process, and finished.

56. **What do accountants call your inventory when you are still manufacturing it?**
    A. Finished goods
    B. Raw materials
    C. Work in progress
    D. Incomplete
    E. Undone

57. **Revenues and expenses are**
    A. permanent accounts.
    B. temporary accounts.
    C. zeroed out at the end of the year.
    D. A and C.
    E. B and C.

58. **FASB stands for**
    A. Financial Accounting Settings Body.
    B. Financial Accounting Standards Board.
    C. Federal Accounting Standards Board.

59. **The principle that prevents accountants from putting a value on brand names is**
    A. conservatism.
    B. a business entity.
    C. objectivity.
    D. cost.

60. **Data are relevant when they**
    A. make a difference to the decision maker.
    B. make a difference during the fiscal year.
    C. are free of errors or bias.

61. **Fiscal years always end on December 31. True or false?**
    A. True
    B. False

62. **The matching principle asks that**
    A. revenues be matched to the depreciation expense from prior periods.
    B. expenses be matched to the revenue they generate.
    C. income from the income statement be matched to retained earnings on the balance sheet.

63. **Sarbox is the nickname that accountants and auditors have given to the new law that requires all public companies to document their internal controls over financial reporting and have their financial reports audited. True or false?**
    A. True
    B. False

64. **The ending balance of cash one year becomes the beginning balance of cash the next year. True or false?**
    A. True
    B. False

65. **The accrual method of accounting asks us to record expenses that we owe but have not yet paid in cash. True or false?**
    A. True
    B. False

66. **Public utilities and airports are examples of what kind of funds?**
    A. Proprietary
    B. Enterprise
    C. General
    D. Internal service

67. *Proprietary* **means**
    A. owned.
    B. not for profit.
    C. governmental.

68. GASB stands for
    A. Government Accounting Setting Board.
    B. Government Actuarial Standards Board.
    C. Government Accounting Standards Board.

69. *Commingling* means that
    A. the government is being friendly.
    B. the government has mixed up its objectives with the objectives of a proprietary entity.
    C. the government has used money out of one fund to pay for a program of another fund.

70. Fiduciary funds can be spent by the government. True or false?
    A. True
    B. False

71. Agency funds are monies held on someone else's behalf. True or false?
    A. True
    B. False

72. A government should have several general funds. True or false?
    A. True
    B. False

73. Governmental financial statements have which two layers?
    A. The entity-wide layer and the fund layer
    B. The user-friendly layer and the proprietary layer
    C. The fund layer and the superfund layer
    D. The superfund layer and the fund category layer

74. The FASB sets standards for the way financial ratios and metrics should be calculated for public companies. True or false?
    A. True
    B. False

75. The balanced scorecard has the following four components.
    A. Financial, compliance, operations, and internal control
    B. Financial, customer, internal business processes, and learning and growth
    C. Financial, customer, internal controls, and business metrics

76. The internal business processes component of the balanced scorecard looks at whether the organization's employees have the training and skills to help the company achieve its goals. True or false?
    A. True
    B. False

77. The balanced scorecard model argues that businesses should create goals and metrics in how many categories?
    A. Two
    B. Four
    C. Six
    D. Eight

78. You can tell a lot about the priorities of an organization by looking at its budget. True or false?
    A. True
    B. False

79. Investors are concerned primarily about what facet of financial health?
    A. Sales
    B. Profitability
    C. Debt
    D. Production

80. Banks want assurance that the organization
    A. sells lots of product.
    B. has a cool product.
    C. can repay a loan.

81. Privately held organizations may not undergo an audit of their financial statements. True or false?
    A. True
    B. False

82. Use dollars and percentages in your financial analysis because they lend perspective to each other. True or false?
    A. True
    B. False

83. In using horizontal analysis, compare outlying years with the base year only. True or false?
    A. True
    B. False

84. **The three categories of ratios are**
    A. profitability, liquidity, and financing.
    B. revenue, liquidity, and financing.
    C. liquidity, financing, and debt.

85. **Ratios should be customized for your particular business. True or false?**
    A. True
    B. False

86. **Gross profit margin is the result of subtracting cost of good sold from**
    A. net profit.
    B. sales revenues.
    C. operating margin.

87. **Operating profit margin is the result of subtracting operating expenses from**
    A. net profit.
    B. sales revenues.
    C. gross profit.

88. **Net income/(long-term debt + equity) is which ratio?**
    A. Return on investment
    B. Return on equity
    C. Cost of goods sold
    D. Cost of debt

89. **If the current ratio and the acid test are similar, it shows that the company has very little money tied up in what?**
    A. Cash
    B. Accounts receivable
    C. Inventory

90. **Working capital turnover measures**
    A. how many times working capital is used to generate accounts payable.
    B. how many times working capital is used to generate sales.
    C. how many times working capital is turned into inventory.

91. **Which of the following metrics do you want to minimize in terms of days?**
    A. Days' supply of inventory
    B. Days' sales outstanding
    C. Days' payables outstanding
    D. All of the above
    E. B and C
    F. A and B

92. **Which of the following is the correct equation for the cash conversion cycle?**
    A. DSO + DSI − DPO
    B. DSO + DSI + DPO
    C. DPO − DSO − DSI

93. **Which ratio helps to indicate the age of fixed assets?**
    A. Depreciation to total fixed assets
    B. Depreciation impact ratio
    C. Cash to working capital

94. **The ratio of cash to current maturities of long-term debt indicates whether a company has enough cash to cover current debt payments. True or false?**
    A. True
    B. False

95. **The cash method of accounting is used when you have receivables and payables. True or false?**
    A. True
    B. False

96. **What do governments call their income statement?**
    A. An income statement
    B. A P&L
    C. A statement of revenues, expenditures, and changes in fund balance

97. **The shorter the cash conversion cycle the better. True or false?**
    A. True
    B. False

98. **Revenues and expenses affect net income and thus affect equity. True or false?**
    A. True
    B. False

99. **The cash method of accounting can result in**
    A. a mismatch of revenues and expenditures.
    B. a miscalculation of true cost.
    C. a misstatement of investment market value.

100. **International accounting standards categorize both the cash-flow statement and the income statement into operating, financing, and investing categories. True or false?**
    A. True
    B. False

Answers to Quizzes and Final Exam

Chapter 1

1. A
2. C
3. B
4. A
5. D
6. B
7. D
8. A
9. B
10. C

Chapter 2

1. B
2. B
3. A
4. B

5. C
6. A
7. B
8. B
9. C
10. A

Chapter 3

1. D
2. A
3. A
4. C
5. C
6. C
7. B
8. A
9. D
10. D

Chapter 4

1. B
2. A
3. B
4. A
5. A
6. B
7. E
8. A
9. C
10. A

Chapter 5

1. C
2. A
3. C
4. A

5. D
6. B
7. A
8. B
9. C
10. A

Chapter 6

1. A
2. B
3. C
4. A
5. B
6. A
7. D
8. B
9. B
10. B

Chapter 7

1. B
2. D
3. A
4. C
5. B
6. C
7. B
8. B
9. B

Chapter 8

1. B
2. C
3. A

4. A
5. A
6. A
7. B
8. A
9. B
10. B

Chapter 9

1. B
2. B
3. A
4. C
5. A
6. C
7. A
8. B
9. B
10. C

Chapter 10

1. B
2. B
3. A
4. A
5. B
6. B
7. A
8. A
9. B
10. B

Chapter 11

1. D
2. C

3. C
4. A
5. B
6. B
7. C
8. A
9. A
10. A

Chapter 12

1. C
2. C
3. B
4. D
5. D
6. A
7. D
8. C
9. C
10. A

Chapter 13

1. B
2. B
3. A
4. B
5. A
6. B
7. A
8. D
9. B
10. E
11. A

Chapter 14

1. B
2. D
3. A
4. B
5. B
6. B
7. D
8. A
9. A
10. A

Chapter 15

1. C
2. B
3. B
4. D
5. C
6. C
7. A
8. A
9. D
10. B

Chapter 16

1. D
2. A
3. B
4. A
5. A
6. B
7. C
8. A
9. A
10. A

Chapter 17

1. B
2. A
3. B
4. B
5. B
6. D
7. B
8. B
9. A
10. B

Chapter 18

1. B
2. B
3. C
4. B
5. A
6. C
7. B
8. A
9. B
10. A

Final Exam

1. D
2. D
3. B
4. C
5. D
6. C
7. D
8. A
9. D
10. D
11. A
12. C
13. D
14. B
15. B
16. B
17. C
18. B
19. C
20. C
21. C
22. C
23. B
24. A
25. B
26. G
27. C
28. B
29. A
30. B
31. A
32. A
33. B
34. E
35. A
36. E
37. G
38. A
39. C
40. A
41. B
42. B
43. A
44. E
45. C
46. A
47. B

48. B	66. B	84. A
49. C	67. A	85. A
50. B	68. C	86. B
51. B	69. C	87. C
52. A	70. B	88. A
53. A	71. A	89. C
54. A	72. B	90. B
55. C	73. A	91. F
56. C	74. B	92. A
57. E	75. B	93. A
58. B	76. B	94. A
59. A	77. B	95. B
60. A	78. A	96. C
61. B	79. B	97. A
62. B	80. C	98. A
63. A	81. B	99. A
64. A	82. A	100. A
65. A	83. A	

Index

Note: Boldface numbers indicate illustrations.